AF378489

Painting Animals on Stones

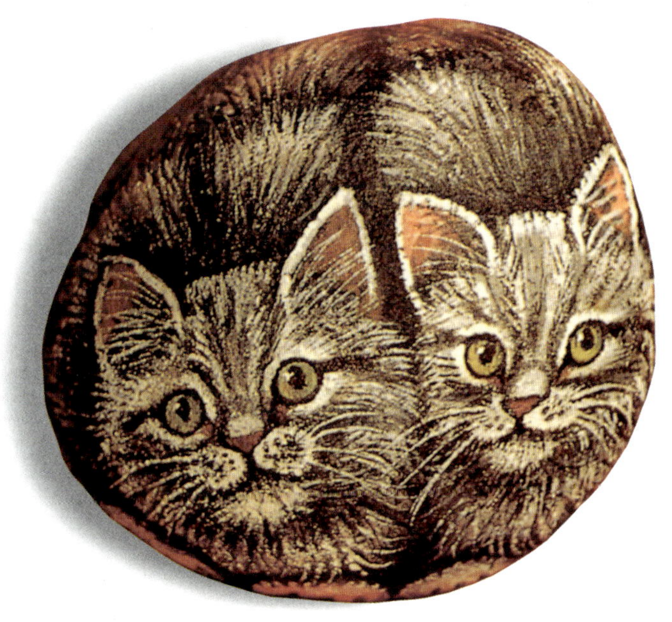

First published in Great Britain as *Painting on Stones* in 1998 by
Search Press Limited
Wellwood, North Farm Road,
Tunbridge Wells, Kent TN2 3DR

Originally published by North Light Books, Cincinnati, Ohio as
The Art of Painting Animals on Rocks. Copyright © 1994 by Lin Wellford
Painting More Animals on Rocks. Copyright © 1998 by Lin Wellford

All rights reserved. No part of this book, text, photographs or illustrations
may be reproduced or transmitted in any form or by any means by print,
photoprint, microfilm, microfiche, photocopier or in any way known or as
yet unknown, or stored in a retrieval system, without written permission
obtained beforehand from Search Press.

ISBN 0 85532 884 3

Readers are permitted to reproduce any of the items/patterns in this book
for their personal use, or for the purposes of selling for charity, free of
charge and without the prior permission of the Publishers. Any use of the
items/patterns for commercial purposes is not permitted without the prior
permission of the Publishers.

Suppliers
If you have any difficulty in obtaining any of the materials and equipment
mentioned in this book, then please write to the publishers for a current list
of stockists, which includes firms who operate a mail-order service:
Search Press Limited, Wellwood,
North Farm Road, Tunbridge Wells,
Kent TN2 3DR, England

Colour separation by P&W Graphics, Singapore
Printed and bound in Malaysia.

PAINTING
ANIMALS
ON STONES

Lin Wellford

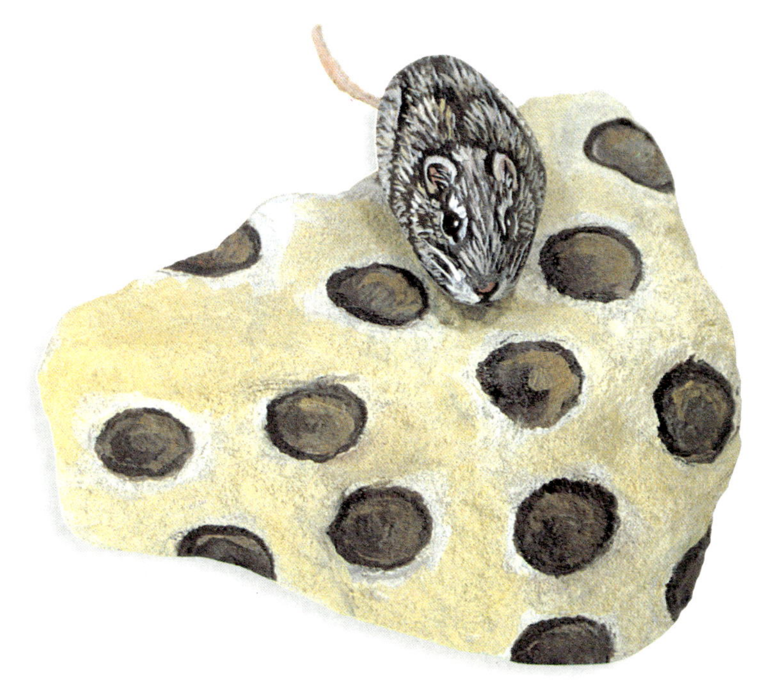

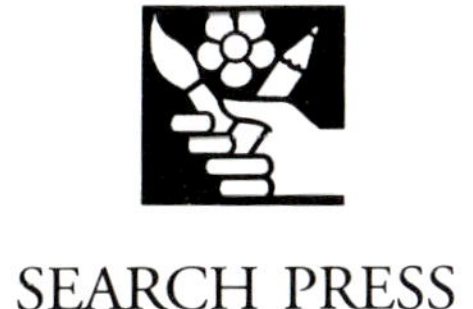

SEARCH PRESS

Table *of* Contents

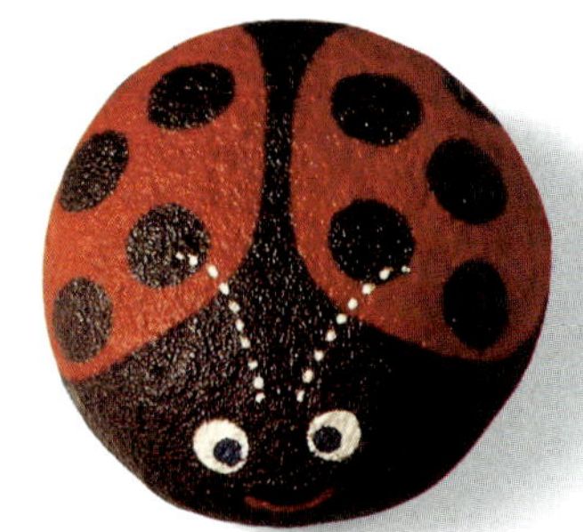

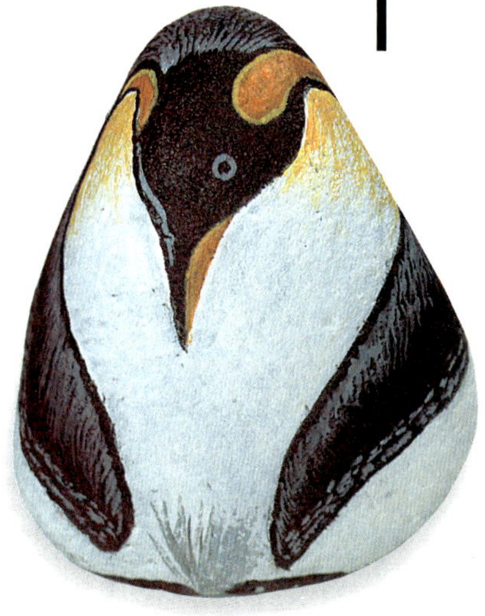

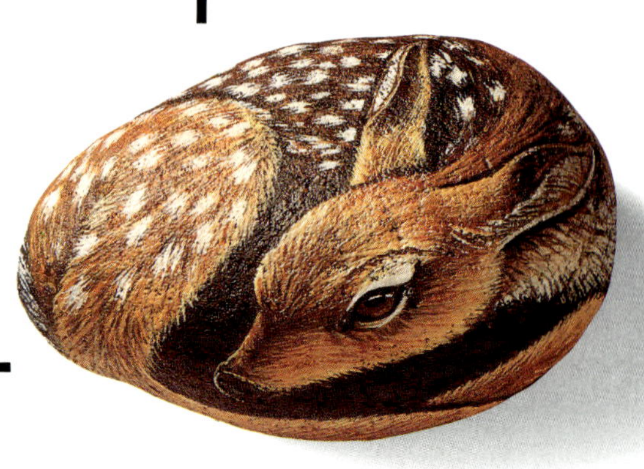

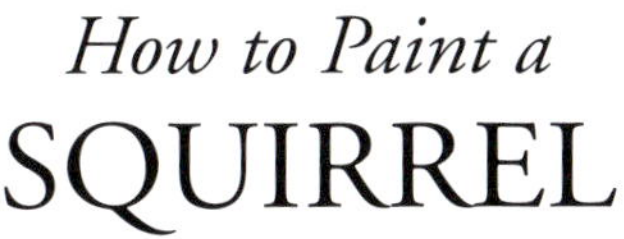
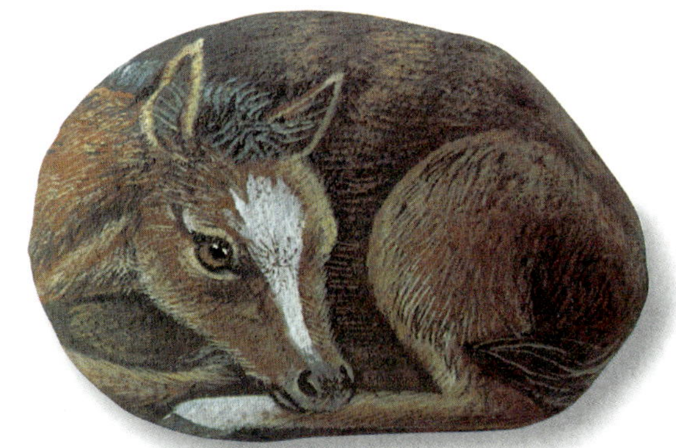
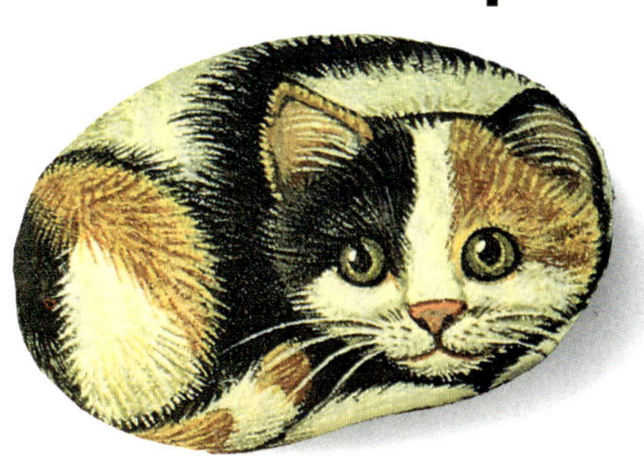
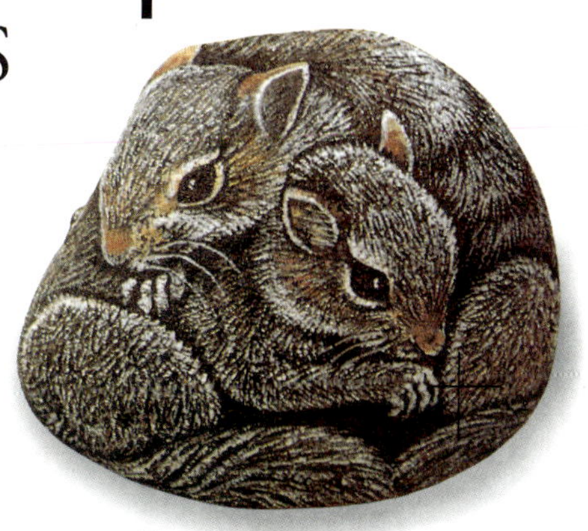

INTRODUCTION

Art has undergone countless evolutions since man executed those first paintings on cave walls. Modern artists can choose from a dizzying array of mediums and methods. At the same time, the use of natural, non-manufactured materials has a growing appeal in this age of ecological awareness.

Stone painting represents the perfect marriage of old and new. Technological advances have given us tough, inexpensive acrylic paints and finishes; and weathered stones can be found all over the world. They are, in fact, so common and plentiful that they are considered by most people to be of little or no value. But for me, collecting stones to paint is like a treasure hunt.

I stumbled on to the art of stone painting by accident, after years of doing pen and inks and watercolours. I came across a stone the size and shape of a baking potato. It looked so much like a rabbit that I felt moved to take it home and give it eyes, ears and a fluffy cotton tail. From the moment I placed tiny white sparkles in the eyes, I was hooked. The transformation from a dull stone into a rabbit, one that actually seemed to be looking back at me, was almost magical.

Over the past fifteen years I have painted thousands of stone animals. My menagerie has expanded to include creatures as diverse as reptiles, birds and practically anything with a fur coat.

Along the way I have shared my enthusiasm for this unique medium with others. With a little guidance, people of all ages and levels of ability can also experience the magic of 'bringing stones to life'. I believe everyone is born with the seeds of artistic ability, but not everyone is blessed with a nurturing environment where those seeds can germinate. Some people are told as children that they have no talent. This withers their confidence and with it their interest in making art. Painting on stones is an especially good avenue for rediscovering those dormant abilities.

Stones come with clearly defined shapes, so it is easier to make choices about what and where to paint. Also, since stones are three-dimensional, a novice painter is not confronted with the perplexing task of making a flat surface look like it is not. Best of all, stones are a free and plentiful resource, so you can experiment without worrying about 'wasting' anything of value.

I hope that looking through the pages of this book will intrigue, excite and, most of all, inspire you to pick up a paintbrush and reclaim the artist within. Happy painting!

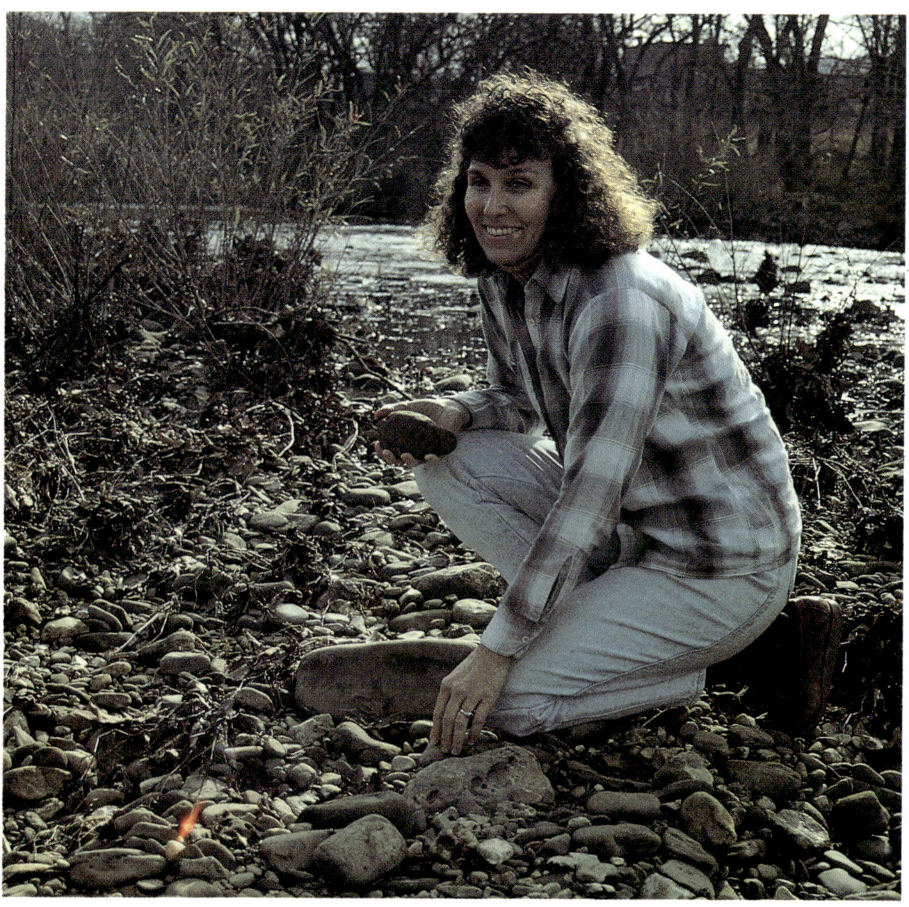

Getting Started

The projects in this book use a variety of stones, which vary in size and shape. I like to use stones with corners and edges that have been smoothed and rounded off by the action of ocean tides or by being tumbled along riverbeds. The logical place to look, therefore, is around moving water. Beaches and riverbeds are sites that offer good pickings. If you are not aware of such places in your area, ask around. Fishermen and other sportsmen can probably offer tips on where to look. You will also find that garden centres often sell stones for rock gardens or landscaping purposes.

The land on which pebbles are found, usually belongs to someone – whether a person, a company, a local authority or the State. Always try to find out who the landowner is, and then get permission for access and to remove stones. If you are unsure whether you can remove stones from a site, it is best to ask first. In all the years I have been collecting them, I have never had a single landowner object, but they do appreciate being asked.

A few stone types should be avoided. If your area offers sandstone, be aware that some pieces may be in the process of final breakdown. I call this condition 'rock rot'. Check for it by rubbing your hand lightly over the stone's surface. If loose particles of sand brush away easily, the surface may not accept paint well and the stone should be discarded.

Also consider overall surface smoothness when choosing stones for painting. Some stones are lightly pitted; you will find that a bit of texture will add to the appeal of your finished work, but overly rough or bumpy surfaces may hinder crisp fur lines and other vital details. Generally speaking, beginners should select the smoothest, most uniform stones available. Odd lumps or cracks do not necessarily make a stone unusable, however (see right). With experience

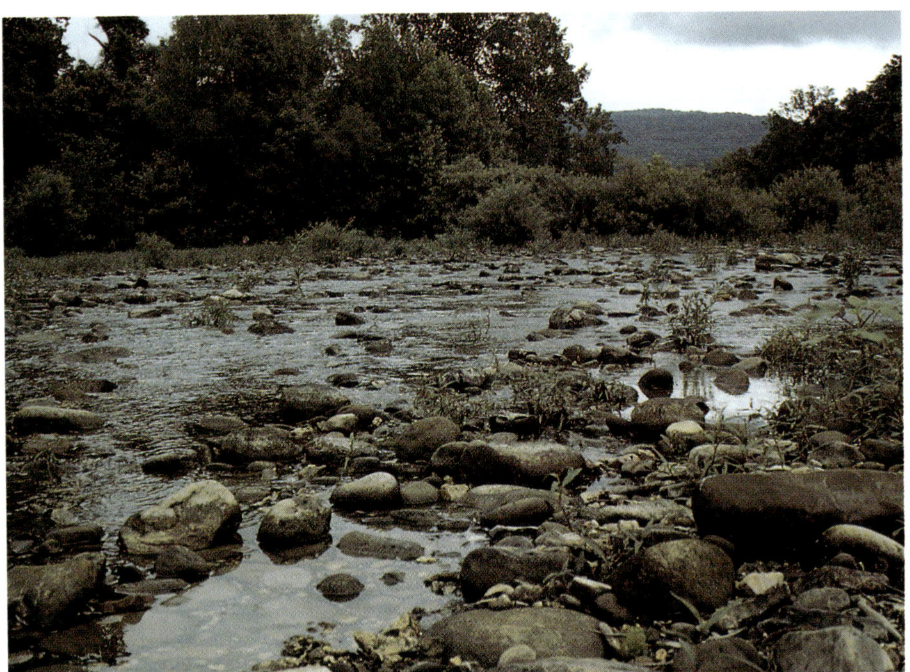

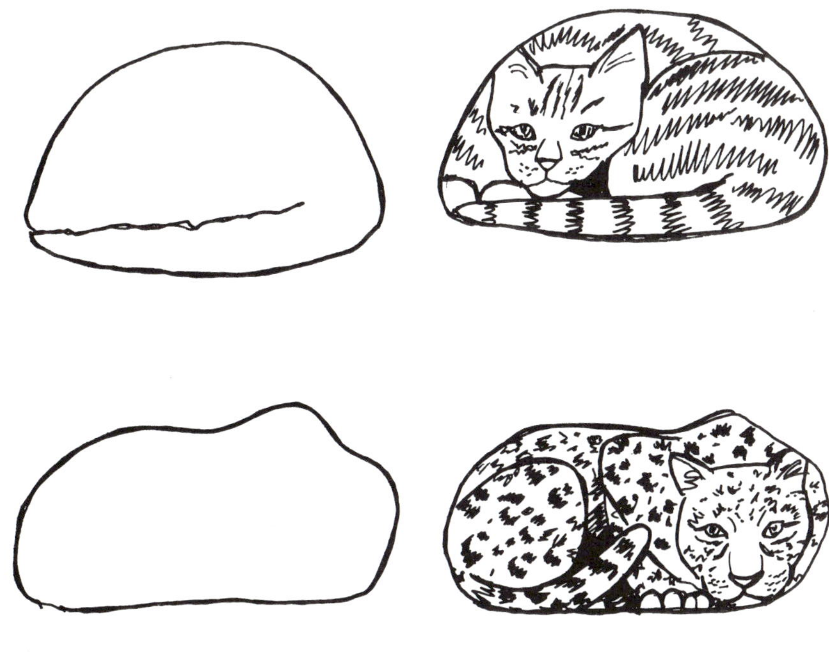

Cracks and lumps on stones can often be used to your advantage.

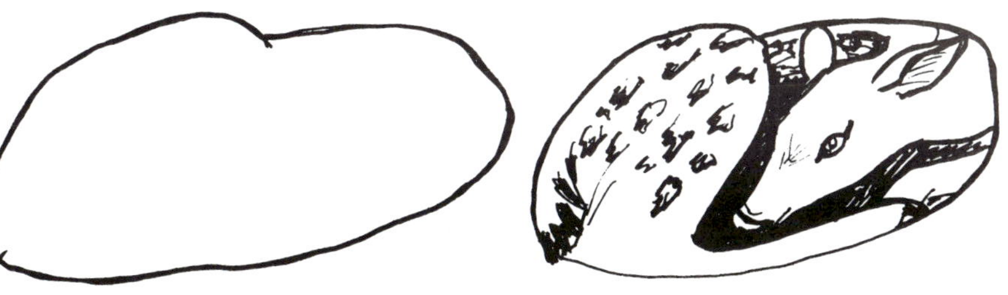

you will learn to see how such defects may actually enhance the realism of your work. For instance, a protruding lump may prove the perfect site for your animal's head, a haunch or even a shoulder blade. A crease or superficial crack might be incorporated to form the tail or define two separate forms. Holes or other small flaws that cannot be worked into the design can be camouflaged by filling them with wood filler, a product that dries quickly and can be painted over.

As a rule, I reject any stone with a harsh angle or jagged, broken edges. Another type of stone I am rarely able to use is the overly flat kind. Such stones simply do not offer enough volume to provide the illusion of contour. Reject any stone that is less than, say 4cm (1^1/$_2$in) thick.

The last requirement is that the stone should rest on one, more or less, flat side. Stones that wobble or fall over do not make good animals. Try turning stones over and around before disqualifying them; many will have one flatter side that works as the base. If the base tips only slightly, you could use wood filler to stabilize it.

It is a good idea to thoroughly clean your stones before you begin painting. Use an abrasive cleaner and a cloth, or a non-abrasive cleaner and a scrubbing brush to remove loose debris and caked-on algae, then allow the stone to dry.

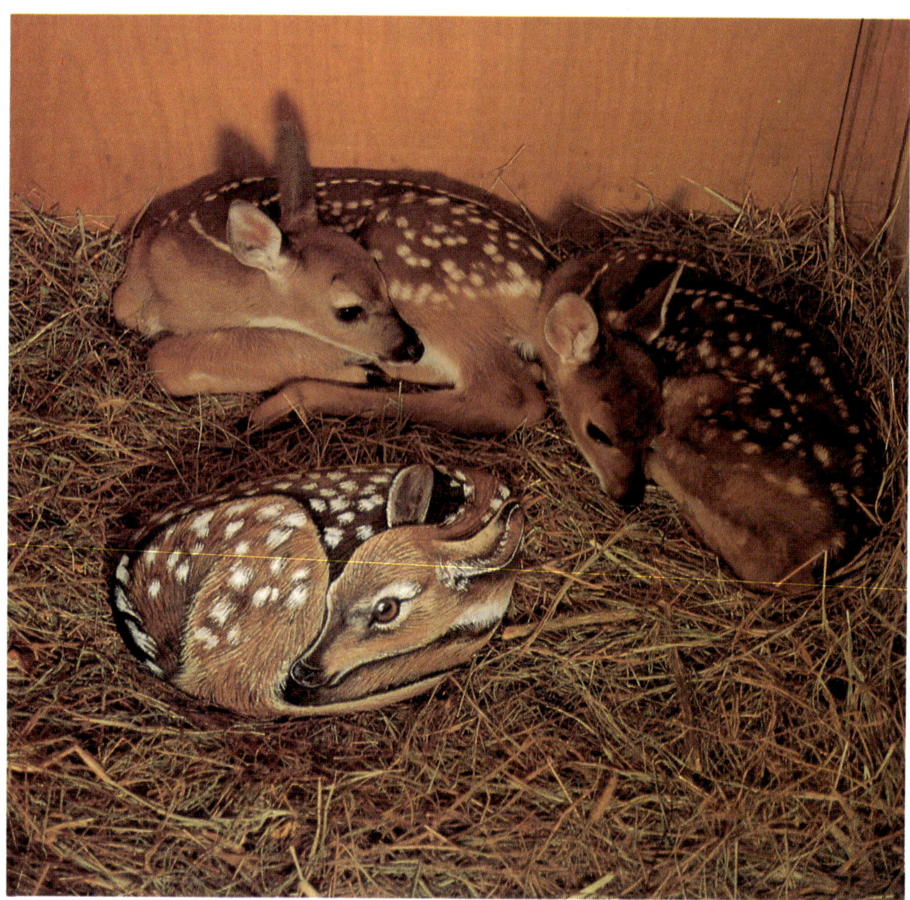

A protruding lump can often prove the perfect site for your animal's shoulder blade, as shown by this fawn. Defects can actually enhance realism – at first glance it is easy to mistake this stone fawn for the real thing.

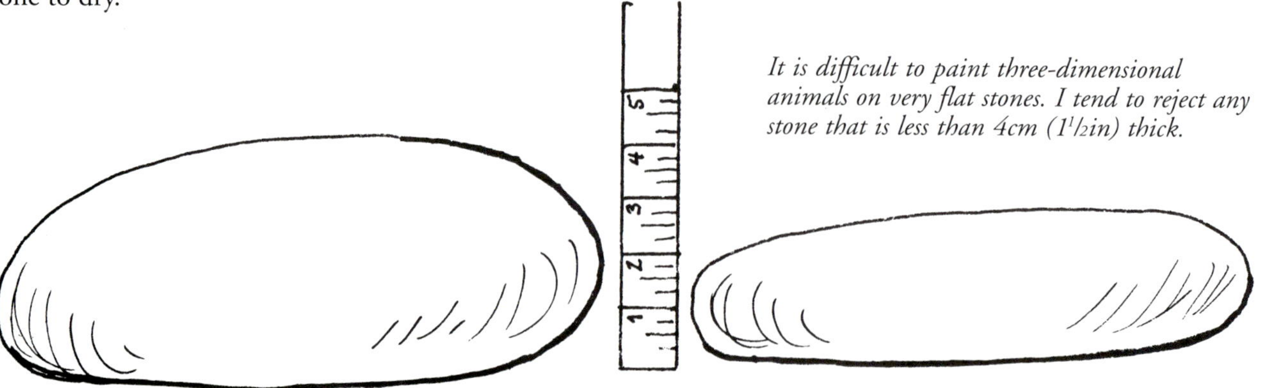

It is difficult to paint three-dimensional animals on very flat stones. I tend to reject any stone that is less than 4cm (1^1/$_2$in) thick.

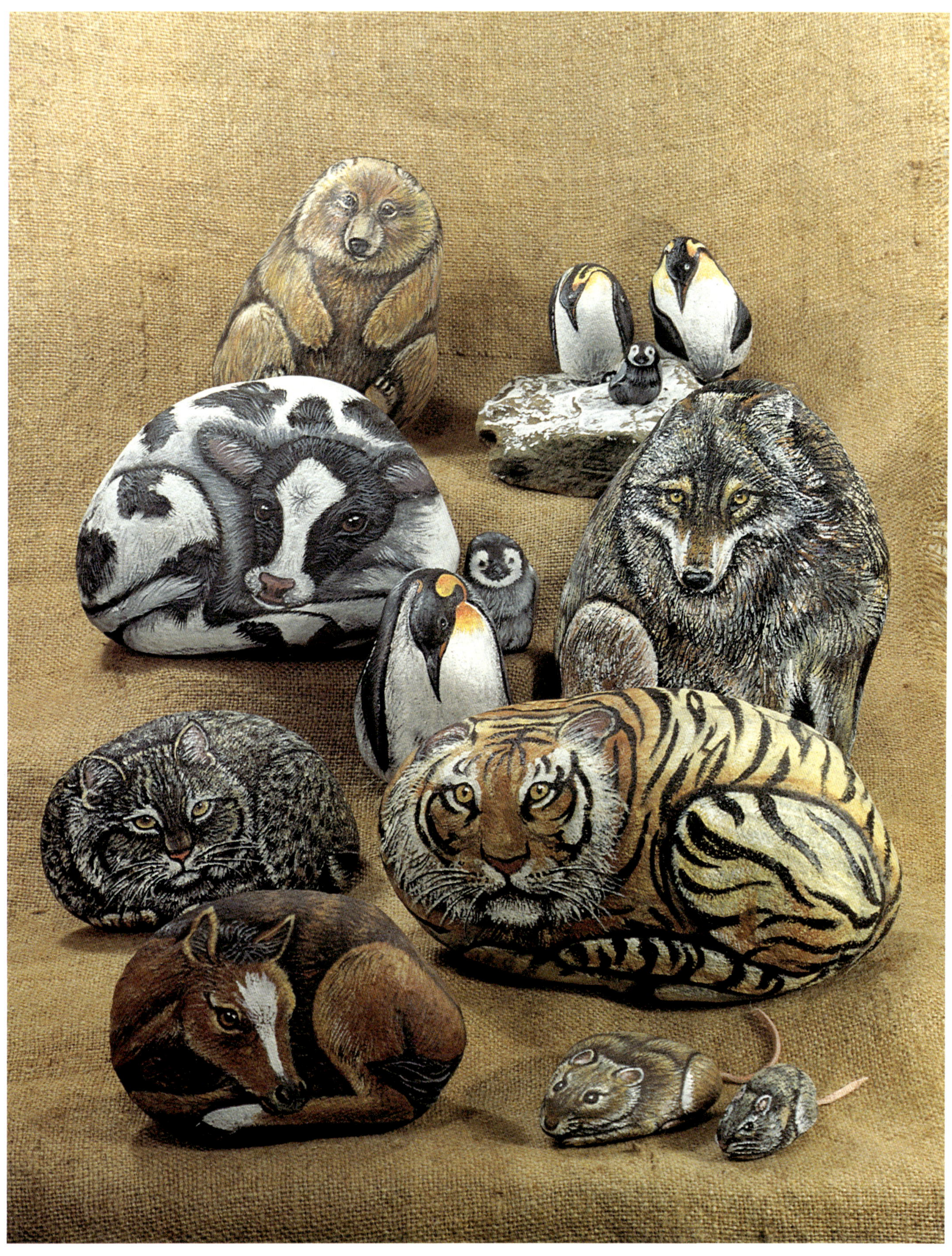

Supplies and Equipment

Most projects in this book can be painted with a limited selection of acrylic paints, available at art or craft shops. You can complete all the projects in this book using just a handful of colours: black, white, red, yellow, golden yellow, yellow ochre, orange, burnt sienna, medium green and blue.

You will also need at least a small selection of brushes. First and foremost is a narrow liner brush – a No. 0 or 1 is ideal. This type of brush is excellent for painting delicate fur lines and fine details which are vital to most stone painting projects. An assortment of other inexpensive brushes in various sizes and shapes will also come in handy, as will any old worn-out brushes you may have, especially ones with separated bristles as these are great for making lots of fur lines if you are in a hurry! If you are going to buy brushes, in addition to a liner brush, it would be worth investing in a medium size square brush for covering large areas quickly, and a couple of small to medium round brushes.

A foil dish or an old plate will make an acceptable palette, and you will also need a plastic cup for rinsing off brushes.

I use varnish to protect painted stones and to enhance the colours. Choose either oil-based or acrylic clear varnish – some are available in spray form which are particularly easy to use.

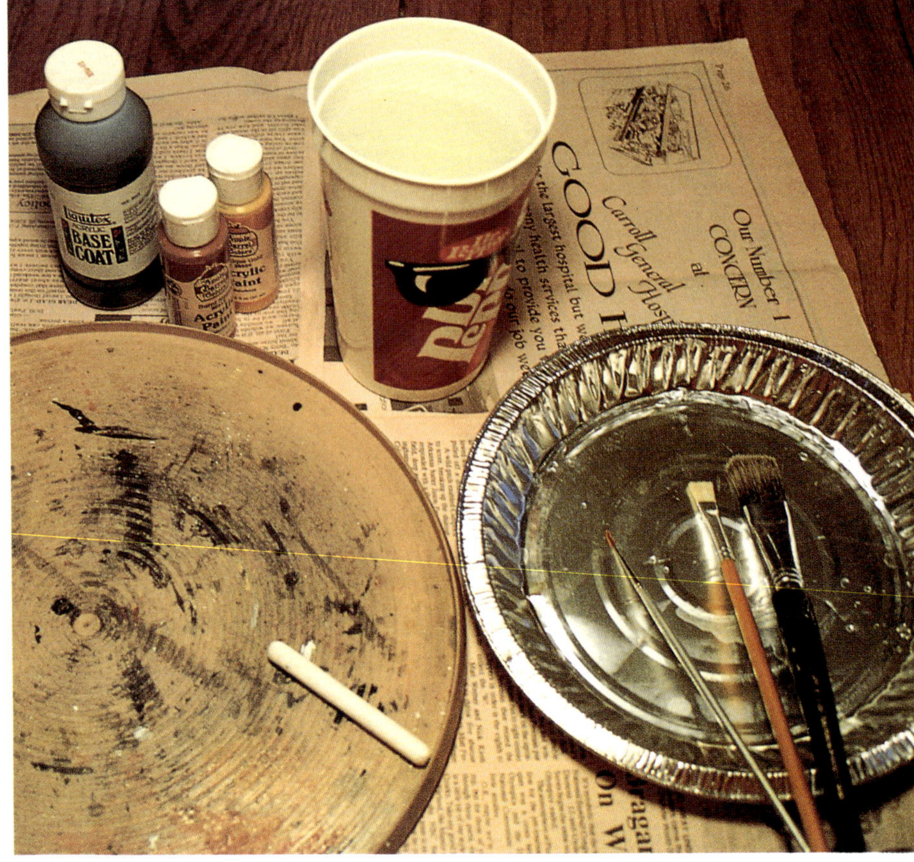

Before you begin, cover your work surface with enough newspaper to protect it. This newspaper will also prove indispensable for wiping excess water from your brushes and for checking paint consistency.

The only other requirements are a good supply of pencils, chalk, a measuring tape, and a bit of imagination.

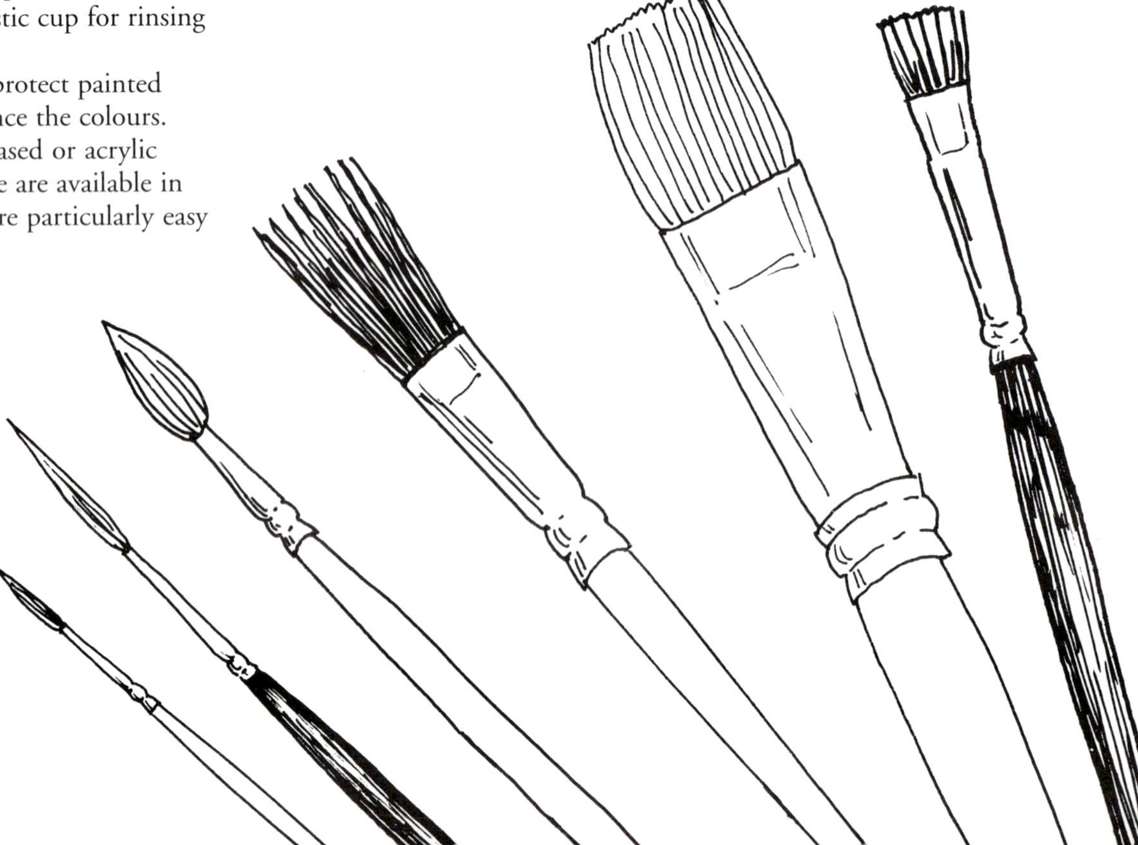

Helpful hints

If you enjoy doing the projects in this book, I recommend you begin building a library of photographs of various animals. Even though I paint many animals over and over again, I find that good photographs are an inspiration and help keep my work fresh. I find it useful to be able to refer to these, and they help me to achieve even more realistic detail, or to discover other poses and expression which I can adapt to suit the pieces I paint.

A final note: All the instructions contained in this book are designed to help creative people get started in an exciting new medium. But remember that artists bring their own unique vision, talent and style to any work they do. There is no 'right' or 'wrong' way to paint stones or anything else. What matters is pleasing yourself. My hope is that these projects will serve as a 'spring board' from which you can go on to develop a style as unique and individual as you are.

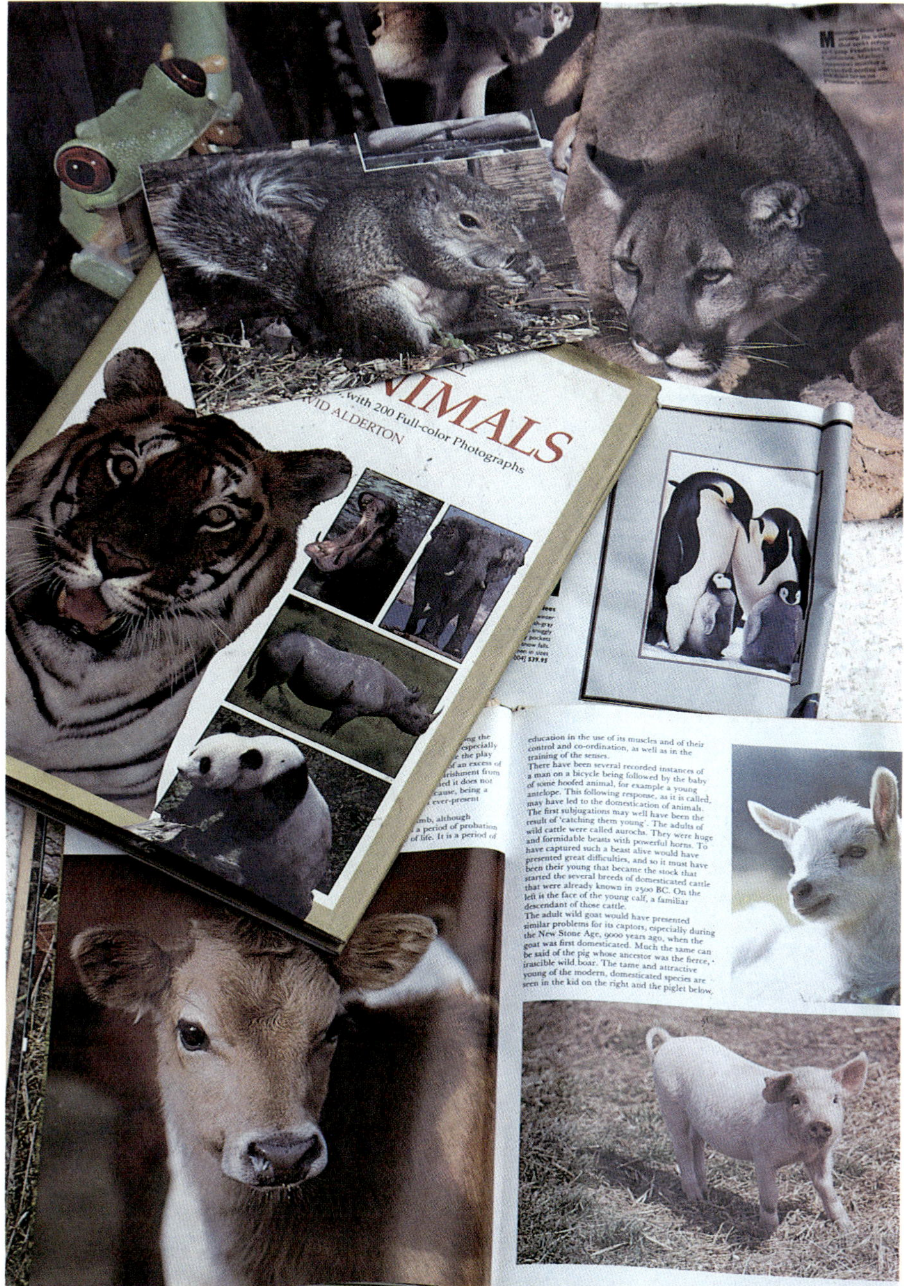

Photographs of animals are a source of inspiration. Try to build up a library of pictures which you can refer to when you are painting. These can help you to achieve more realistic detail, or to discover other poses and expressions which you can adapt to the pieces you paint.

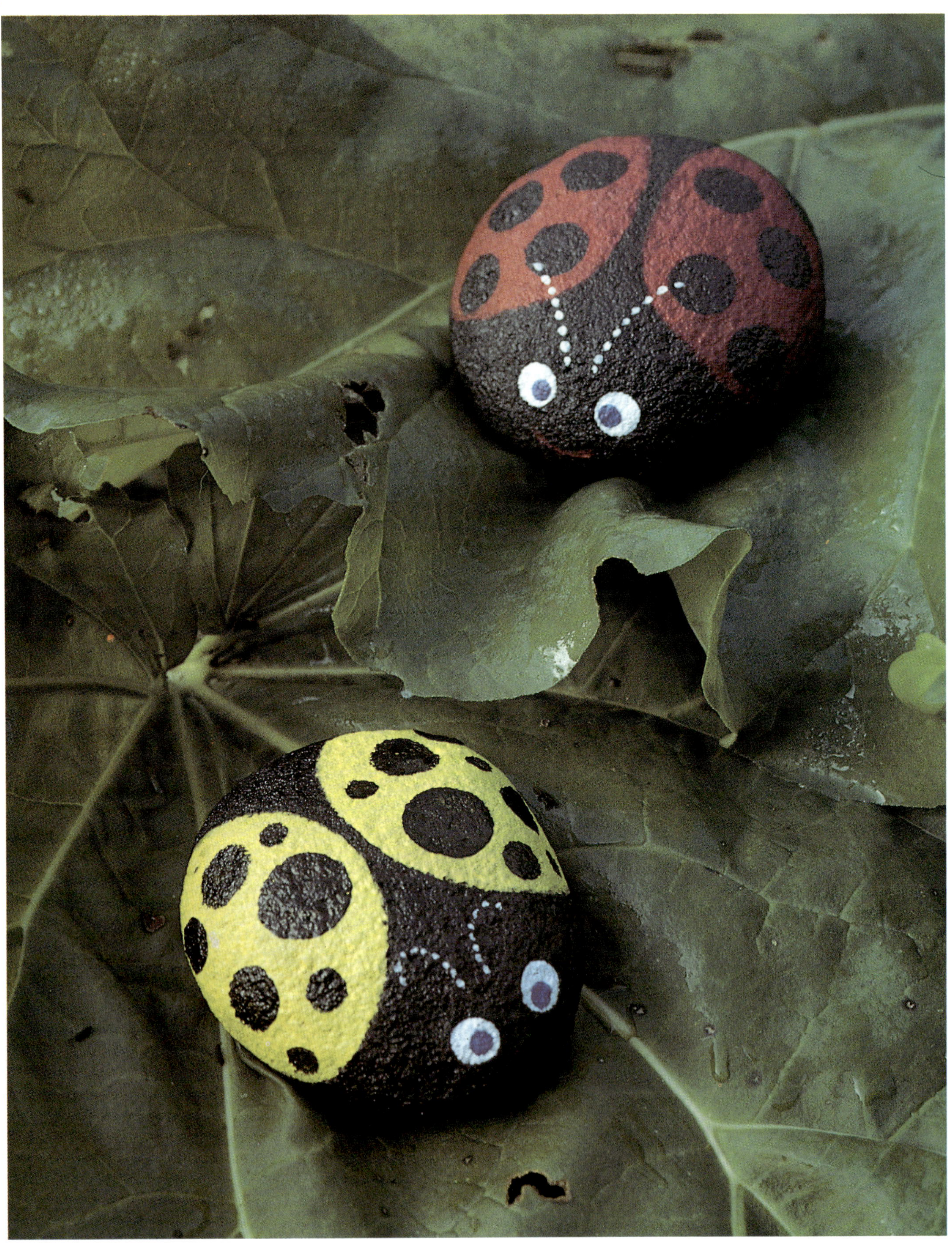

How to Paint a
LADYBIRD

The simple design and bold colours make this ladybird an ideal first stone to paint.

As with every project in this book, success depends on selecting the right stone to begin with. A potential ladybird stone might be as small as a bottle top or as big as a dinner plate, but your best bet is to look for a smooth stone between 5 and 10cm (2 and 4in) in diameter. If your stone is too large, your ladybird risks losing some of its appeal. On the other hand, a stone smaller than 5cm (2in) across will require far more skill and concentration to paint it.

The stone you choose could be either perfectly round or slightly oval in shape, but it must be symmetrical. The best ladybird stones are rounded

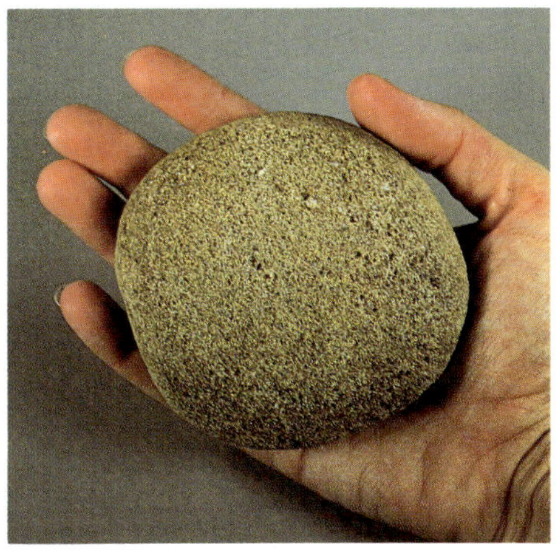

A perfect ladybird stone.

like a dome on top, but your stone could be only slightly curved on top and still work. The bottom side, however, must be fairly flat.

You Will Need

- acrylic paint: black, red, white and blue
- selection of brushes
- pencil
- sheet of paper (optional)
- scissors
- card
- oil-based or acrylic clear varnish

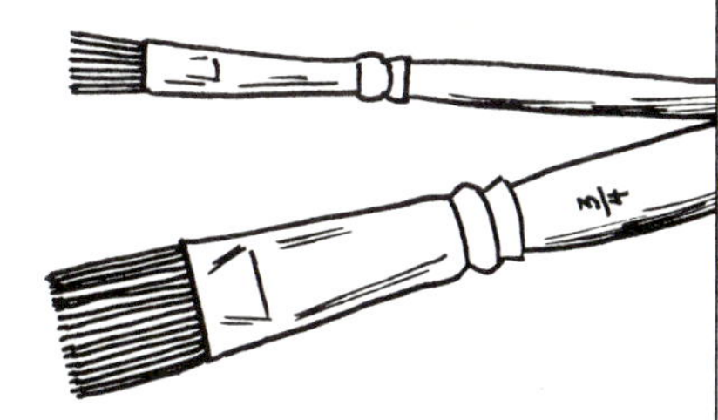

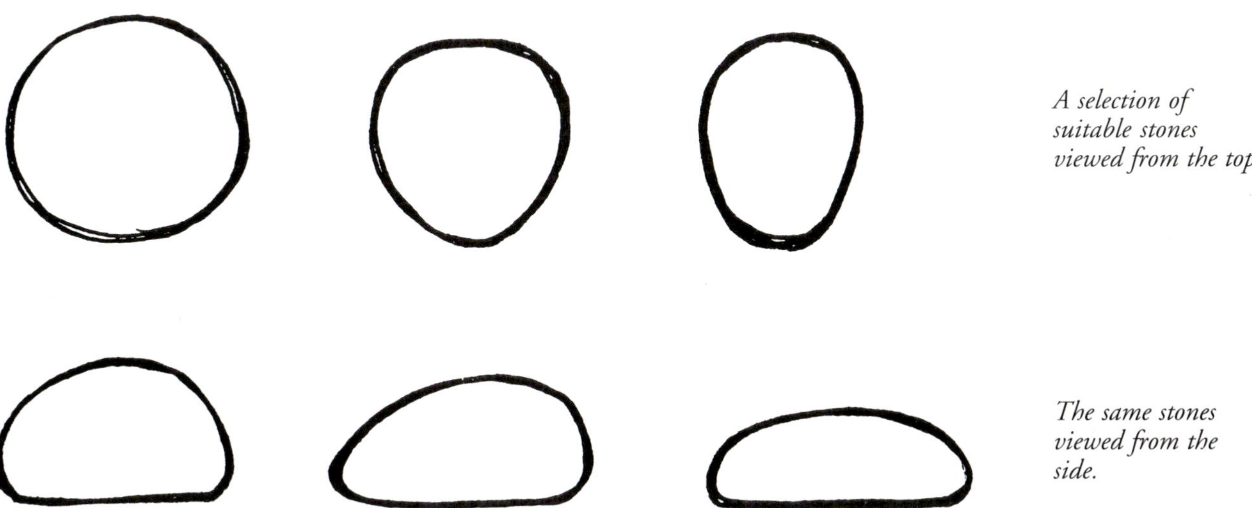

A selection of suitable stones viewed from the top.

The same stones viewed from the side.

Ladybird stones can be round, oval or tear-shaped.

1 Layout

When you have found a promising stone, clean it then let it dry. Sketch the wings on freehand or, if you prefer, use the template method shown here to lay out the wings.

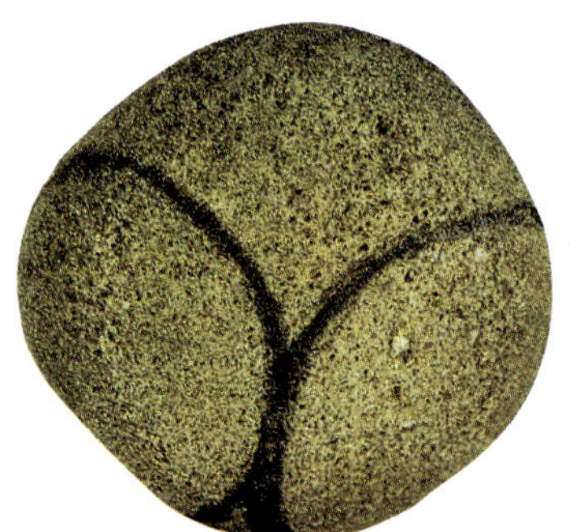

Wing pattern.

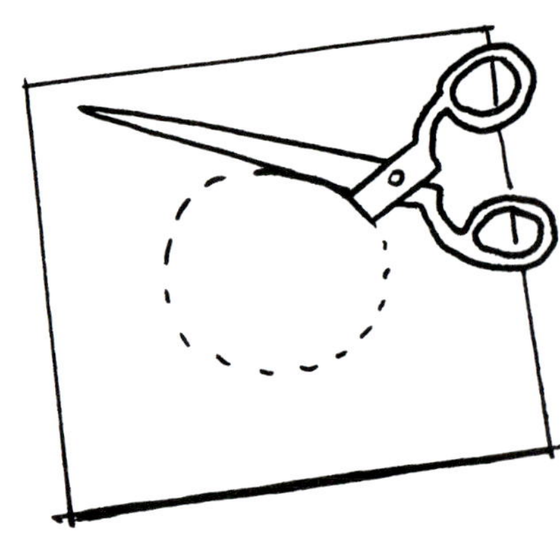

A. Lay your stone on a piece of paper and carefully trace all the way around the edge with a pencil.

B. Cut out the shape you just traced.

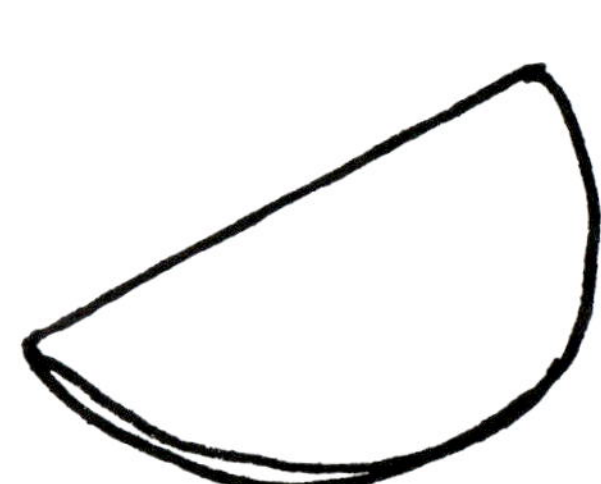

C. Fold the shape in half. The curved side will serve as the template for the ladybird's wings.

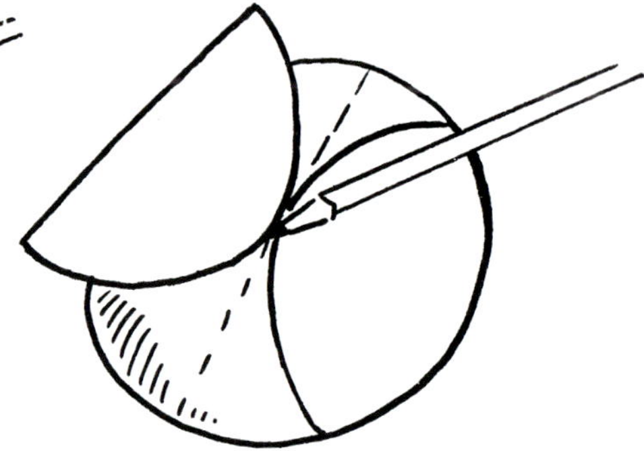

D. Draw a line down the exact centre of your stone using a pencil and ruler or other straight edge.

E. Place the curved edge of the template so it covers half of the stone. Now carefully trace around this curved edge. Flip the pattern over and reposition to make a matching curved line on the opposite side. Round out the wing shapes into ovals.

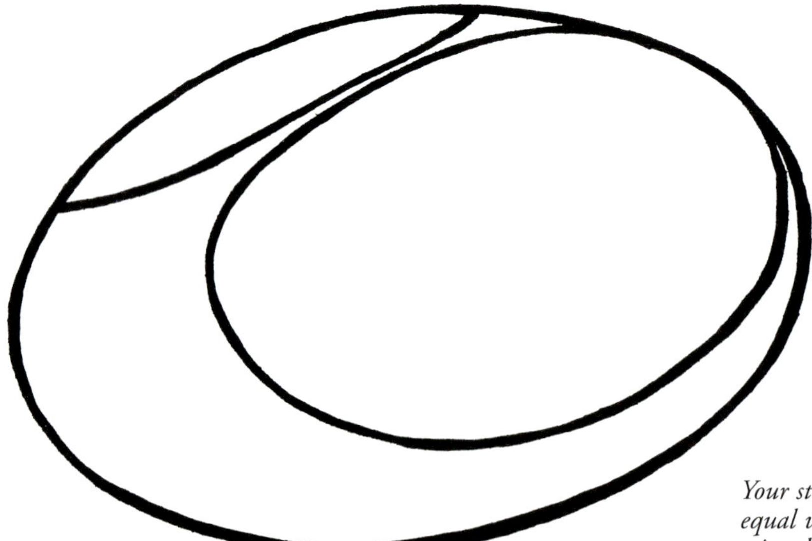

Your stone should be divided into three sections: two equal wings, a slightly smaller head area, and a small triangle at the tail end where the wings curve in opposite directions. If your first attempt is not satisfactory, simply scrub away the pencil marks and try again.

2 Painting the Black Areas

Pour a small amount of black acrylic paint into your palette. Add water if necessary, so that the paint is thin enough to apply easily, but still retains enough body for solid coverage. If your paint is runny or if the stone shows through when dry, your paint is too thin and may require a second coat. If, on the other hand, your brush drags dryly over the stone and coverage is rough and broken, try adding a little more water to the paint.

Use black to cover every part of the stone except the oval wings and the bottom of the stone. You can use a larger brush for most areas, but switch to your smallest brush to paint the line where the two wings come together on top. This line should not be more than 3mm (¹/₈in) wide. Allow the black paint to dry thoroughly before you go on to the next step.

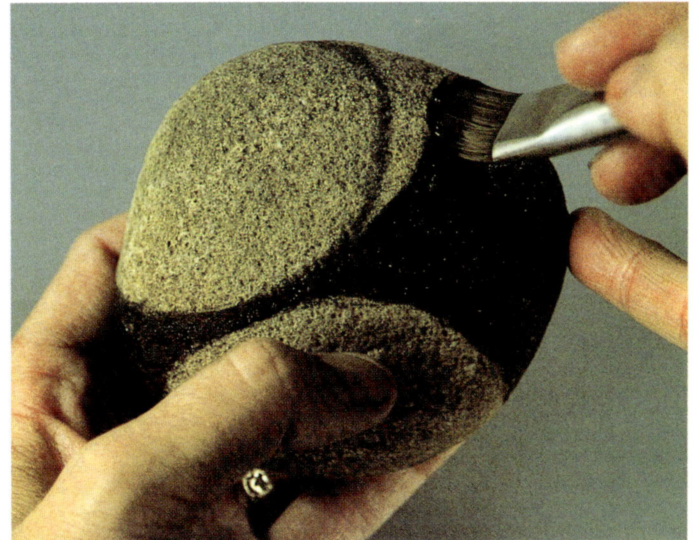

Cover every part of the stone except the wings and the base.

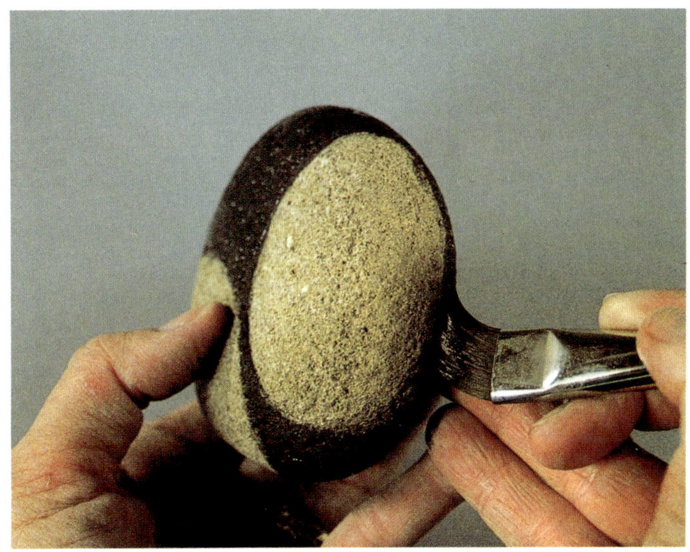

Turn your stone to paint around the wings.

3 Adding Wing Colour

Paint the wings red, keeping your strokes steady. Turn your stone around as you paint, to ensure that the wings are coloured in all the way around. If you need more than one coat, let the paint dry between applications. If you accidentally paint over the black undercoat at any point, do not panic. Simply allow the area to dry, then go over it with a little more black paint to repair the line.

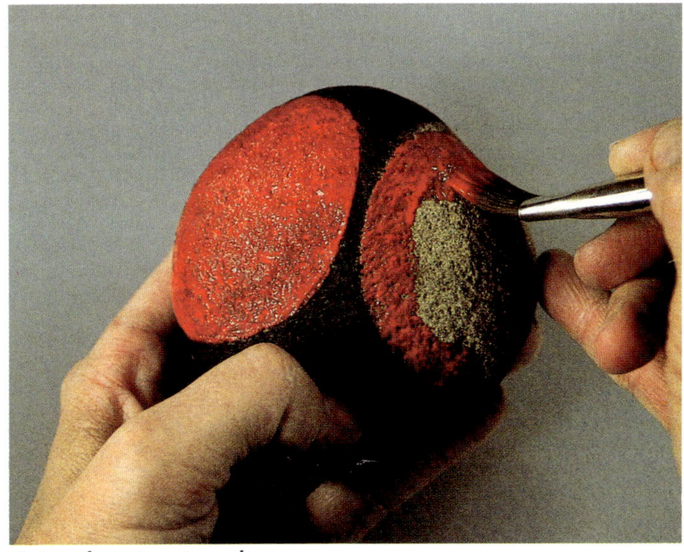

Paint the wings in red.

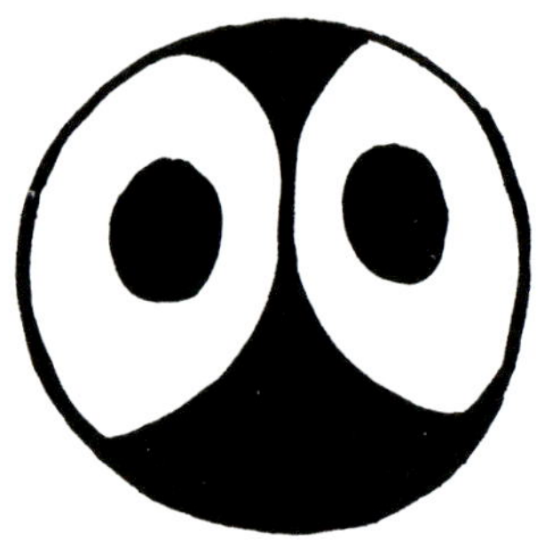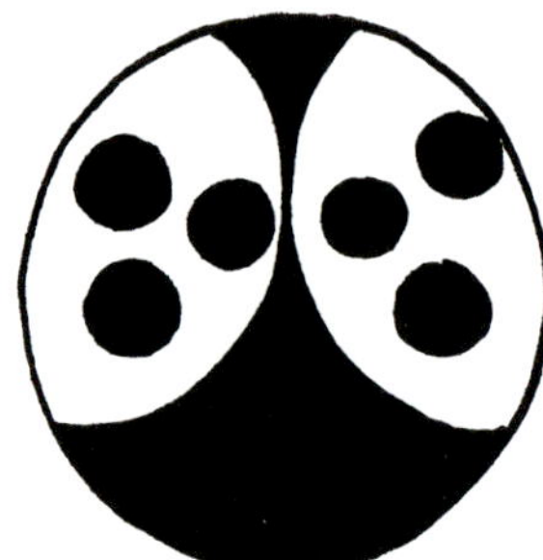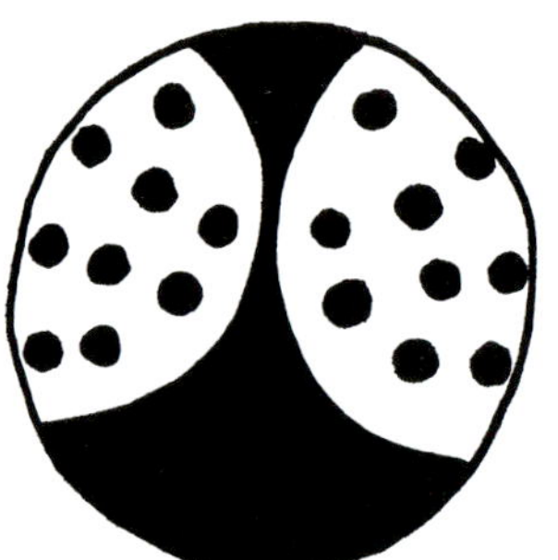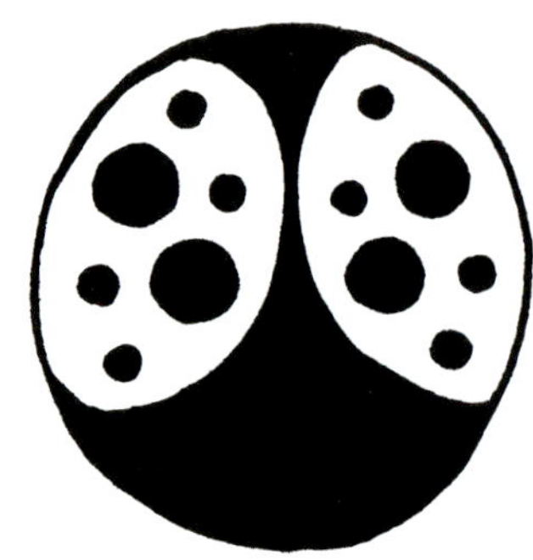

Suggested spot designs.

4 Painting the Spots

The number of decorative spots you paint and where they go is up to you. You may only want a couple of large spots on each side, or you may decide to scatter smaller ones about. However many you choose to paint, be sure to space them uniformly so they do not touch or overlap. Both wings should match. Use a pencil to sketch spots on the dried wing area. Remember that sketch marks can be painted over at any point and redone until you are satisfied.

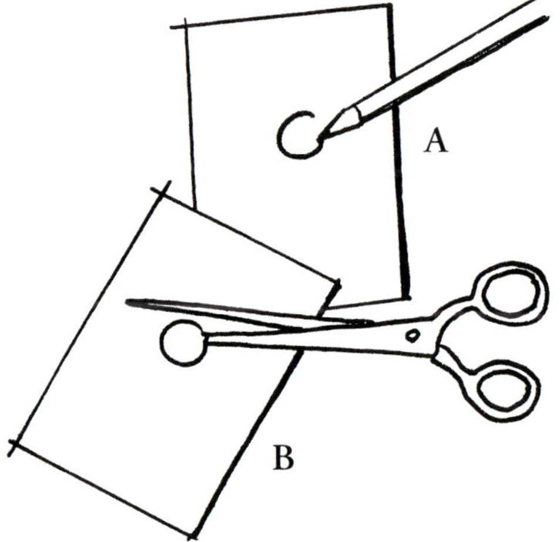

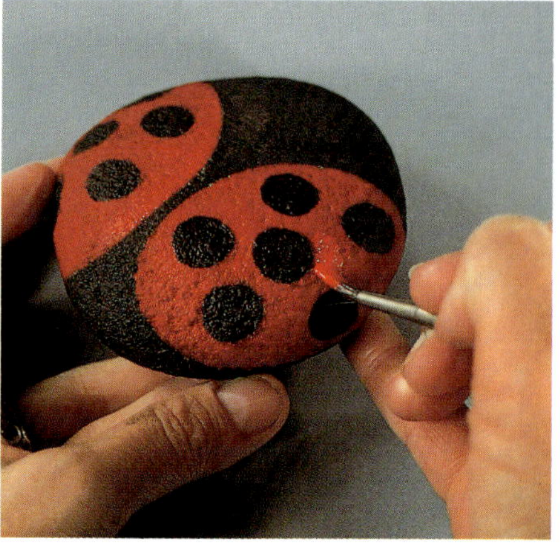

Go around the spots to smooth the edges.

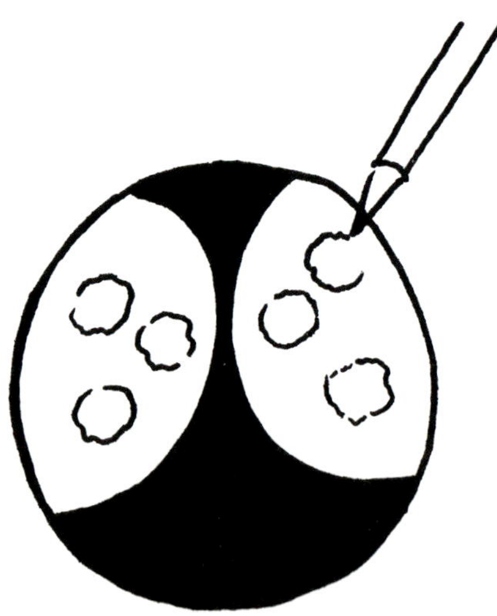

You can sketch the spots on freehand with a pencil.

If you do not feel you can paint a round spot freehand or if you want all the spots exactly the same size, try making a stencil. (A) Trace a circle on to a piece of card. (B) Cut out the centre. (C) Line the hole up over one of the spots you sketched on to your stone. Press firmly around the edges of the stencil to hold it in place and use a medium-sized brush to dab on just enough black paint to fill in the circle. Carefully lift the card straight up to avoid smearing. Allow each spot to dry before going on to the next. To speed things up, switch to the other wing and work on that while waiting.

After you have completed your pattern of spots and let them dry, you may need to go around some of them with the wing colour and a small brush to smooth rough edges.

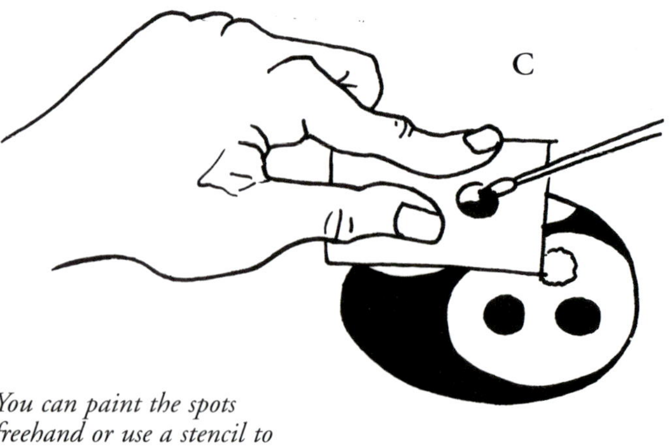

You can paint the spots freehand or use a stencil to create perfect circles.

5 The Face

Your ladybird's personality will be determined by the expression it wears. I prefer a happy look, but there are many other choices.

Whether you use one of my expression designs or make up your own, take extra care when painting your ladybird's features. Use a small brush and be sure the paint is thick enough to show up against the black background of the face. You may have to go over the features more than once to make them stand out clearly. If you are not happy with your first attempt, you can always paint out what you do not like and try again.

To protect your ladybird and make the colours look brighter, you may wish to seal the surface – use an oil-based or acrylic varnish to do this.

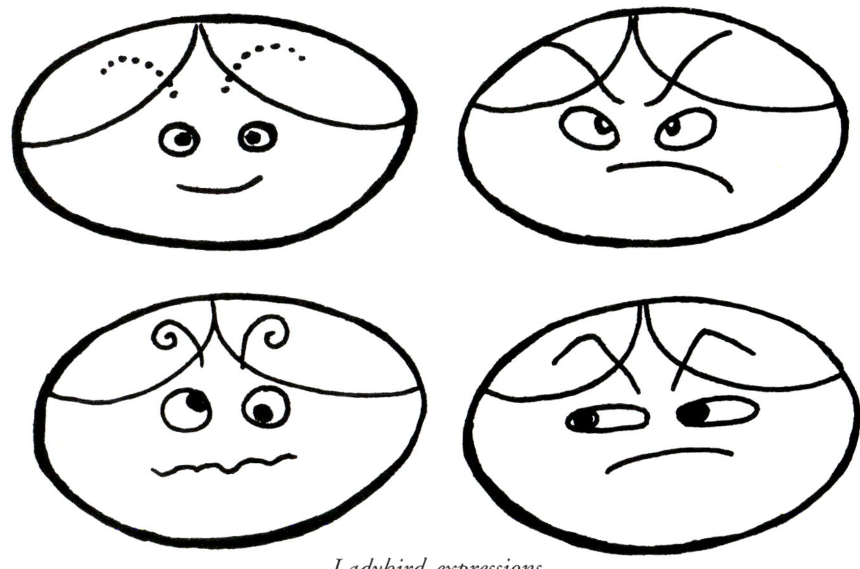

Ladybird expressions.

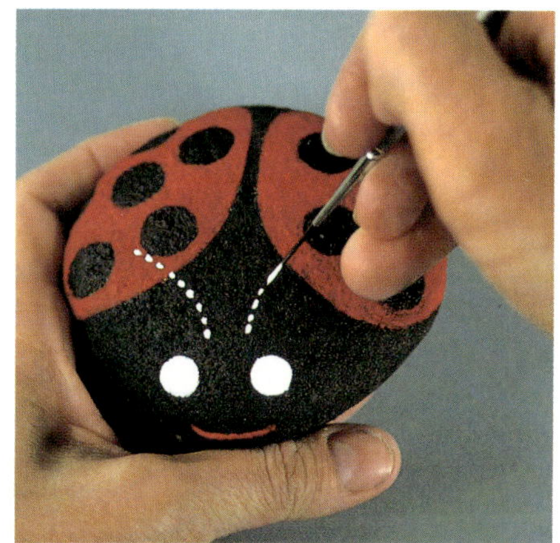

Use thick white paint for the eyeballs.

Add antennae using broken lines of paint.

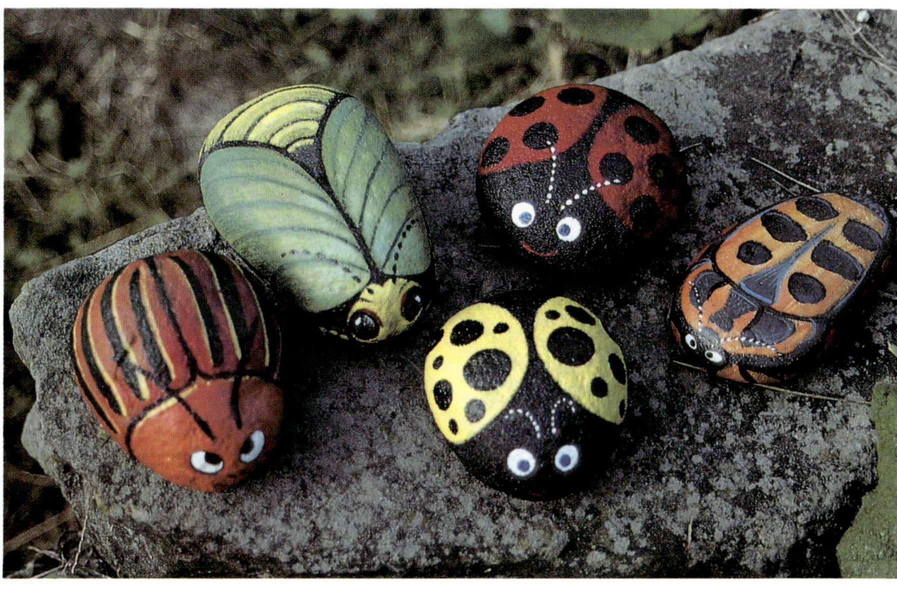

After you have painted a ladybird or two, you may feel like getting more creative. Ladybirds come in an amazing array of shapes and colours. Red, yellow, orange and green are all good choices; if you use lighter colours, you may need several coats of paint for complete coverage. Books are a great place to get ideas for other kinds of insects to paint. Alternatively, use your imagination to come up with your own make-believe insects.

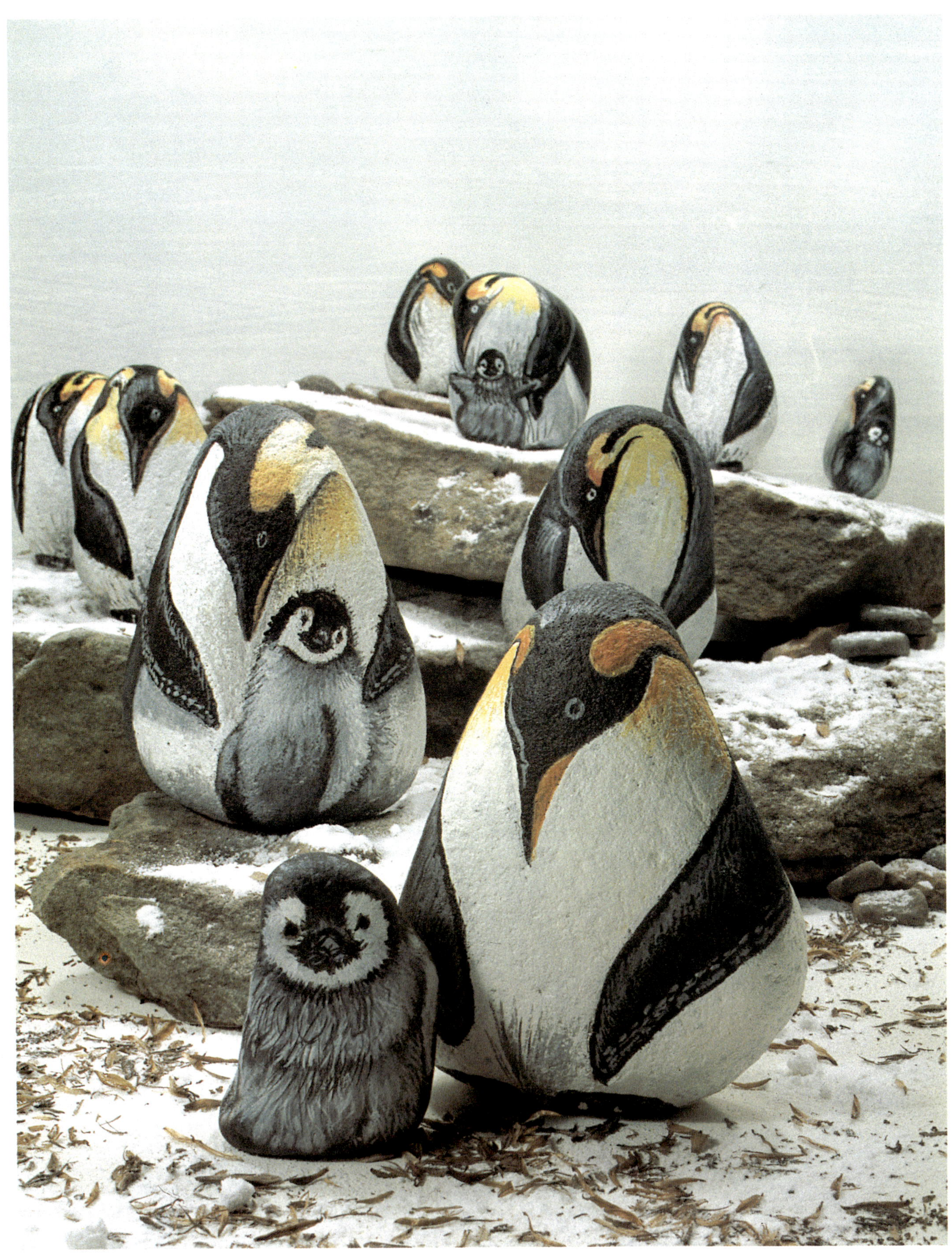

PENGUIN

Perky penguins make a unique subject for stone painting, and their design is so simple that even novice artists will enjoy creating them. For this project choose stones that 'sit up' – in shapes ranging from tall and narrow to plump and squat, or even small, gently rounded pebbles. The stone you select should be taller than it is wide, and while it can be somewhat asymmetrical, it should stand sturdily on its base.

Penguins can be just about any size, from larger-than-life to smaller than your little finger. For this project, I found a stone with two attractive features: it was fairly symmetrical and neatly pear-shaped. Unfortunately, the base was a bit thin, making it prone to tipping. To correct this, I added a line of wood filler to one side of the base. I moulded this firmly into place before smoothing the surface.

You Will Need

- acrylic paints: white, black, yellow, red and orange (optional)
- pencil
- assorted brushes
- wood filler for the base (optional)
- oil-based or acrylic clear varnish

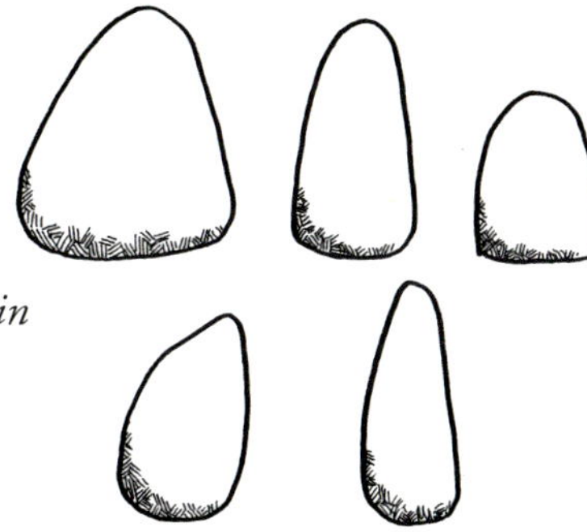

Here are some outlines of penguin stone shapes to look for.

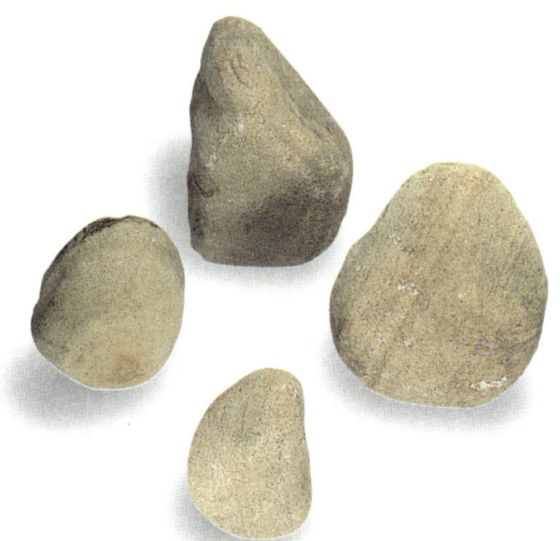

Any of these stones are suitable for a penguin.

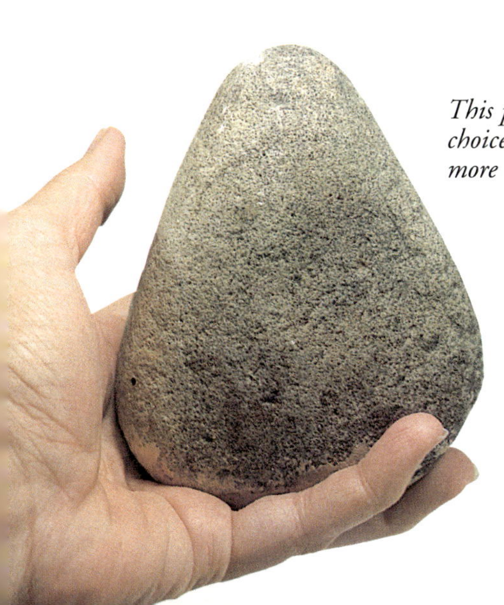

This pear-shaped stone is a good choice. Smaller stones may prove more challenging.

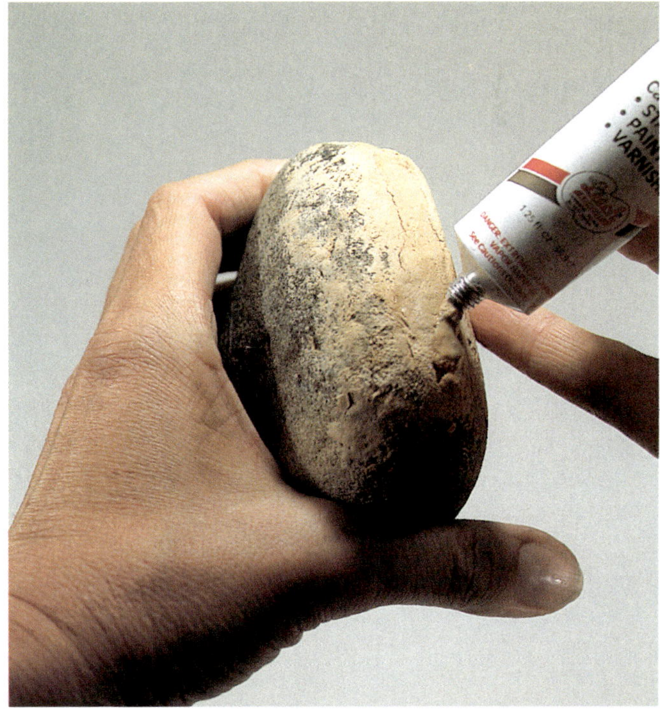

The addition of some wood filler corrects a wobbly base.

1 Layout

Clean your stone then allow it to dry. You are now ready to begin your layout. Placement of the head will depend on how much your stone tapers, so select the design that most closely fits your particular stone shape. Since my stone has a pointed top, the head can be set fairly high. For more rounded, less pointed stones, create a head that droops down as if resting against the bird's chest.

The shape of the head is a simple oval with a long narrow beak. Curve the flipper-shaped wings as shown. On the rear side, the only marking is a large black diamond shape, with the top flowing up to serve as an extension of the neck, while the bottom tapers neatly to a pointed tail. Before continuing to the next stage, look at your layout again to see how it compares to my examples at the top of the page opposite.

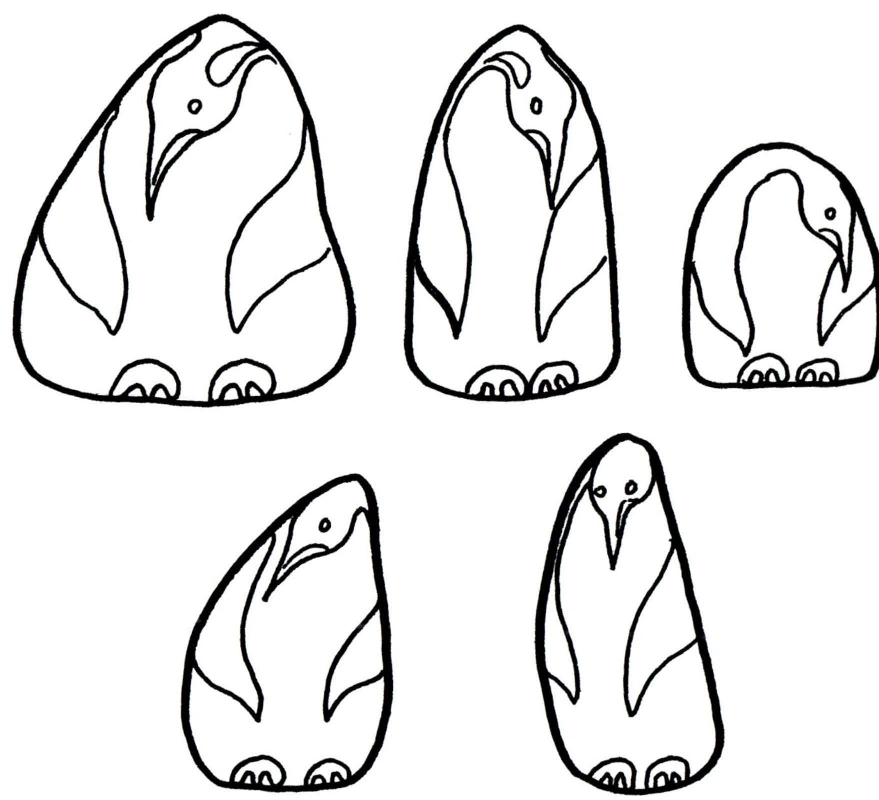

These sketches show how to adapt penguin features to different stone shapes.

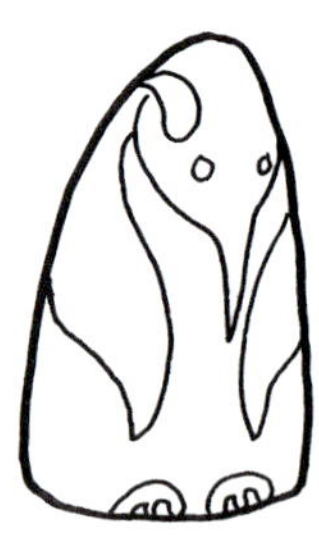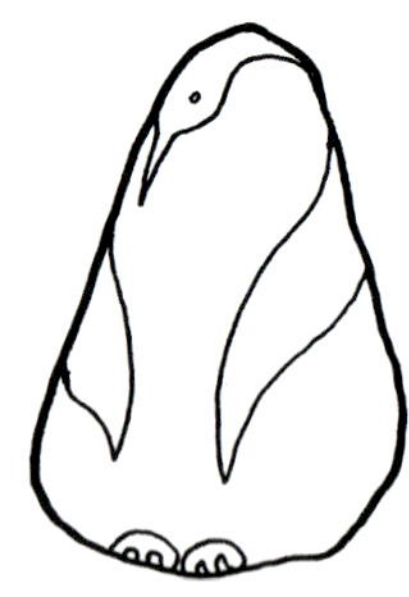

Two common mistakes are making the head too large (left), or making it too small (right).

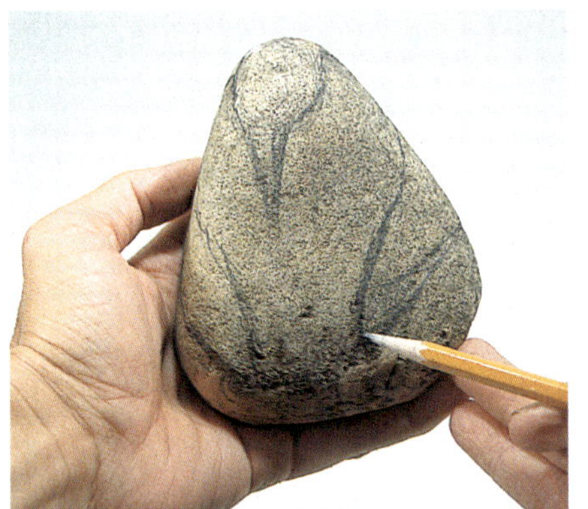

Sketch in the head first, then move on to the wings, curving them in from either side.

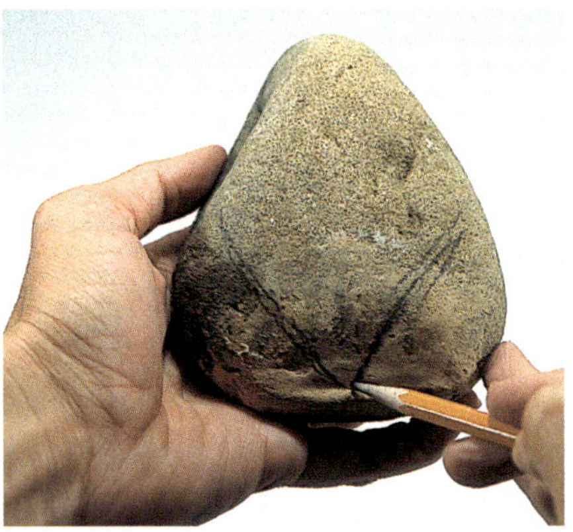

Think of the back as a diamond, with the top end merging into the neck and the other end forming a pointed tail.

2 Base Coat

When you have completed the basic layout, you can base coat the stone. Only two colours are needed for this: black and white. Begin with white and a medium-sized brush. Cover the chest and the areas under the wings and around the head and beak. On the rear side, paint only the area showing below the diamond shape and up under the rear edges of the wings. Allow your white paint to dry, then change to black paint and use the same size brush to fill in all remaining areas, being careful to keep outside edges smooth. Use a small brush for the beak.

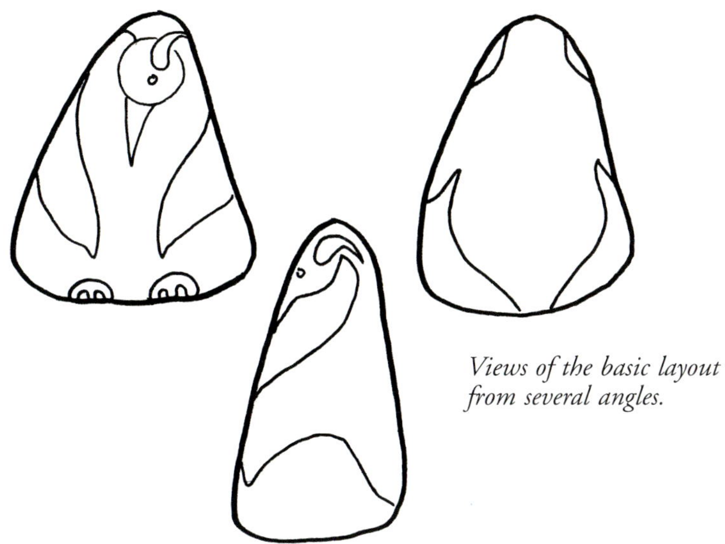

Views of the basic layout from several angles.

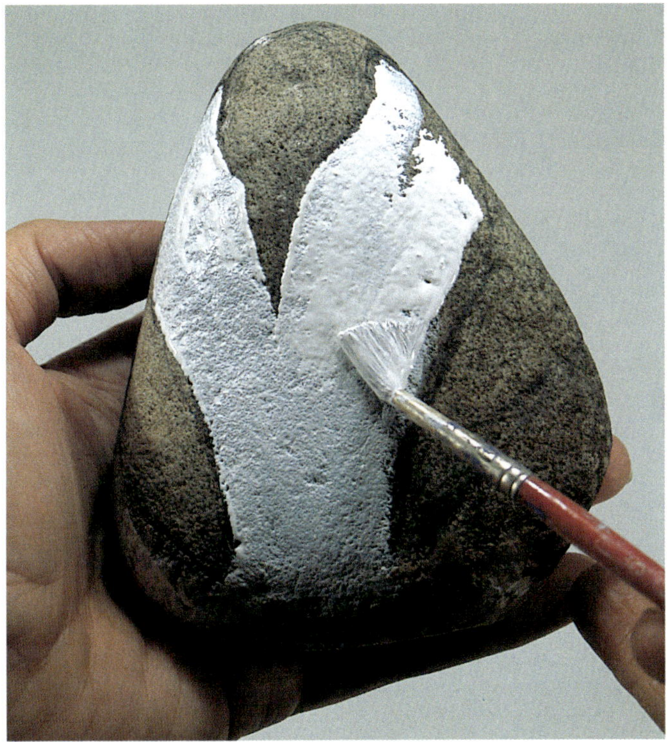

Paint in the white areas of the front and sides. If your stone is dark, it may require more than one coat.

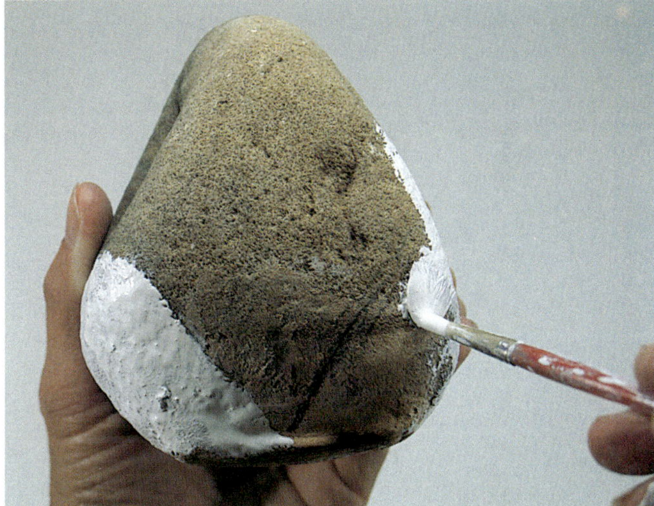

This rear view shows how simple the design is.

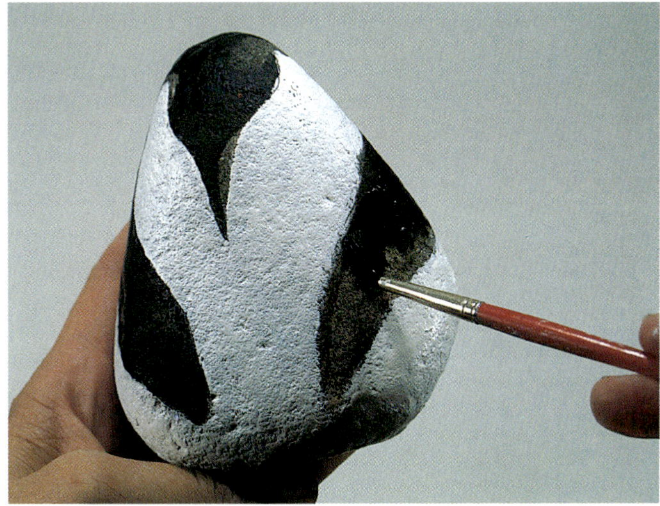

Allow your white paint to dry before you change to black.

3 Feet and Beak

Create black feet that peep out from the base of your penguin. Shape them like rounded M's, but with an extra peak. Next, use a liner brush and a mixture of red and yellow, or a premixed orange, to make a paisley-shaped marking either side of the penguin's head, extending the tapered end back along the contour of the neck. With the same orange, add a narrow curve of colour to the bottom edge of the beak. I have turned my penguin's head slightly to one side, but if yours is looking straight on, make the orange beak markings thinner and ensure that they show on both sides.

Clean your brush then add an outline of bright yellow around the orange head markings to make them stand out. Moisten your brush tip to dilute the yellow paint slightly, then add a little colour to the white area just below the curve of the head. Use your finger to gently smudge and soften this colour so it blends into the surrounding area of the upper chest.

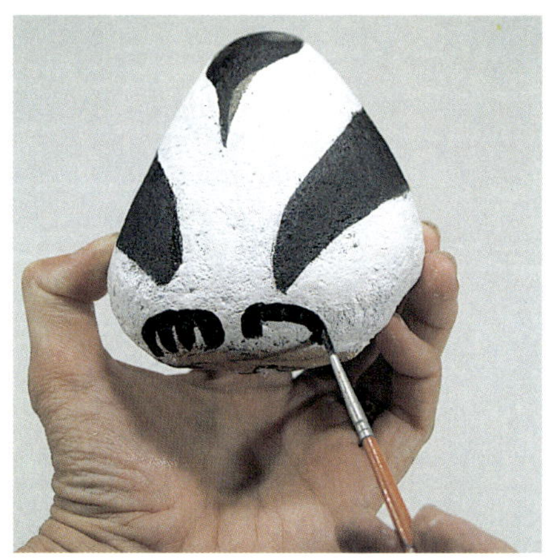

These stylized feet may barely show, but they are a nice touch.

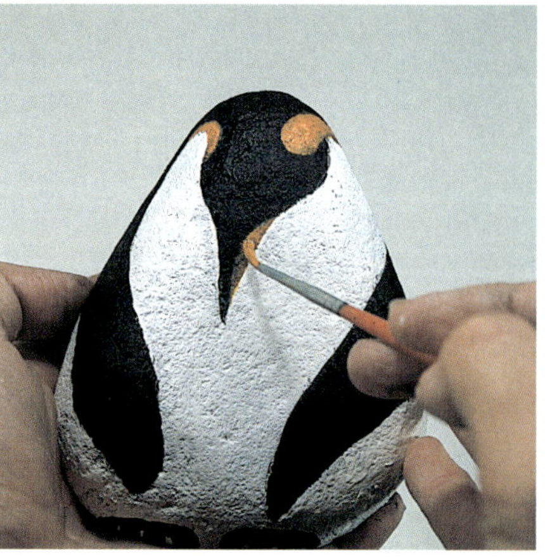

Orange markings add an important visual element. Beak markings are nothing more than a thin crescent of colour. Use a small round brush or the tip of a liner brush for more control .

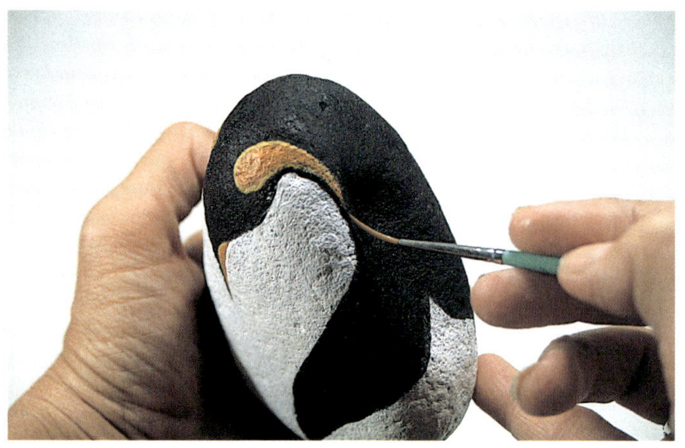

A thin yellow outline around the orange head marking increases the impact.

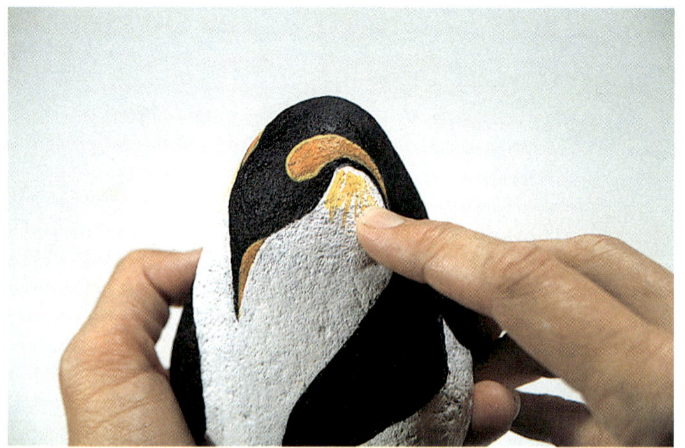

Add yellow paint to the area just below the neck and blend it downward with your finger, softening it to a sunny blush.

4 Brushwork

The remaining brushwork will give your penguin added realism and texture. Use a liner brush and mix equal parts of black and white paint to get a medium grey shade. Beginning at the back of your penguin's head, make a row of very delicate, short lines that taper back and away from the face. Add a second and third overlapping row of strokes, fanning them out and lengthening your strokes down into the upper back area before stopping. To highlight the wings, angle the same kinds of tiny strokes down along the upper and lower edges of the wings. Finish the back by adding more of the same fine lines along the outside edges.

Indicate the eye (or eyes) with a small circle of grey placed midway between the orange head marking and the orange beak marking.

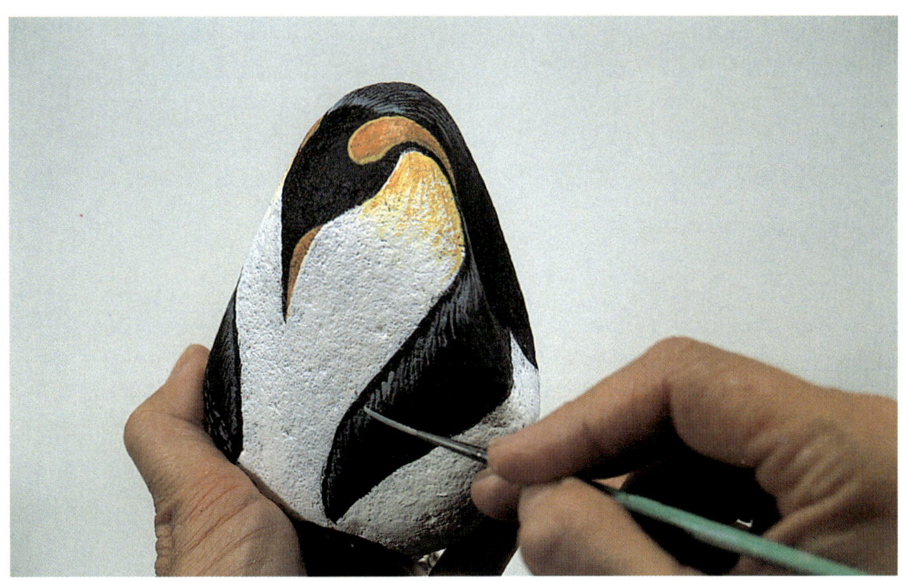

Small highlighting strokes help define your penguin's contours, while suggesting the texture of feathers. More delicate lines along the flipper-shaped wings give them extra substance.

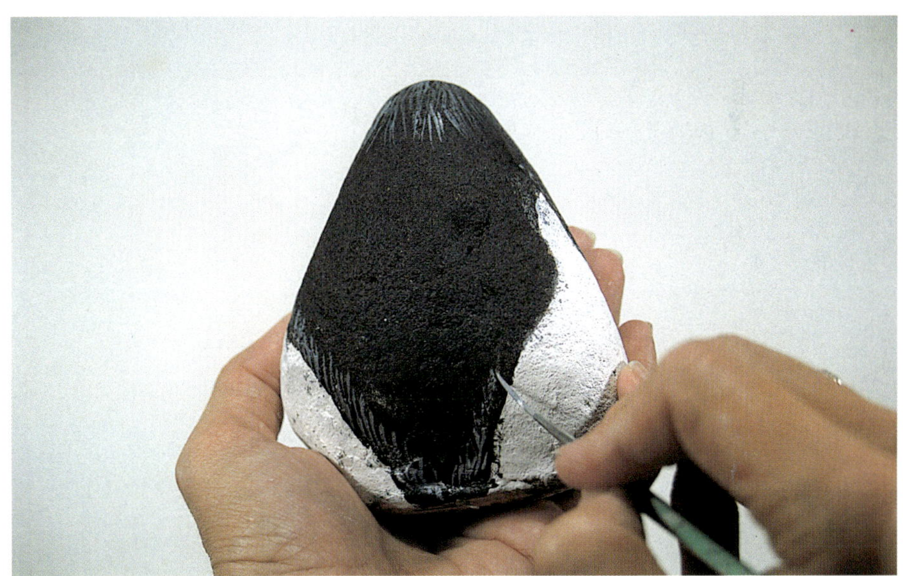

Detail the back of the wings with more tiny strokes.

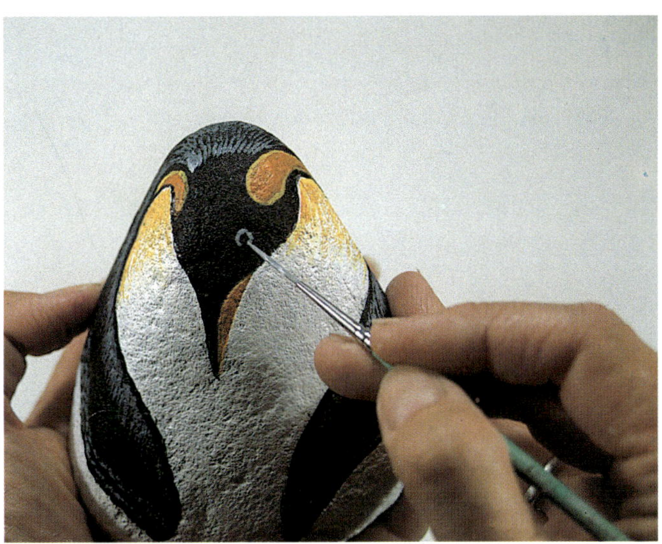

Define the eyes with simple grey circles. Because my penguin's head is turned to the side, only one eye shows.

5 Finishing Touches

Use more of the medium grey paint to indicate shading in the centre of the body, just above the feet. This will help emphasize the shape of the legs on either side. Use feathery strokes in varied lengths, extending the longest ones up beyond the level of the wing tips. Finally, with a relatively dry brush (a brush with very little paint) add one or two long, sketchy lines just inside and following along the contour of the head to give it shape. Now look at your penguin from every angle to make sure you have defined and detailed wherever needed. A coat of oil-based or acrylic varnish will bring out the richness of your colours and protect the finish.

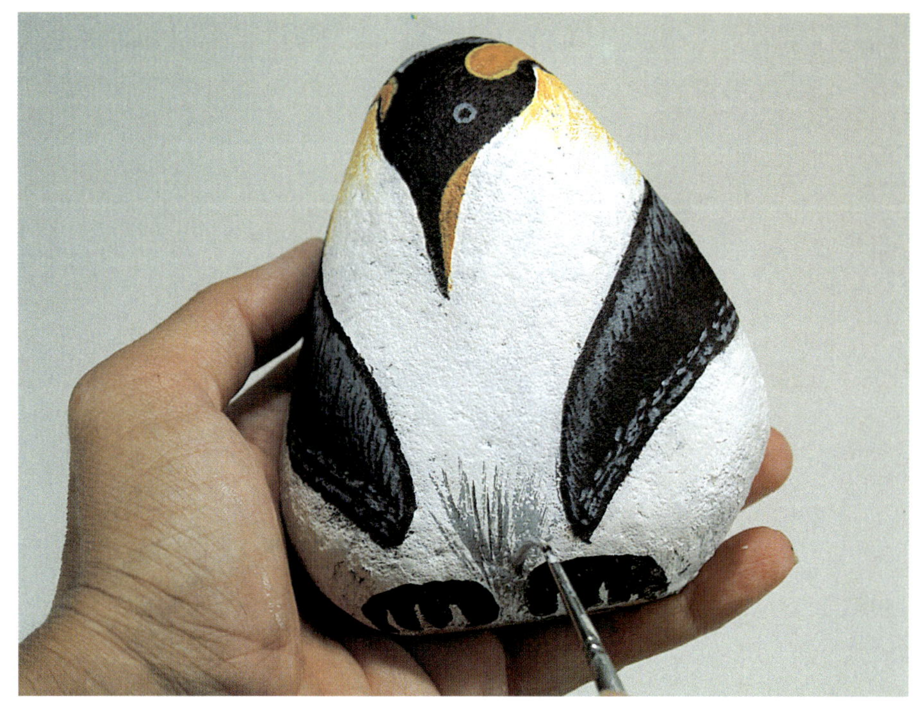

Feathery shadows between the legs create the illusion of contour.

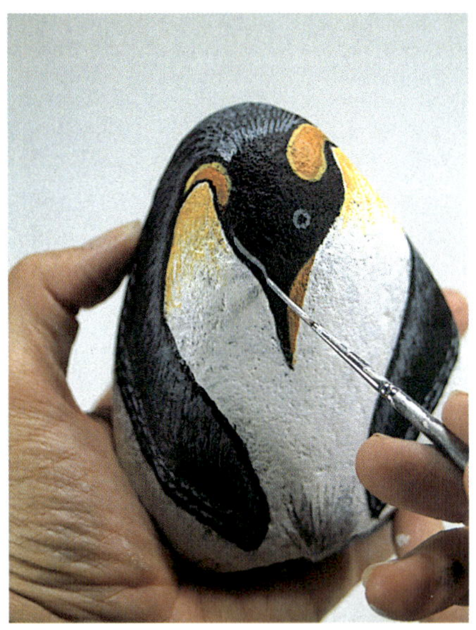

A highlighting line following the shape of the head makes it appear rounder.

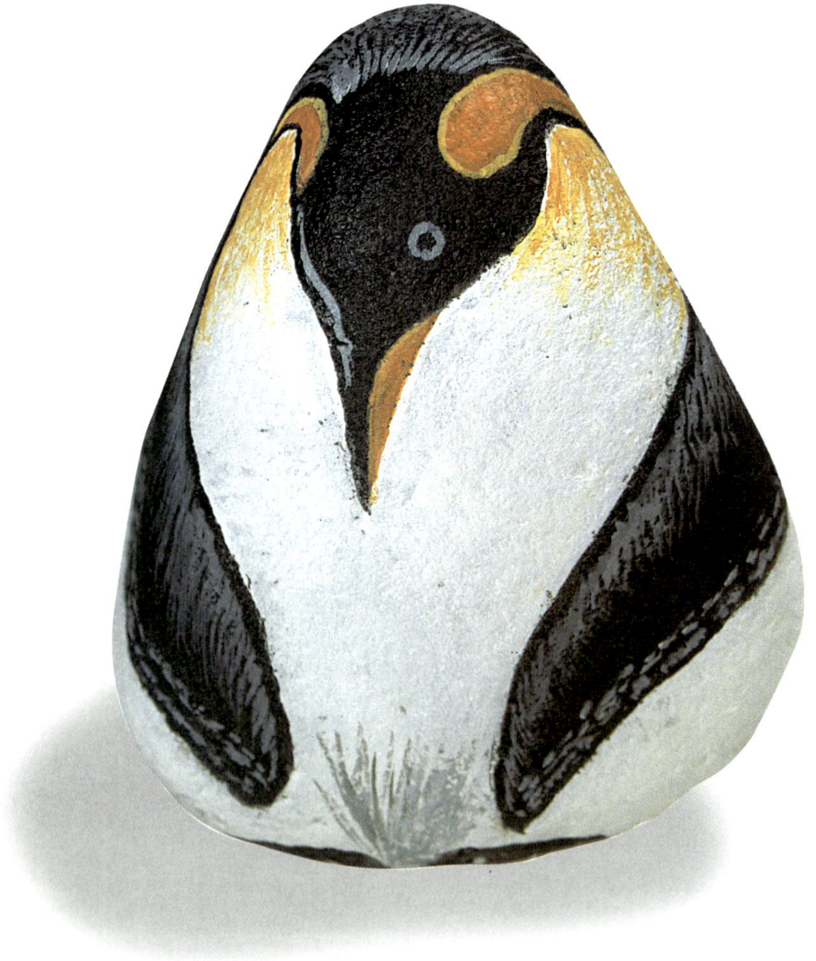

The finished penguin.

You may want to try creating a parent
and chick combination, which makes a
delightful gift or eye-catching conversation
piece. Another fun idea is to create a
snow-covered scene for your penguin,
using white stones to form a base.

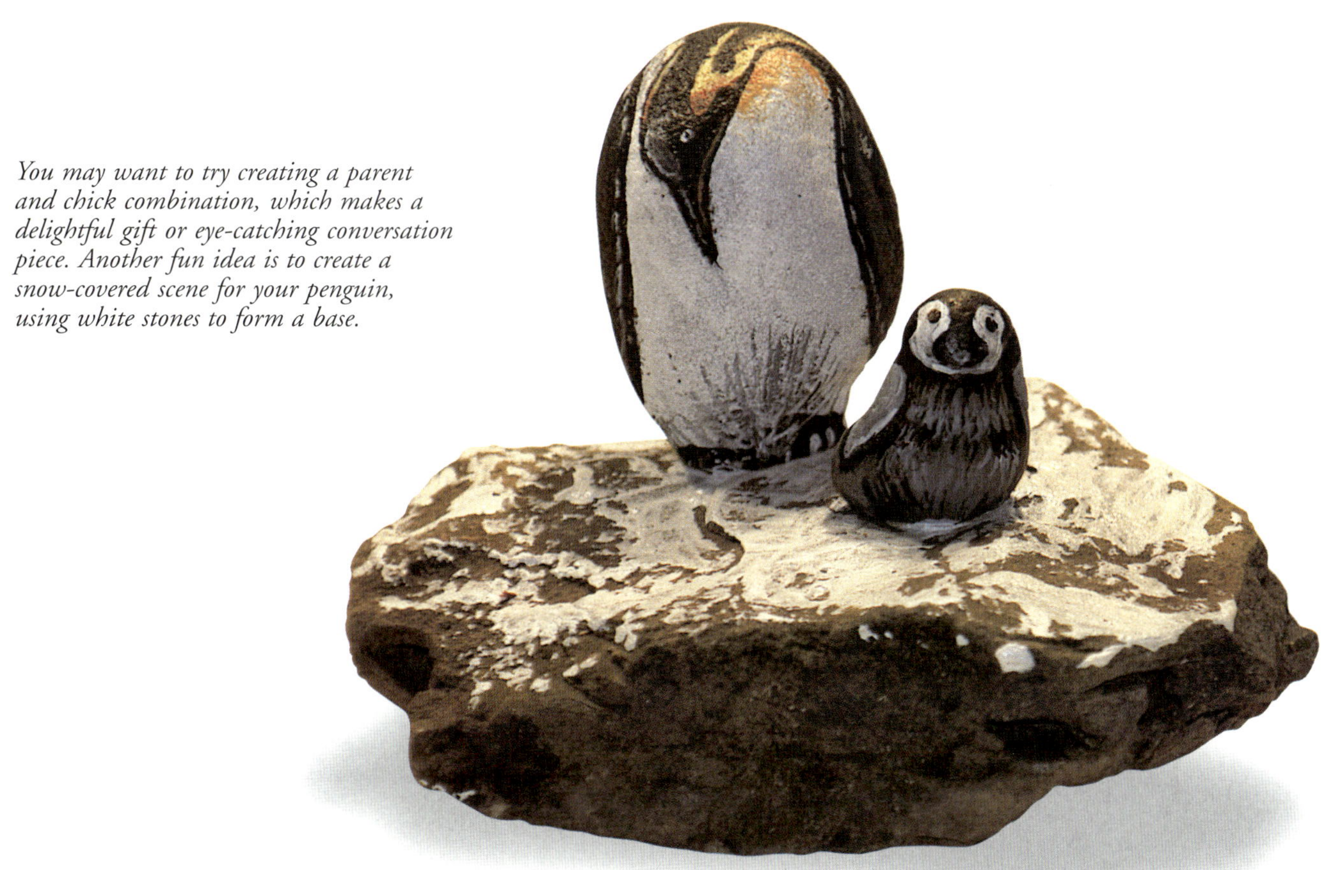

Stone penguins look particularly
attractive when arranged in
small groups. This flock
illustrates just some of the
possible poses and species of
penguin.

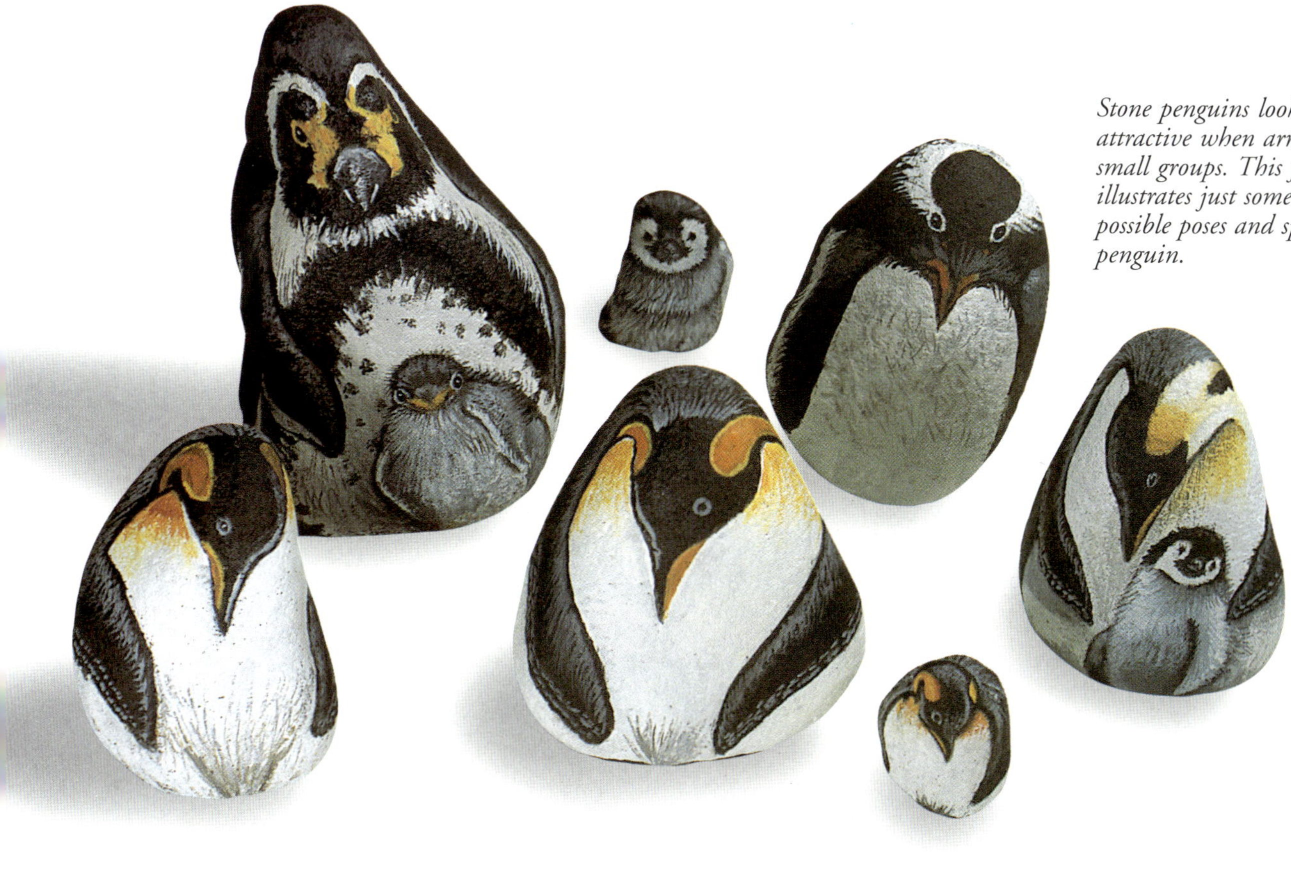

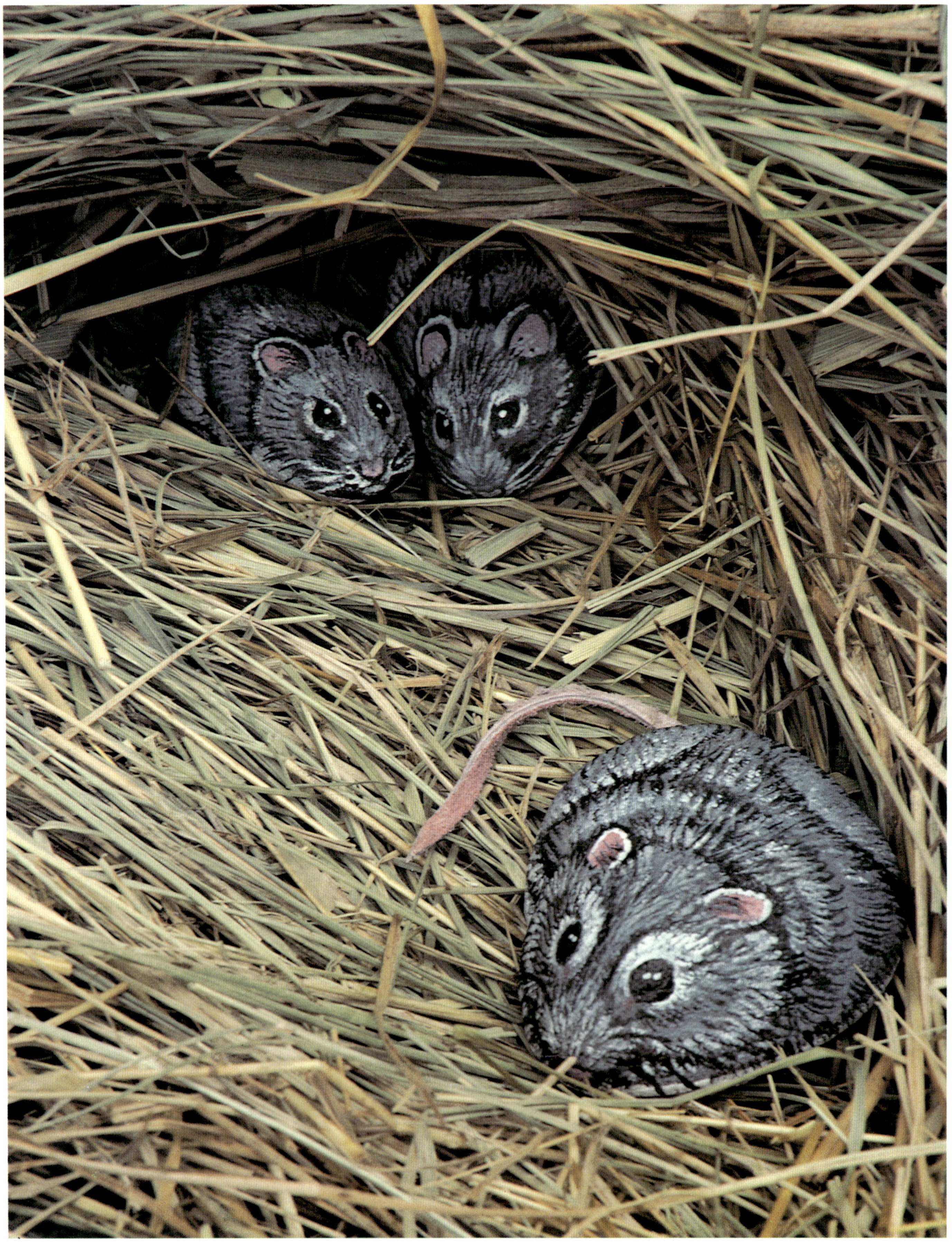

FIELD MOUSE

A furry grey field mouse with bright eyes and a pink tail makes a great subject for anyone new to stone painting. Stone mice can also be painted in white or subtle shades of brown.

Look for stones that are basically oval, either short and plump or more elongated. The best ones will also have one tapered or pointed end to serve as the nose. They can be around 10–13cm (4–5in) long (any bigger and they look more like rats), or much smaller if you want to make a baby mouse. Remember, though, that painting very small details on a very small stone can be quite difficult – I advise trying a larger size mouse first. For the tail, leather lacing is available at many craft stores and some shoe shops, or you can cut a tail from a thin strip of pink felt.

<table>
<tr><td>You Will Need</td></tr>
</table>

- acrylic paints: black, burnt sienna, white and red
- pencil
- assorted brushes
- 7–10cm (3–4in) of pink leather lacing or pink felt strip
- PVA glue or wood filler
- oil-based or acrylic clear varnish

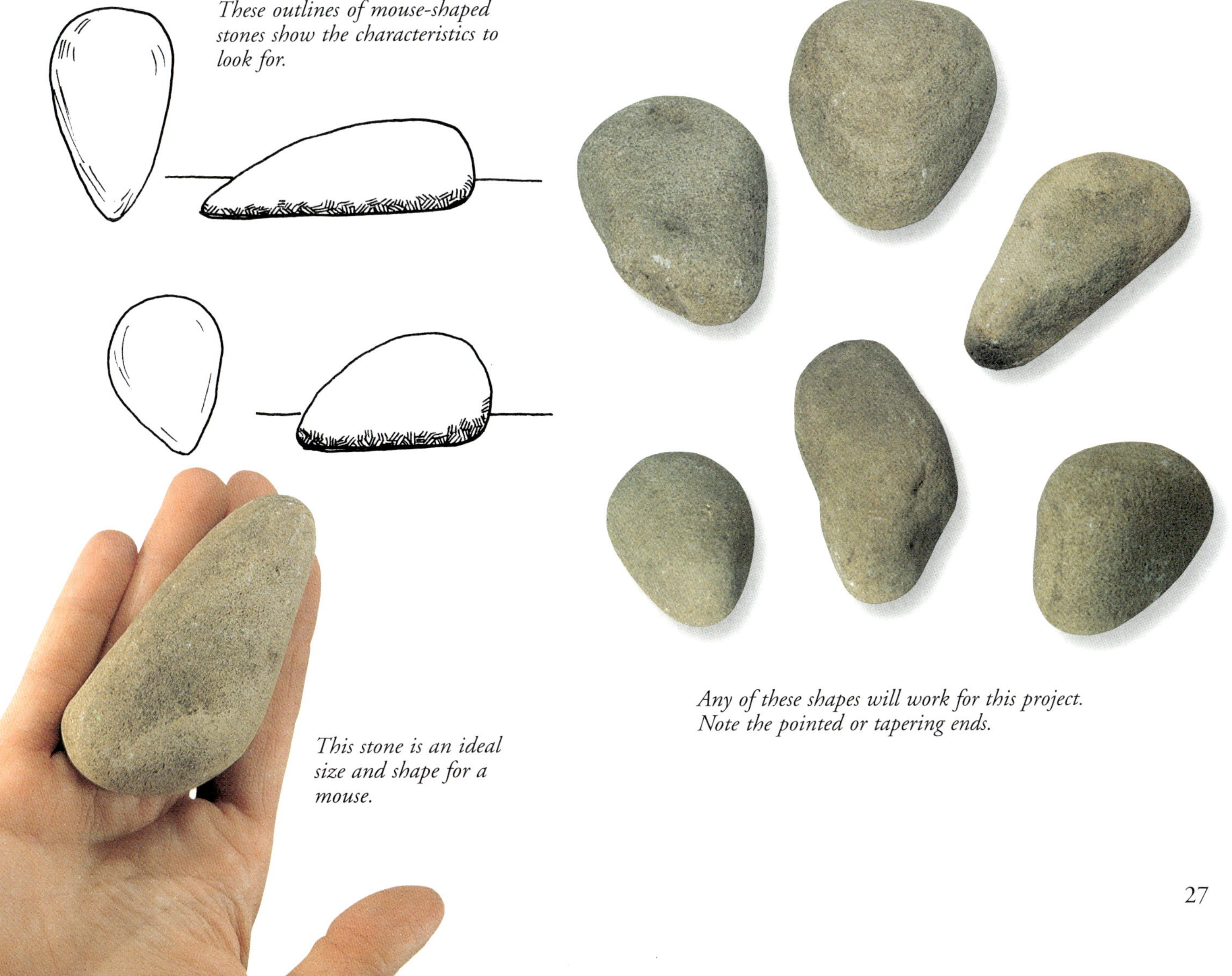

These outlines of mouse-shaped stones show the characteristics to look for.

This stone is an ideal size and shape for a mouse.

Any of these shapes will work for this project. Note the pointed or tapering ends.

1 Base Coat

Make sure the stone you have chosen is scrubbed clean before you begin painting. Mix together roughly equal parts of black and white paint to get a medium shade of grey. Use a large brush to quickly cover the top and sides of the stone, leaving a narrow strip around the bottom edge unpainted. Leave to dry, then use a clean brush and white paint to cover the entire bottom of the stone and the unpainted strip around the sides. Leave to dry.

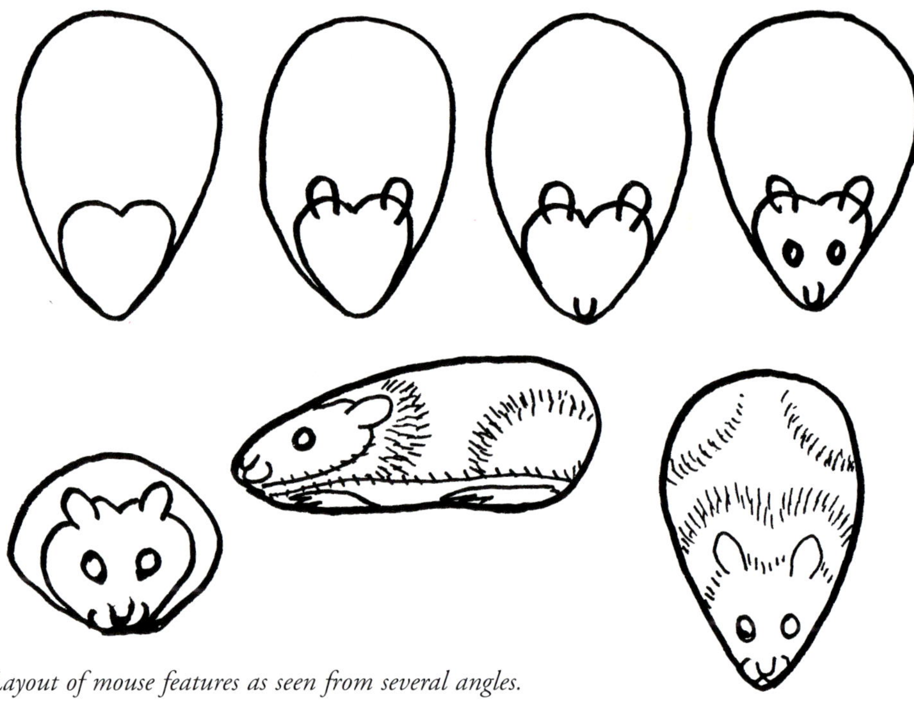

Layout of mouse features as seen from several angles.

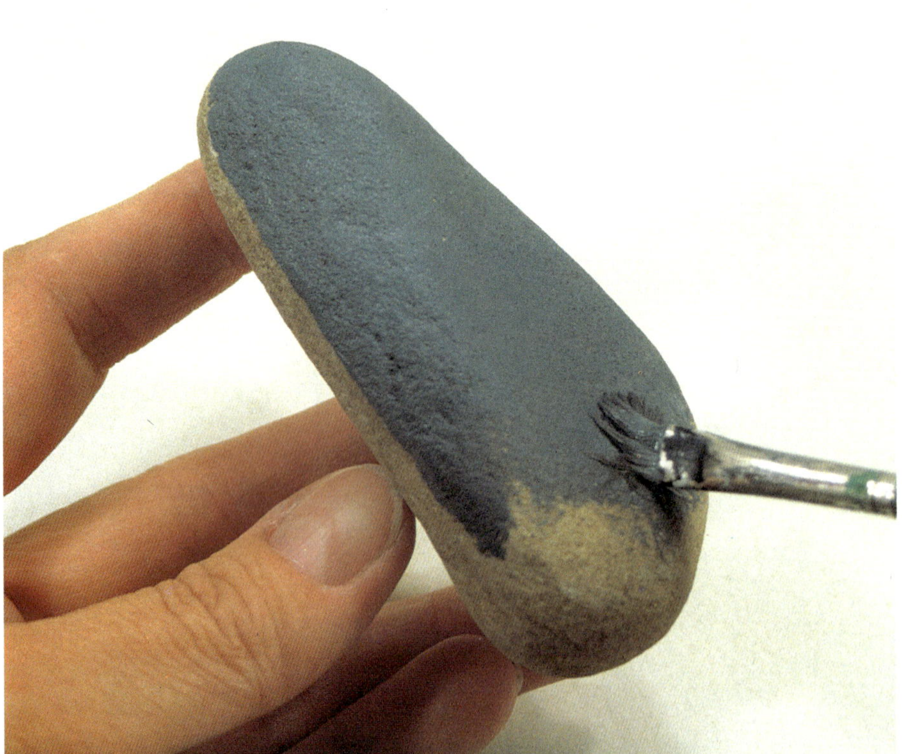

Paint the top and sides a solid grey. Leave an unpainted edge along the base.

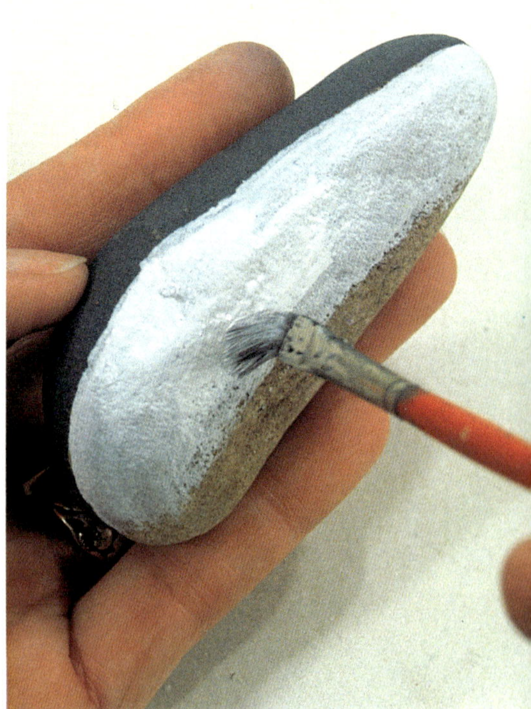

Paint the entire bottom and lower edge of the sides white.

2 Layout

Use a pencil to sketch in the features. Begin by outlining the head in an elongated heart shape. Place small round or oval ears along the top curves of the head. Add a small, U-shaped nose at the pointed tip of your heart shape. Two round eyes should be spaced at least one eye-width apart and situated midway between the nose and the ears. Indicate semicircle muzzle shapes on either side of the nose.

Next, turn your mouse over and sketch the long, narrow front and rear feet. Try to position the feet so that they are partially visible from the sides.

3 Fur

Use black paint and a liner or other small brush to outline the ears, eyes, nose and muzzle lines to make them stand out clearly. Go around the entire head with a series of tiny fur lines. Use more closely spaced, dense strokes to create the curves of shoulders and the round shapes of the haunches. Once these basic contours are in place, make more short, tapering strokes along the back and sides, overlapping and crisscrossing these delicate strokes randomly to simulate fur, as shown in the fur directional guide on the next page. Turn your stone as necessary to make it easier to apply the brushstrokes. Add even shorter, more delicate strokes to the forehead and up along the centre of the muzzle from just above the nose. Encircle the area below each eye with tiny black fur lines, too. While you have black on your brush, this is a good time to fill in the eye circles, giving your mouse its bright, beady-looking eyes.

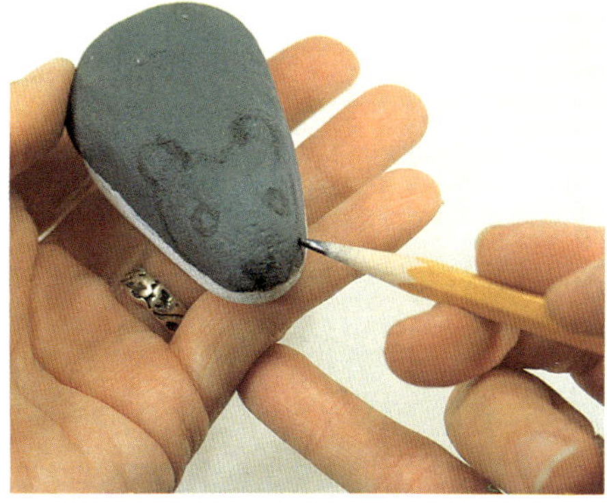

Sketch in the face. Set the eyes midway between the top of the head and the tip of the nose.

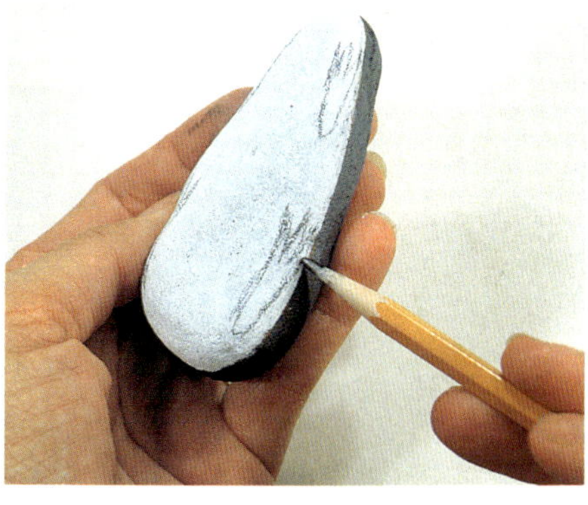

Place the front and rear feet so they show along the sides of the stone.

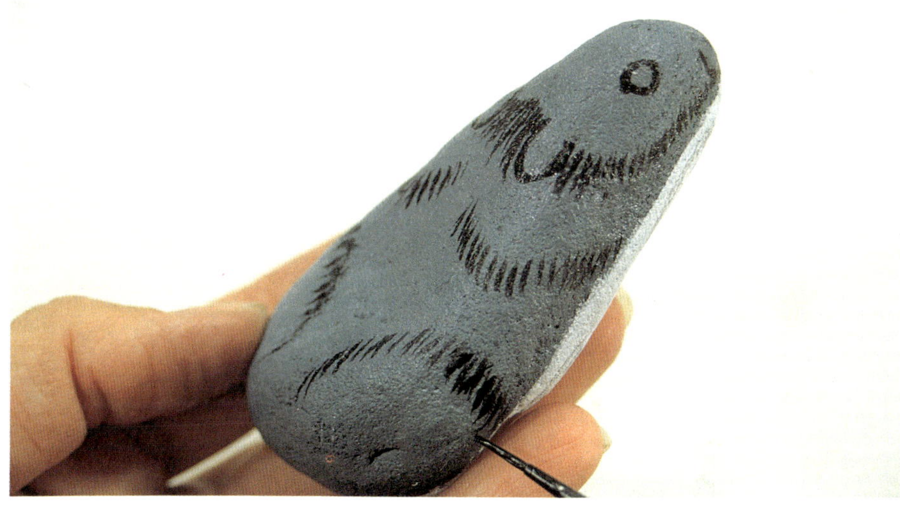

Carefully outline facial features with black paint. A series of short, tapering lines emphasize body contours while beginning to build up a fuzzy, furry texture.

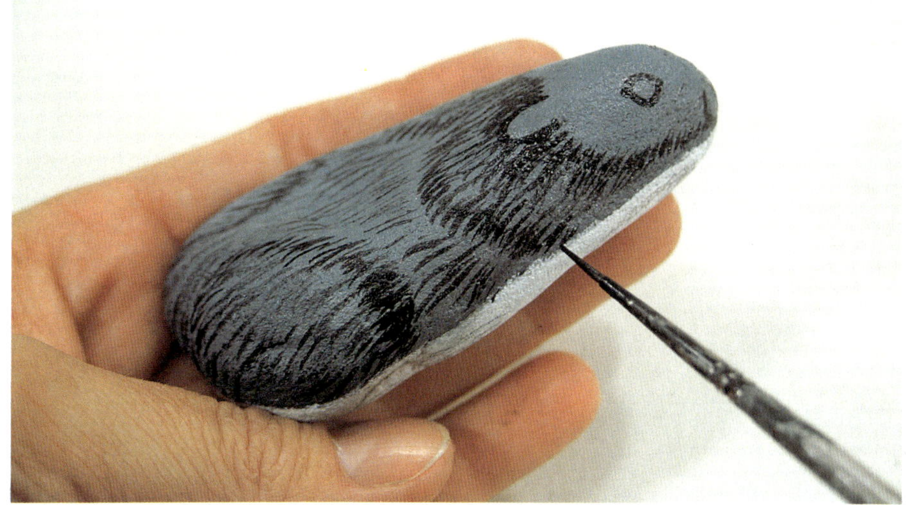

Vary the length and direction of your strokes as you add layers of detail — this will contribute to the realistic look of your mouse.

4 Pink Areas

Clean your brush and mix a small amount of red into a large amount of white paint to get a soft pink shade. Use pink to colour the sketched-in front and back feet. Also use pink to fill in the U-shaped nose and the centres of the ears.

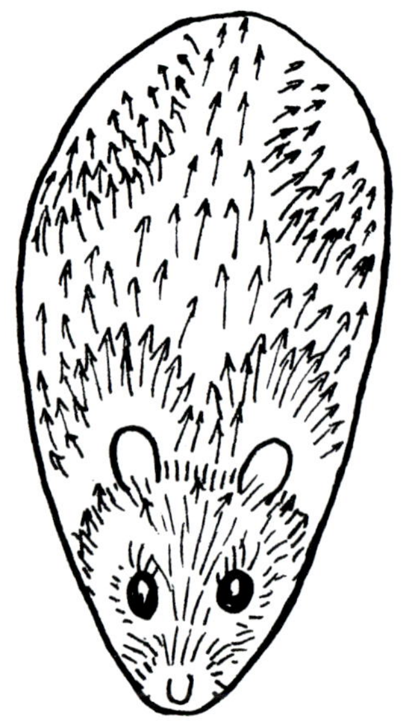

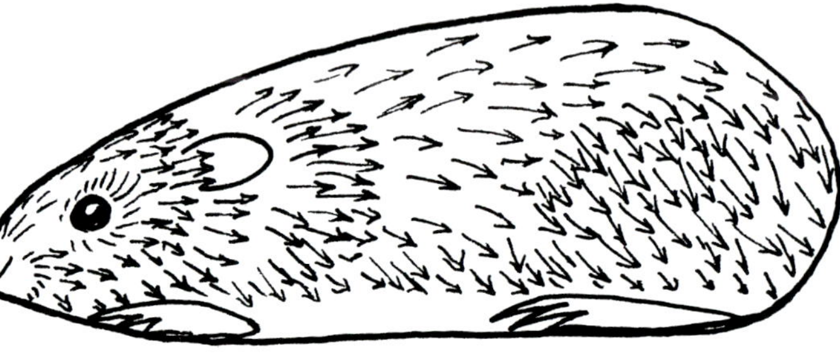

These sketches show the directions in which mouse fur naturally grows. Begin by detailing the face above the nose and work your way up, allowing the delicate fur lines to splay out as the head widens. Then scatter tiny fur lines into the area between the muzzle and eye.

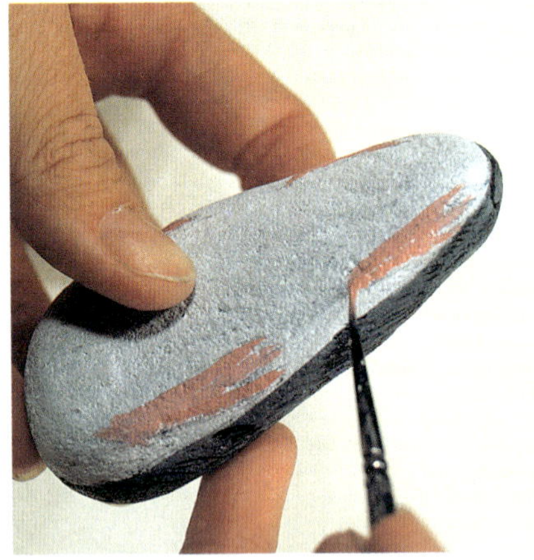

Paint the front and rear feet pink. Three or four narrow toes are all you need.

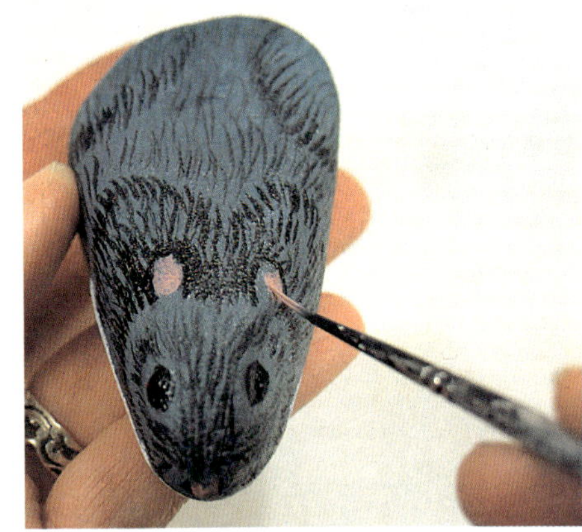

Fill in the U-shape of the nose and the centres of the ears.

This detail shows the eyelash strokes clearly – these are a finishing touch that help to frame the eyes.

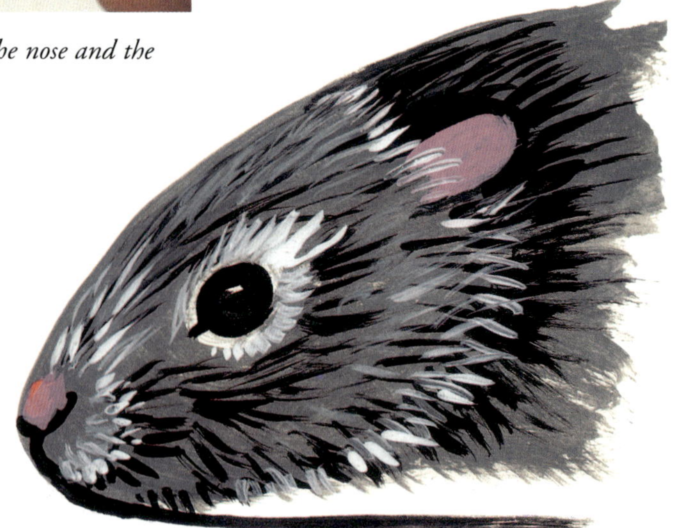

5 **Finishing Touches**

Still using a liner or small brush, change to white paint and add the details that will bring your little mouse to life. First, highlight the top of each eye with a series of eyelash-like strokes; start with an outline from the front that sweeps around to the back as shown at the bottom of the opposite page. Fan out another row of much shorter lash lines along the bottom of the eye. Then, just above the edge of the head shape, overlap a series of light fur strokes outward, tapering them off before they completely cover the black fur lines. Do the same across the top of the head, along the base of and between the ears. Paint a half circle of very small strokes around either side of the muzzle.

If there are any plain grey areas left, soften them by adding pale fur strokes; remember to angle the strokes away from the head. Emphasize the shoulder and haunch contours in particular, highlighting the darker fur lines with a matching series of white ones. Scatter a few thin fur lines randomly over the back and sides. Soften the white strip along the bottom by stroking some paler fur lines down from the grey areas above.

With the tip of your brush, place a white dot in each eye to give it a sparkle.

Experiment on scrap paper to ensure the paint is not too thick or thin before adding several sweeping whiskers on each side of the muzzle.

Go around the bottom of the paws with a thin outline of burnt sienna to clearly define them. Now look carefully at your mouse to see if there are any other areas that require more detail or definition. If you are satisfied, use PVA glue or wood filler to secure the tail to the bottom of the stone at the rear edge. A light coating of clear acrylic or oil-based varnish will protect the finish and enrich the hues of your paint.

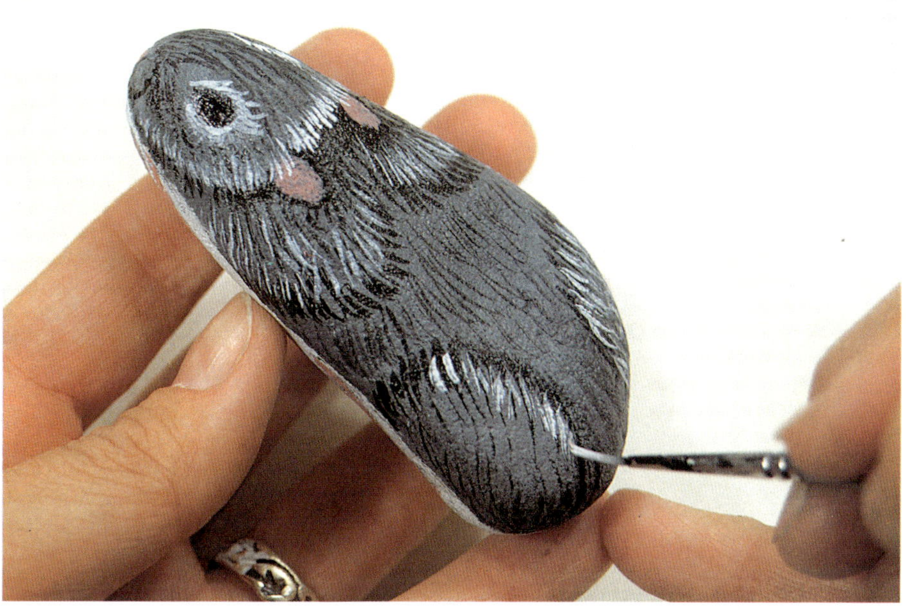

White brushstrokes accentuate the contours and add texture. Cluster white fur lines along curves to suggest highlighting.

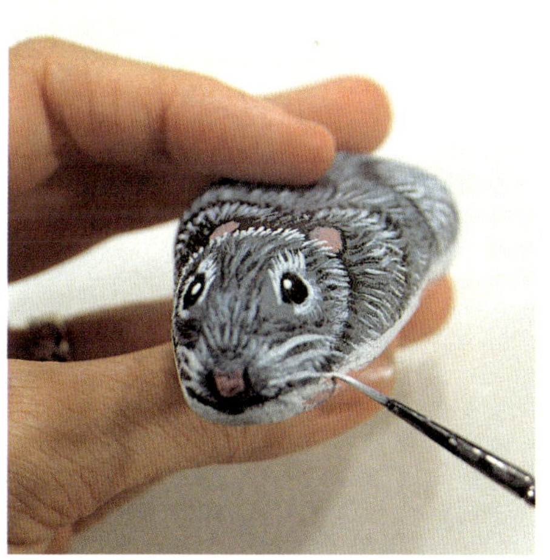

White dots lend a bright sparkle to the eyes. Test your paint consistency before sweeping narrow whiskers out from either side of the muzzle.

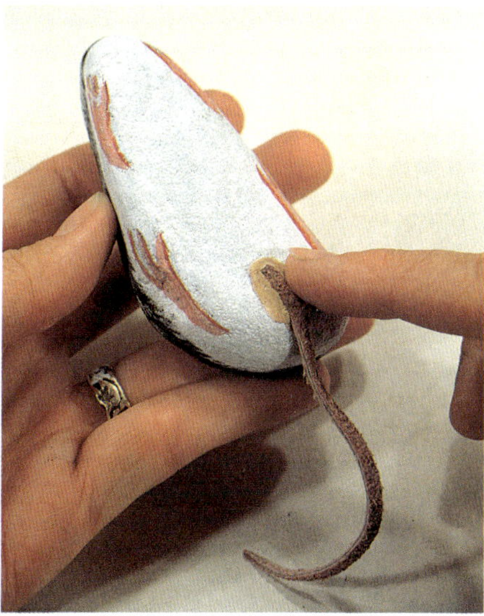

Attach a short tail to the bottom of the stone, close to the rear edge.

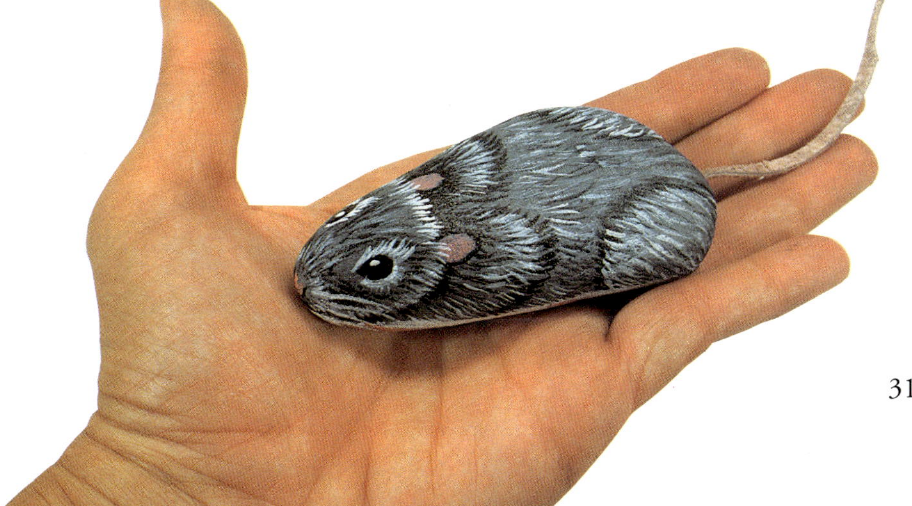

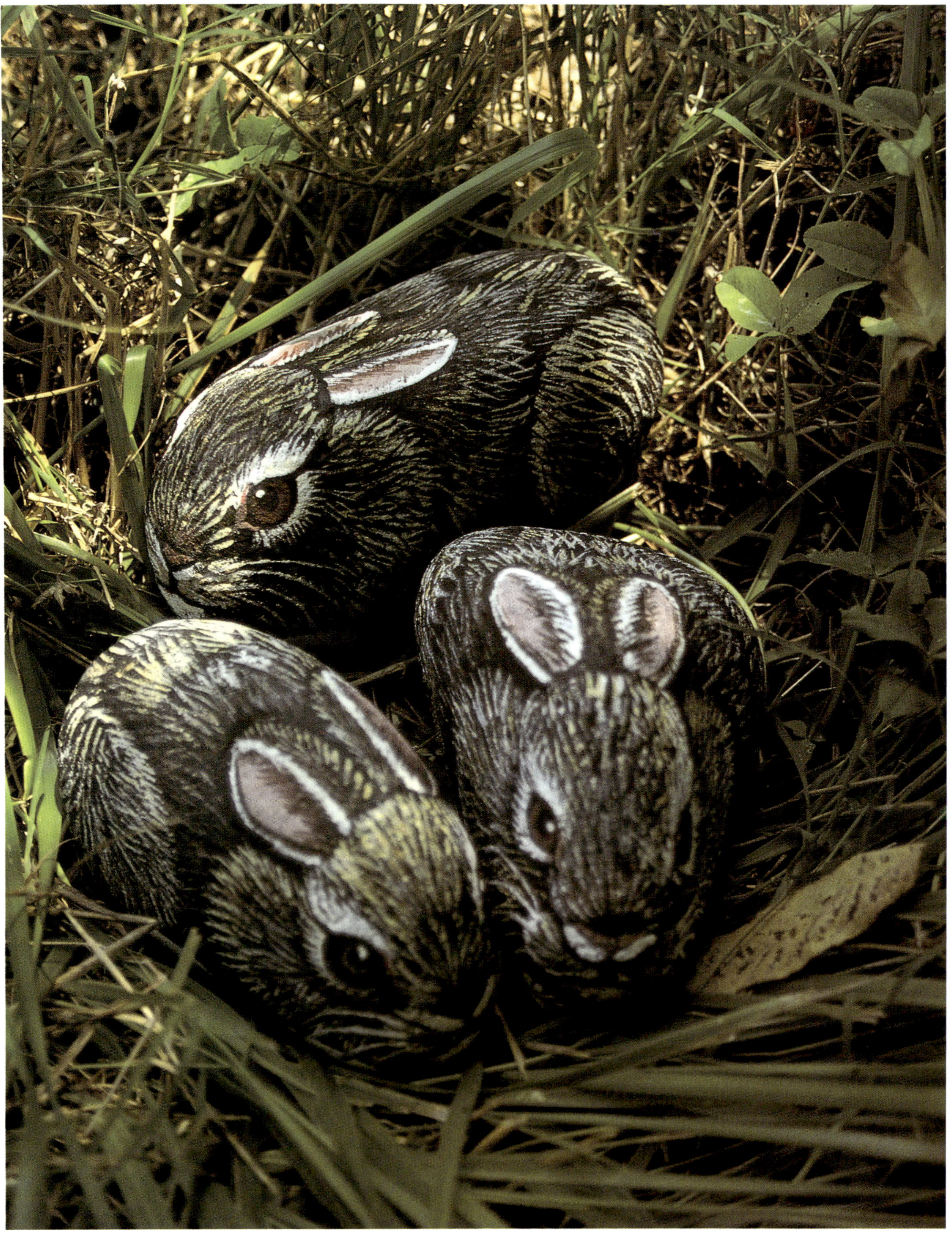

RABBIT

When you are ready to tackle a more detailed project, this rabbit is a good place to start. Select a smooth stone, similar in shape and size to a large baking potato. The stone should have a flat bottom so that it will sit without rolling over.

While the ideal rabbit stone is oval as shown by stone A, there are many variations that will also work. Your stone may be taller and narrower (B), it may have a blunt, somewhat squared shape (C), or it may taper off slightly at one end (D). The most important features are a flat bottom for stability and overall symmetry of shape.

Beginners will find it easier to paint on a stone with a smooth or fine-grained surface. It is much more difficult to achieve fine detail on a rough or pitted surface. Once you have found a promising stone, clean it well and then allow it to dry.

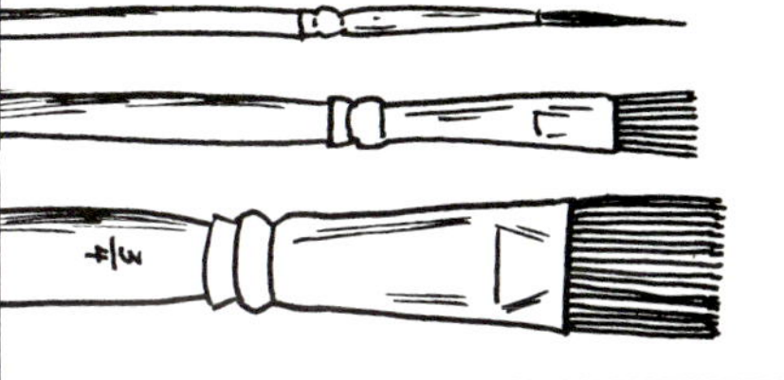

You Will Need

- acrylic paints: black, white, golden yellow, red and burnt sienna
- selection of brushes
- white-lead pencil or chalk
- oil-based or acrylic clear varnish

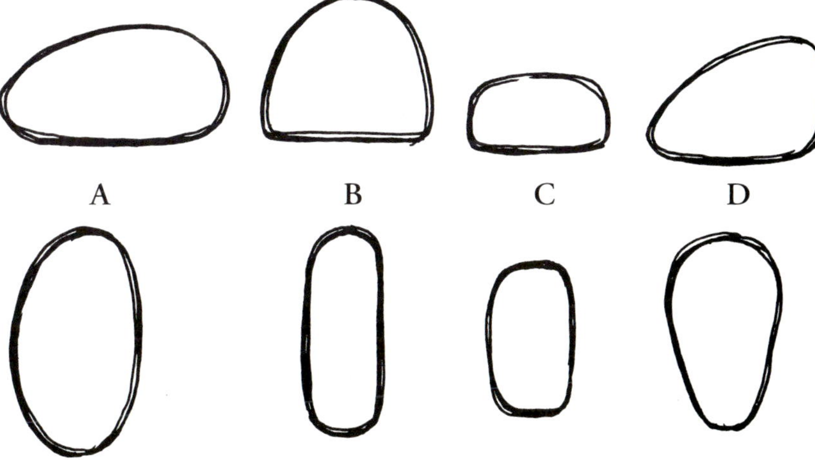

Side views.

A   B   C   D

Top views.

A variety of stone sizes and shapes are suitable for rabbits.

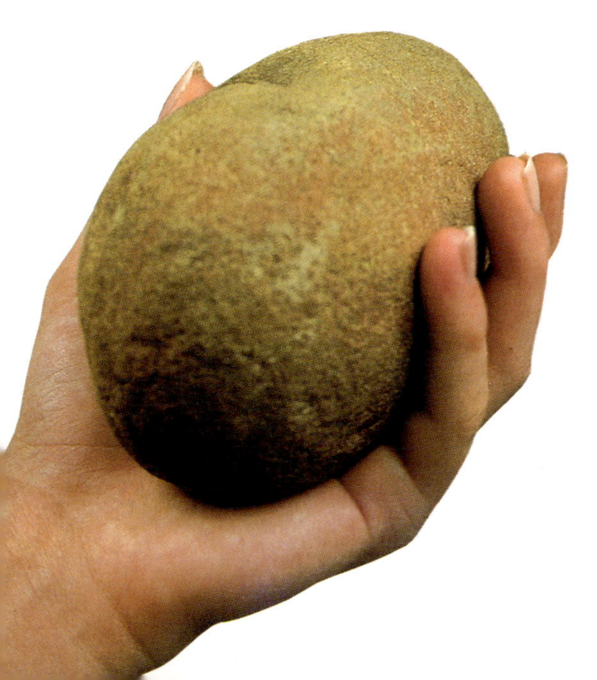

A perfect rabbit stone.

1 Layout

Use your largest brush to cover all but the very bottom of your stone with a coat of black paint. If the stone dries with a greyish cast, apply a second, thicker coat. When the paint is dry you can begin sketching in basic shapes.

A. Imagine your stone is divided into thirds. The first third encompasses the jowl area, and the back third is the haunch area. With a sharpened pencil or white chalk, lightly sketch in these guidelines. Sketch curving jowl lines on both sides of the head end; check from the top to make sure both jowls are the same shape.

B. At the top of the stone these two lines must meet to form the forehead. The ears begin at the top of the forehead, extending backward towards the middle of the stone.

C. Now move to the face. Imagine the front of your stone is divided into quarters. The bottom of each eye will rest on a bisecting horizontal line. Eyes that are too large in proportion to the stone will give your rabbit a 'cartoon' look, so keep them small. Allow a minimum of one and one-half eye widths between them. Check for symmetry by lining up a pencil with the bottom of the eye circles.

Next, centre a nose triangle on the vertical bisecting line. It should not be much wider across the top than one of the eyes.

D. Turn your stone around and add an oval-shaped tail to the rear end. Tuck two sets of paws along the bottom edge of either side.

If you are not satisfied with your guidelines at any point, simply dab them away with a damp rag or go over them with more black paint and try again.

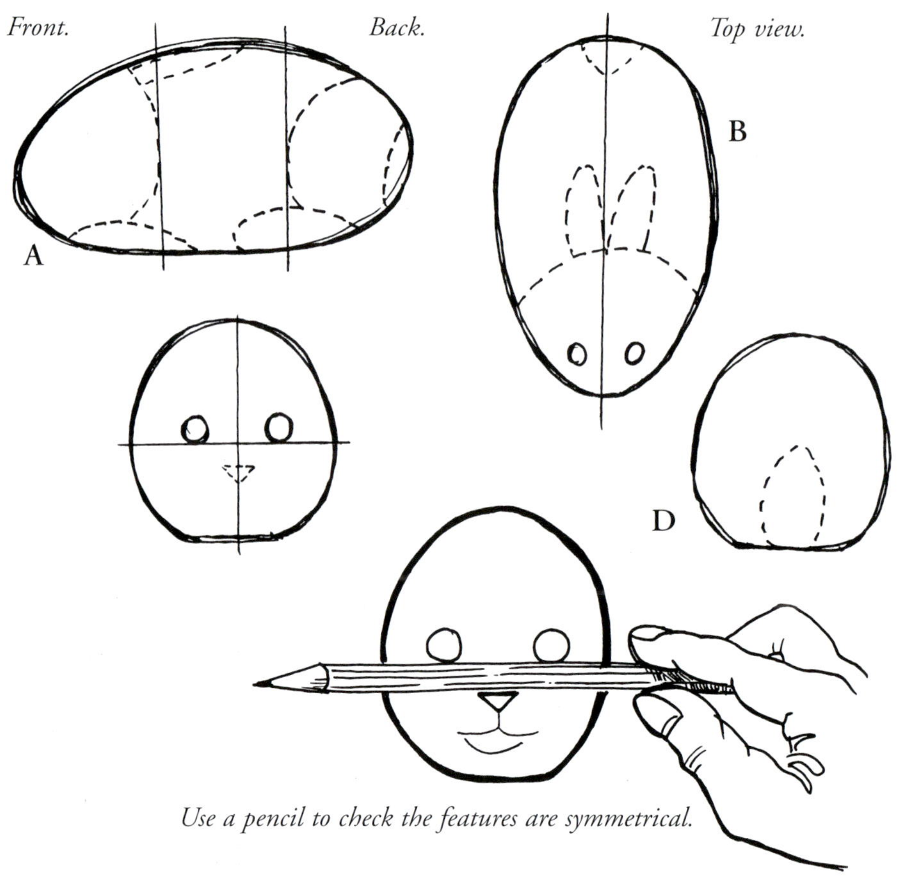

Use a pencil to check the features are symmetrical.

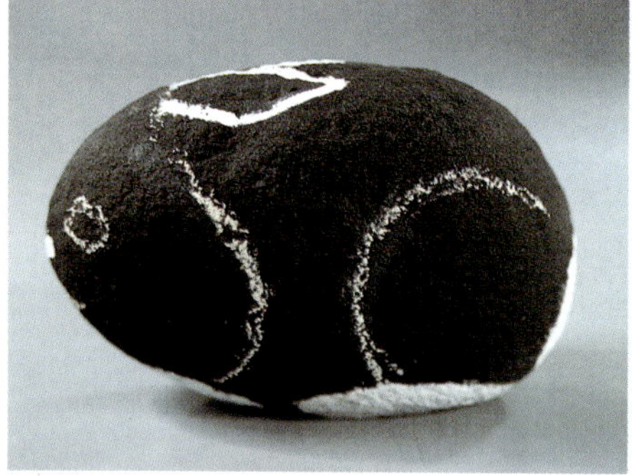

The paws should be easily visible but not too big.

Add a line to the inside of each ear to indicate a flap.

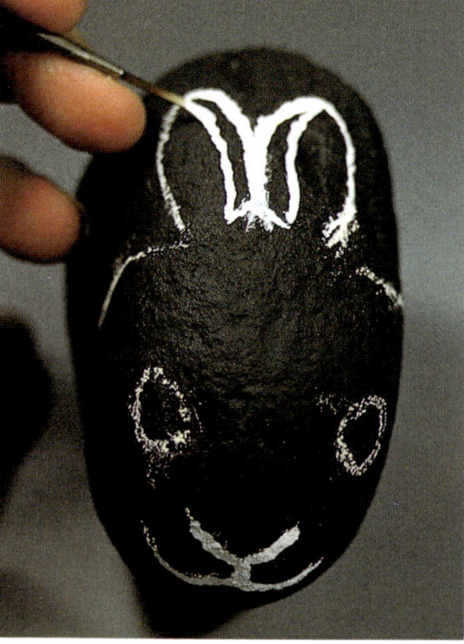

2 White Contrasts

Fill in the paws and tail with white, using enough paint for solid coverage; these areas look fluffier if you feather your strokes outward along the edges. Next, change to a smaller brush to paint in two short white lines along the bottom angles of the nose. Outline the basic shape of the ears. Paint a second, parallel line inside the upper edge of each ear to indicate a flap.

3 Eyelashes

Still using white paint and a small brush, stroke in a series of delicate 'eyelash' lines. Begin at the outside upper corner of each eye and stroke in a long, curved line extending nearly to the base of the ear. Add more lashes, shortening them as you work towards the inside of each eye. Make a fringe of shorter, curving lashes along the bottom edge of both eyes.

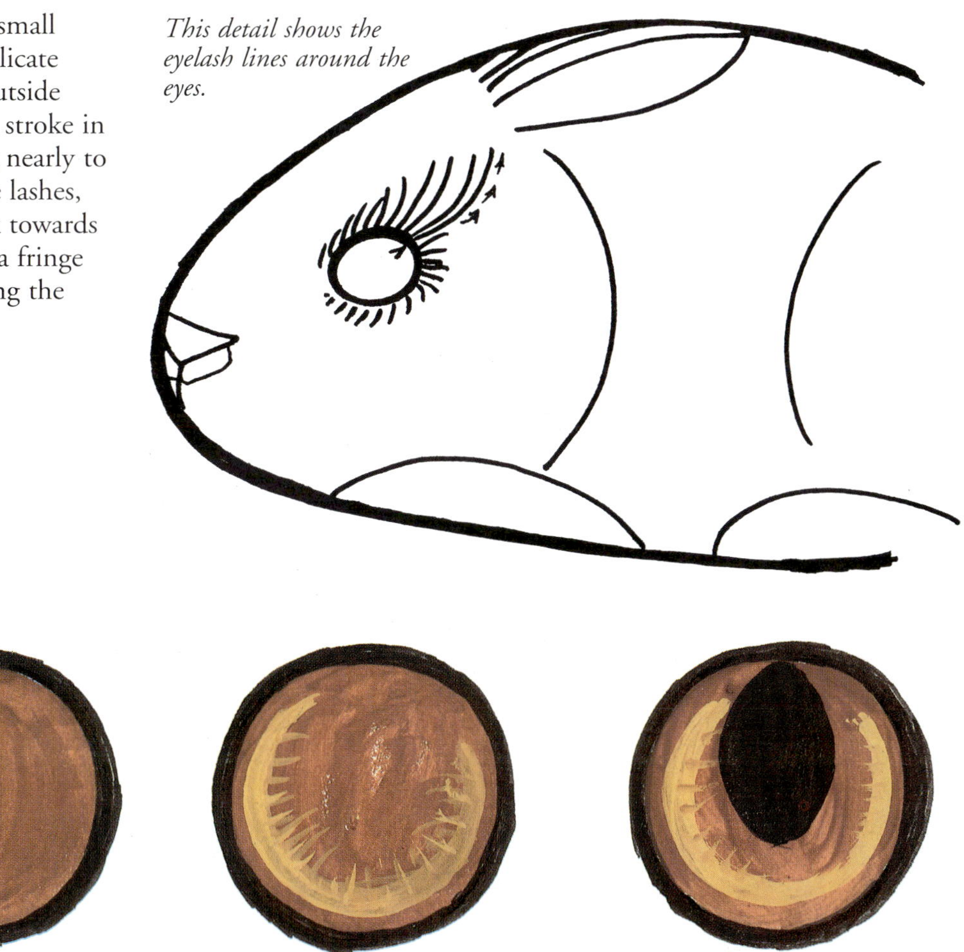

This detail shows the eyelash lines around the eyes.

These three illustrations show how the eye is built up.

4 Eye and Ear Colour

Paint both eye circles with burnt sienna. Keep the eyes neat and round. If they look uneven, or if you accidentally paint over the eyelash lines, let the brown paint dry, then use black to redefine the eyes later. Add a touch of golden yellow paint to the sienna on your palette and blend to get a lighter shade of brown. With this colour, form a half-circle inside the bottom portion of each eye – this will give the eyes a more lifelike depth. When the eyes are dry, use black paint to make two oval irises; these should touch the top of each eye circle.

Work on the ears next. Clean your brush well and mix small amounts of red with white until you have a medium shade of pink. Add just enough golden yellow to soften it to a pale flesh tone. Use this colour to fill in the insides of the ears, not quite meeting the white outlines you painted earlier. Leave the ear flap unpainted for now. Add burnt sienna to darken the flesh tone on your palette. Use this new colour to create a shadowed effect along the upper edges of the ears just below the ear flaps.

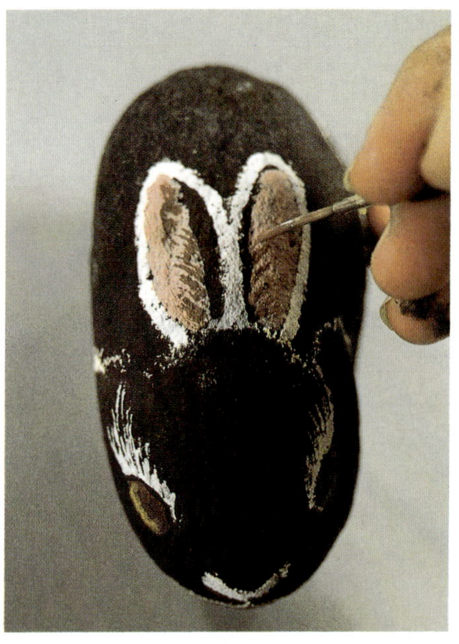

Shade the insides of the ears .

5 Fur Lines

You are now ready to paint the fur lines that will give your rabbit a soft, realistic look. Fur lines should be as fine and delicate as possible. Dilute the paint so that it flows on easily but is not transparent – you want the fur lines to dry crisp and clear. Begin the fur by making a series of short, perpendicular strokes, following the curved line of the jowl. Refer to the fur directional guide, shown right, for guidance in placing your strokes.

Add a second row of longer strokes just inside the first set. Allow each line to taper into a point by easing the pressure on the brush as you lift. Try to ensure that your rows overlap slightly, and vary the direction and size of your strokes for realism.

Three or four sets of overlapping fur lines should bring you close to the bottom eyelashes. Be sure to stop before reaching these lash lines so that some dark contrast remains around the eye areas. Repeat the process with the other jowl, then move on to the haunches.

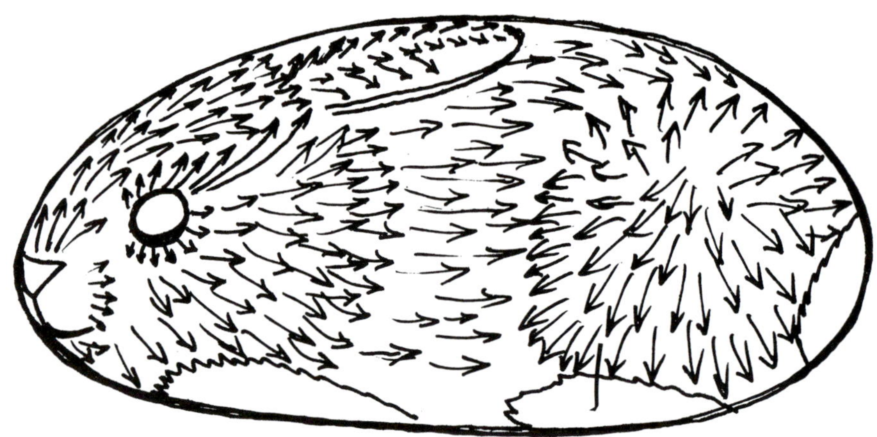

Follow the arrows on this guide for realistic fur.

Fill in the haunches with rows of strokes that angle out like spokes on a wheel. Start on the outside and work towards the centre of each haunch, overlapping your strokes.

Next, move to your rabbit's back. Start between the ears, leaving a narrow area of black paint surrounding the ears for contrast. Work back towards the tail, varying the length and angle of your strokes.

Indicate shoulders by allowing your strokes to form an M-shaped row behind the head. Skip a space and start a fresh row of fur further back. Leave several other similar spaces showing as you continue to work towards the back of the stone. Stop just short of the tail. Paint less lines as you move down the body so that much of the bottom remains plain black above the paws.

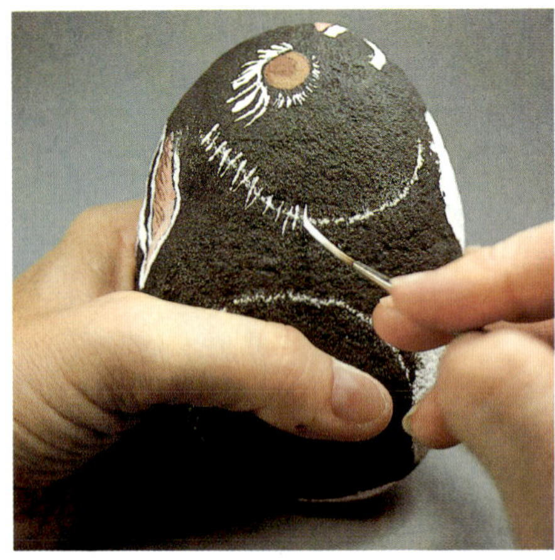

Start painting the fur with a series of tiny fine brush strokes across the curved line of the jowl.

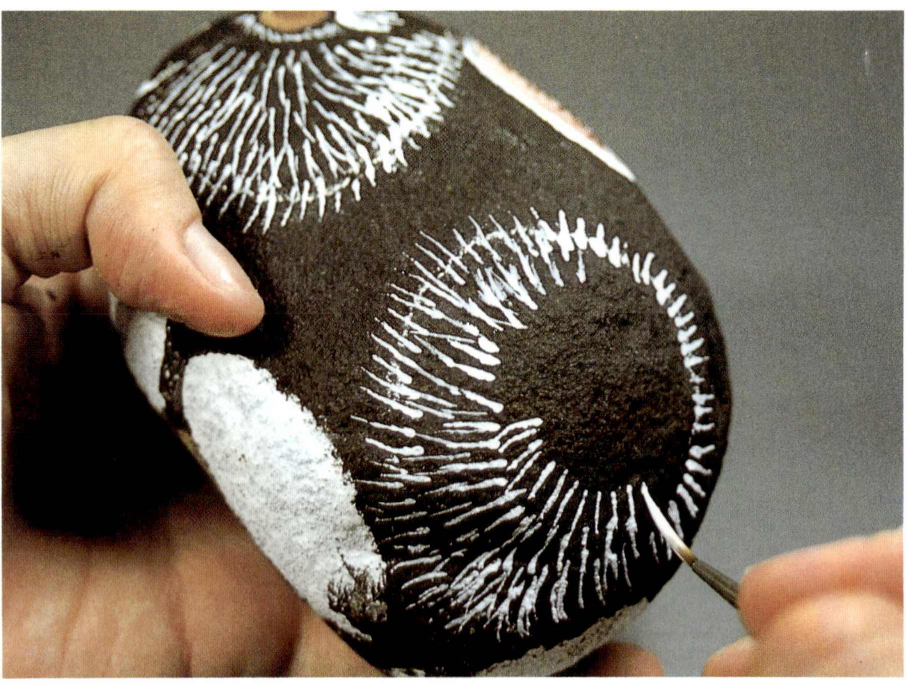

Fill in each haunch with strokes that angle out like spokes in a wheel.

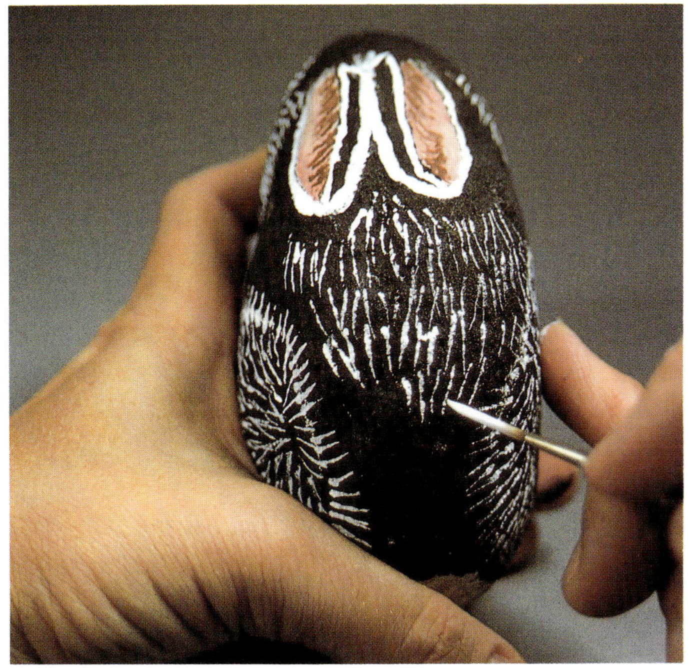

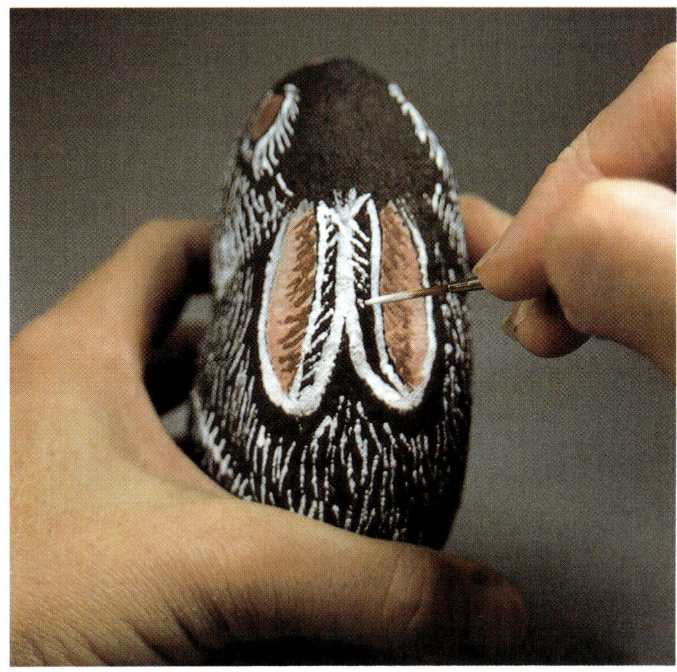

Remember to leave spaces around the ears and other features.

Add tiny fur lines to soften the ears.

6 Facial Features

Paint the nose, muzzle and forehead next. To do this, darken a little deep pink paint with some burnt sienna. Fill in the centre of the nose triangle, leaving a black outline. Now scatter some whisker lines in the pink part of each ear. Clean your brush and change to white paint. Make a series of tiny fur strokes along the outsides of the ears to make them softer and more natural looking.

The forehead fur begins just above the nose and fans upward and outward in uneven overlapping rows.

Stop before you reach the base of the ears and make one final row of dense, short lines along the top of the head. Leave an area of black showing between these lines and the base of the ears for contrast.

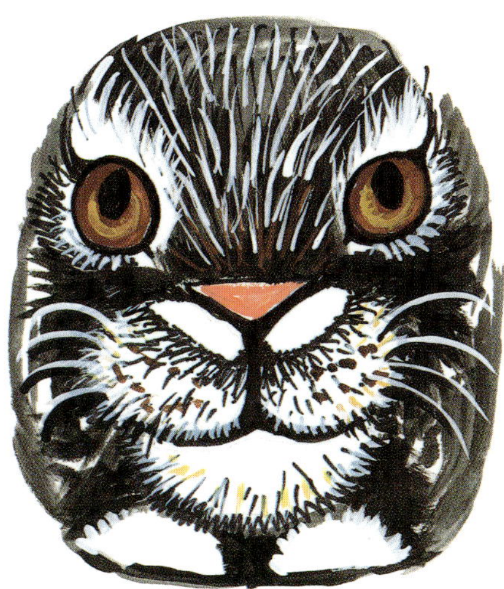

This detail shows the facial features.

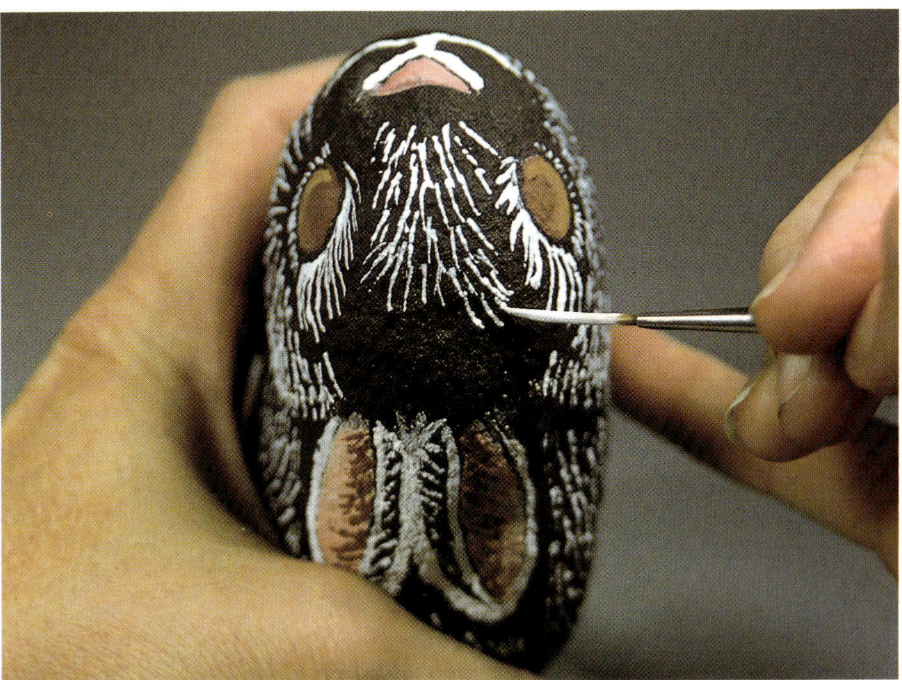

You may find it easier to paint the forehead fur if you hold your stone upside down.

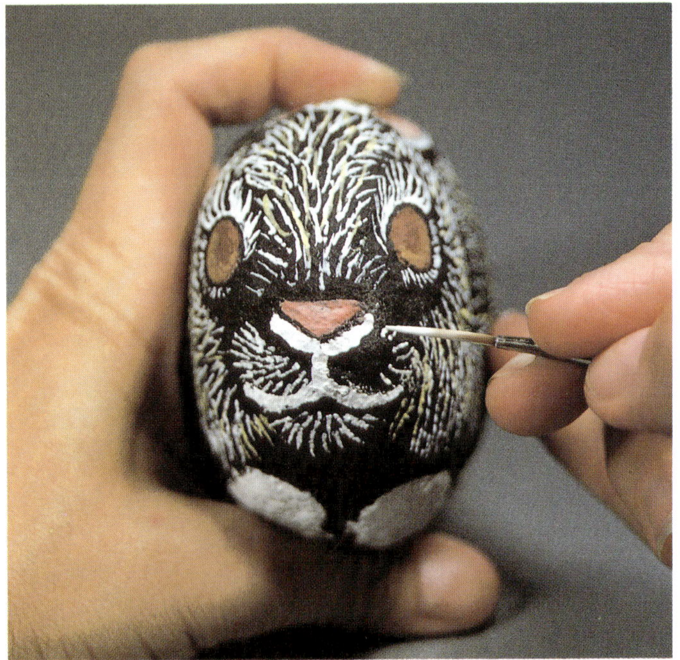

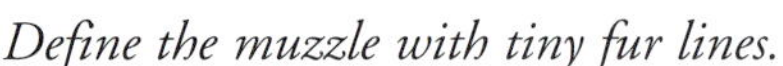
Define the muzzle with tiny fur lines.

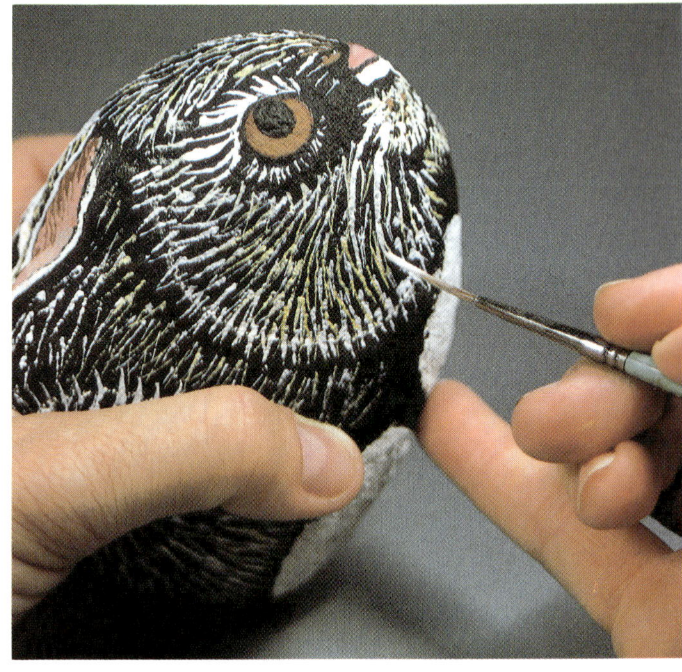
Paint in a few long, curving whiskers on each side of the muzzle.

7 Finishing Touches

Define the muzzle area below the nose by stroking in two matching semi-circular shapes of tiny fur lines on either side. Leave a narrow line of dark paint between each muzzle circle. Stroke in a semicircle of white fur for the chin beneath the muzzle, also leaving a narrow line of black between the chin and muzzle; these dark lines form the mouth in an anchor shape. Go over the mouth lines with black if necessary.

Change to golden yellow and highlight the outside edges of the muzzle with more tiny fur lines. Add realism by scattering golden yellow fur lines among the white fur elsewhere on your rabbit, including the forehead. Add a touch of sienna to the golden yellow and stroke the colour back along the ear flaps, but leave plenty of black showing.

With more sienna, create a fan-shaped set of lines just above the nose triangle and encircling the outside edges of the muzzle. Add a touch of black to the sienna and use this darker shade to dot the muzzle with whisker follicles.

Rinse out your brush and carefully mix white paint with just enough water so that it will flow easily. Draw three or four long, curving whiskers from each side of the muzzle. Finally, dab a dot of white paint in the iris of each eye   this sparkle will make your rabbit come alive. Be sure to place the dot in the same spot in both eyes or your rabbit may appear cross-eyed.

Look at your rabbit from every angle. Do you have enough fur lines for a soft, fuzzy look? If not, add a few more. If some of your fur lines have run together to form a distracting blotch, use a hairline stroke of black to redefine them. You may want to emphasize the whiskers by carefully underlining them with a narrow, parallel line of black paint.

When you are satisfied, apply a coat of clear varnish to seal the paint and bring out the rich colours of your piece.

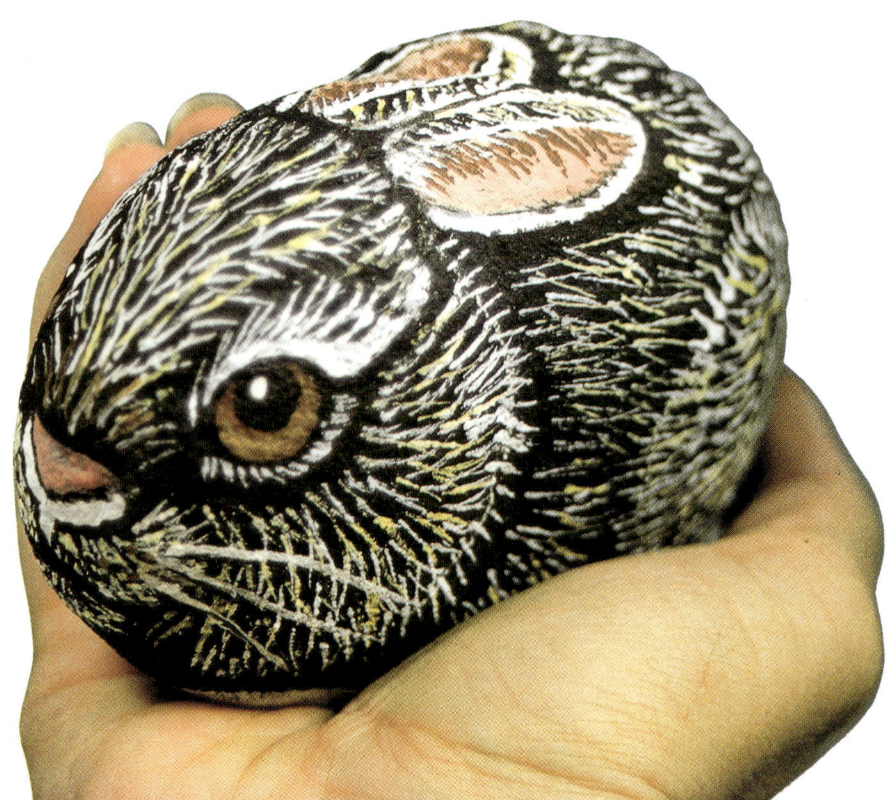

38

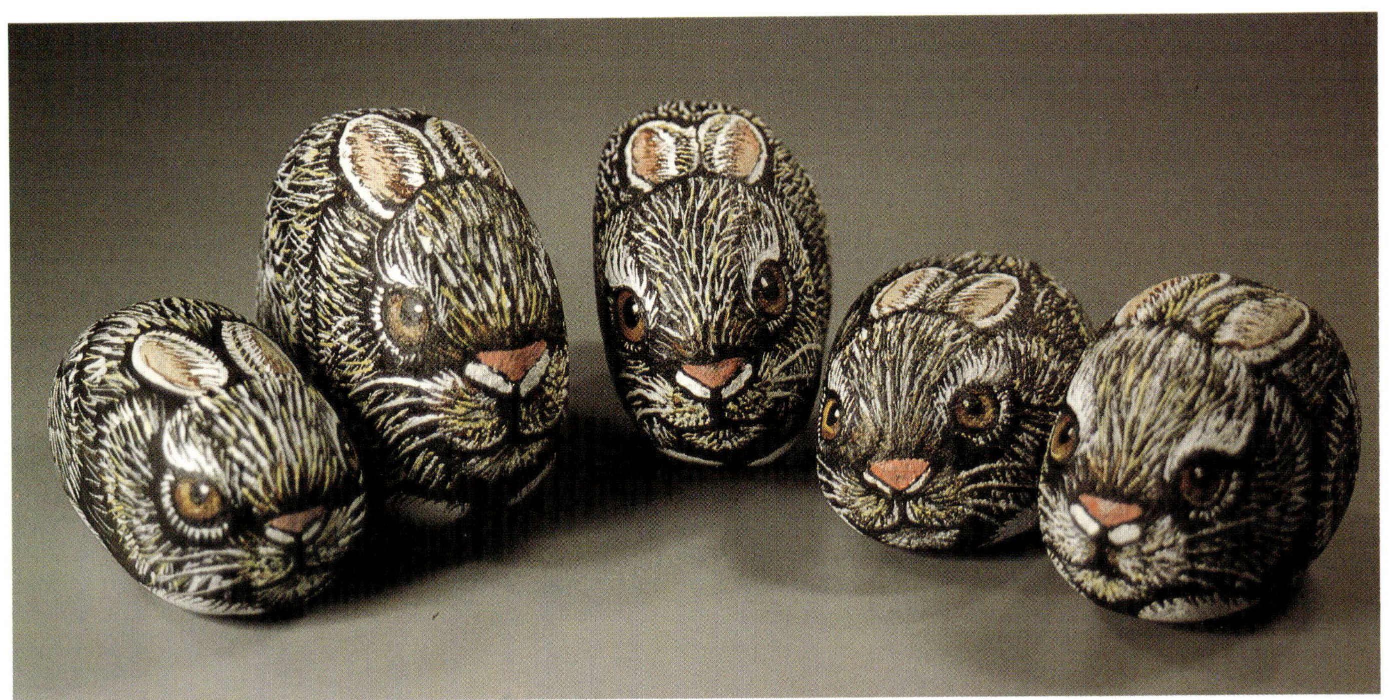

*Stone rabbits make great gifts –
particularly at Easter. They can be used at
work or home as paperweights or
doorstops, or they can be grouped in
'litters' to create an irresistible centrepiece.
If you display your stone artwork on a
table or other polished surface, it is a good
idea to glue a circle of dark felt around
the bottom of each piece to prevent
scratching. Alternatively, try displaying
your rabbit in a basket or nestled in
amongst your potted houseplants.*

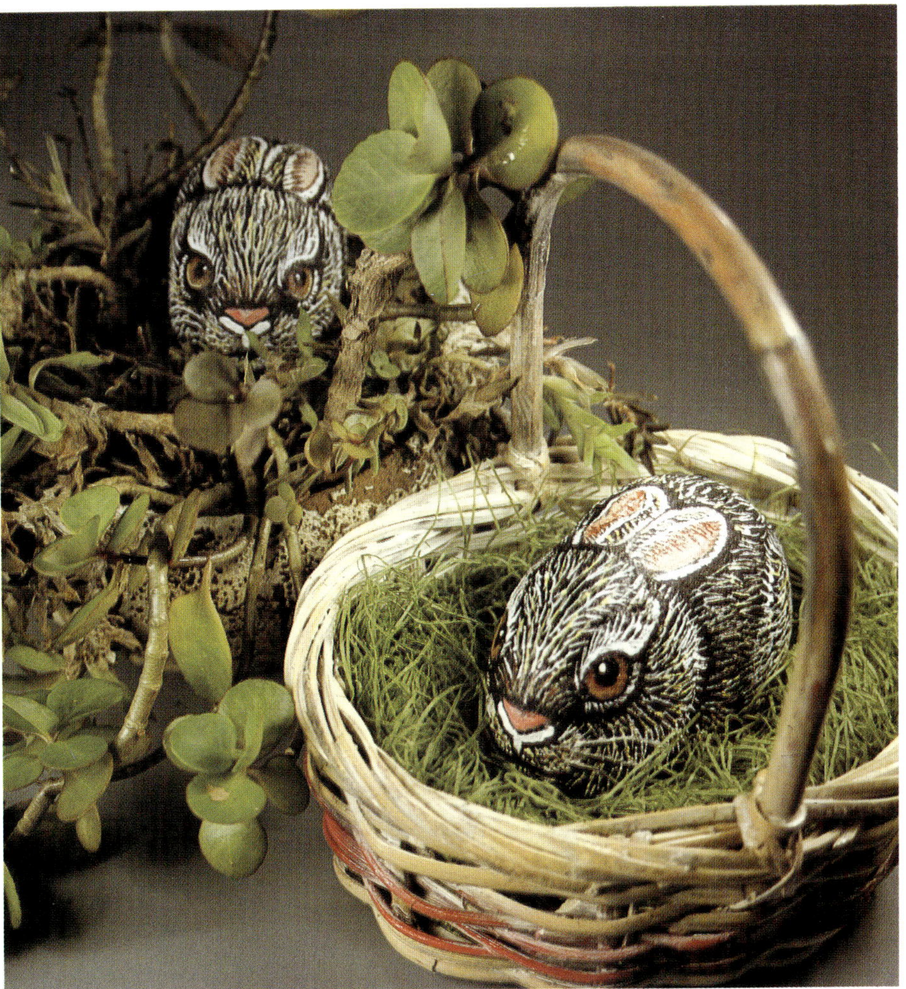

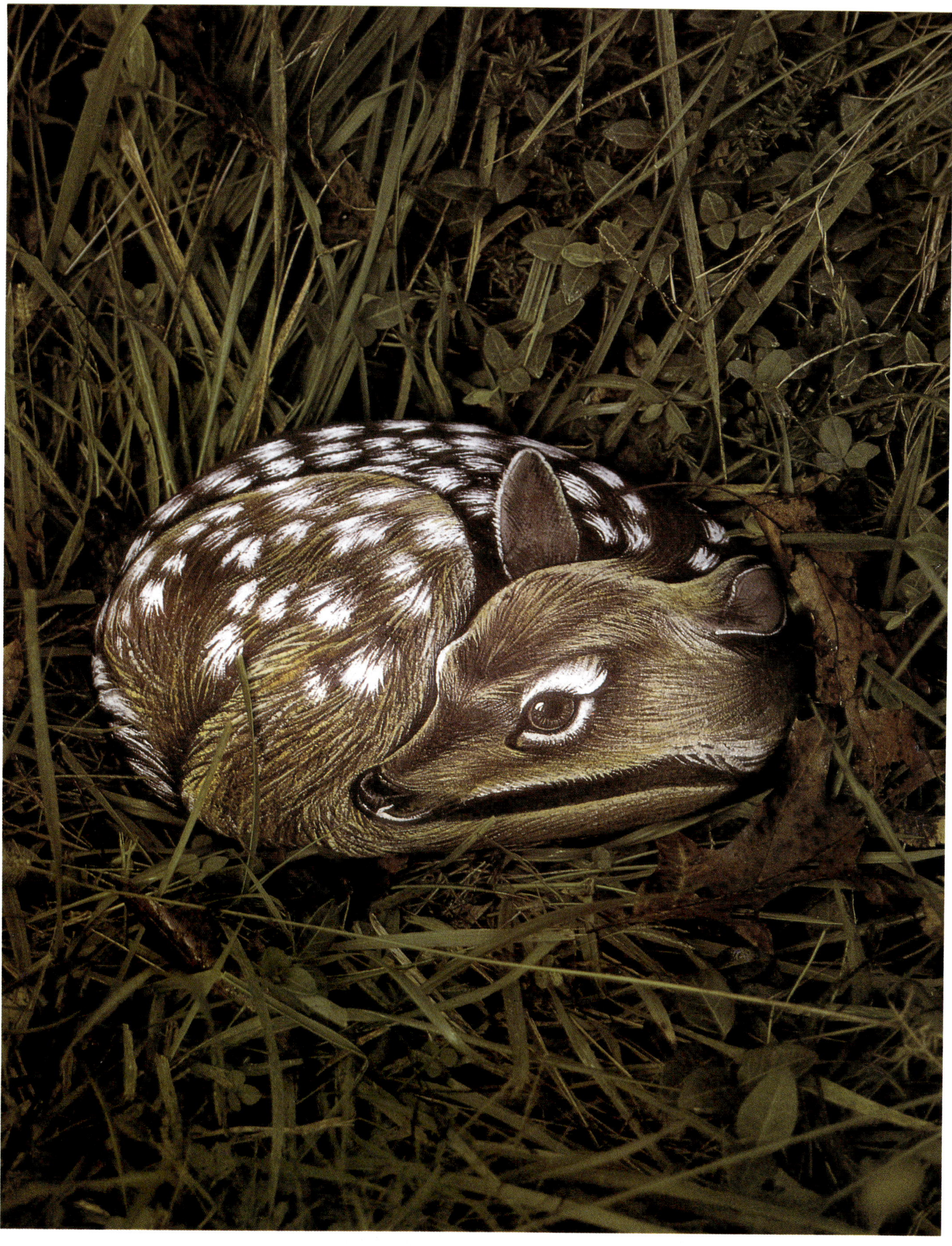

FAWN

Fawns fold themselves into exquisitely compact positions – you could hardly ask for a better subject to paint on a stone.

I am particular about the stones I use for fawns. The ideal shape is a plump oval, angled at one end to simulate the crook of the fawn's back leg. Unfortunately these stones are not always easy to find. For this demonstration, I have chosen a plain, elongated oval-shaped stone that is much more common.

Fawns can be worked on fairly flat stones or more rounded ones. Flat stones look best when viewed from above, while rounder stones look good from several angles. Like so many stone animals, they can be painted in a wide range of sizes, from a pebble that fits in an outstretched palm to near boulder size. I once painted a fawn on a huge granite rock. The fawn turned out really well, but lifting it required two people – I would not recommend working that large! Most of my fawns measure between 23 and 61cm (9 and 24in) in length. The one in this demonstration is 33cm (13in) across.

You Will Need

- acrylic paint: black, burnt sienna, golden yellow, white and red
- assorted brushes
- pencil and measuring tape
- oil-based or acrylic clear varnish

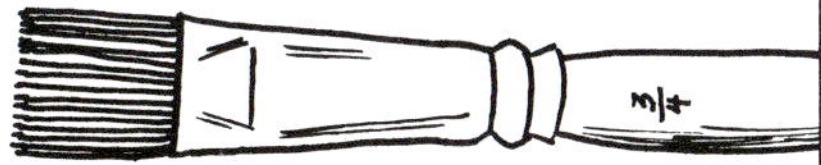

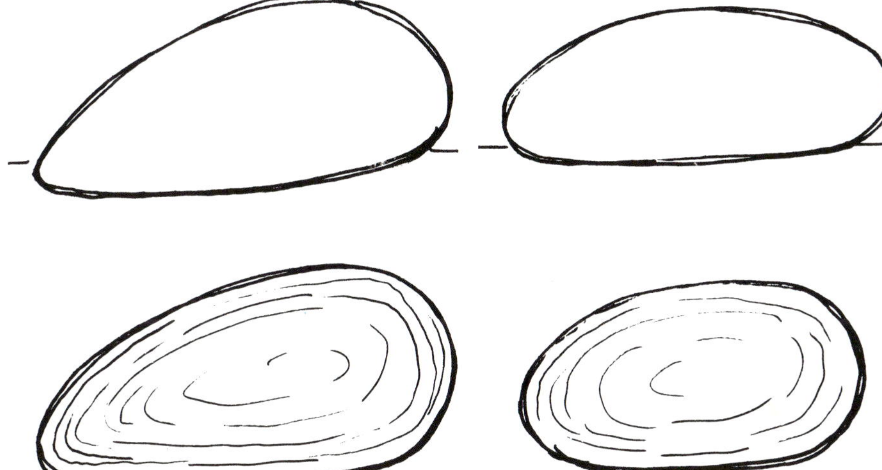

The best fawn stones are oval or egg-shaped.

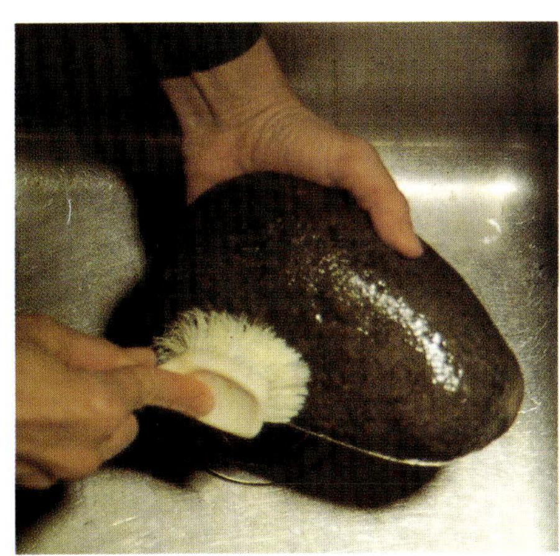

When you have selected your stone, clean it thoroughly, then let it dry.

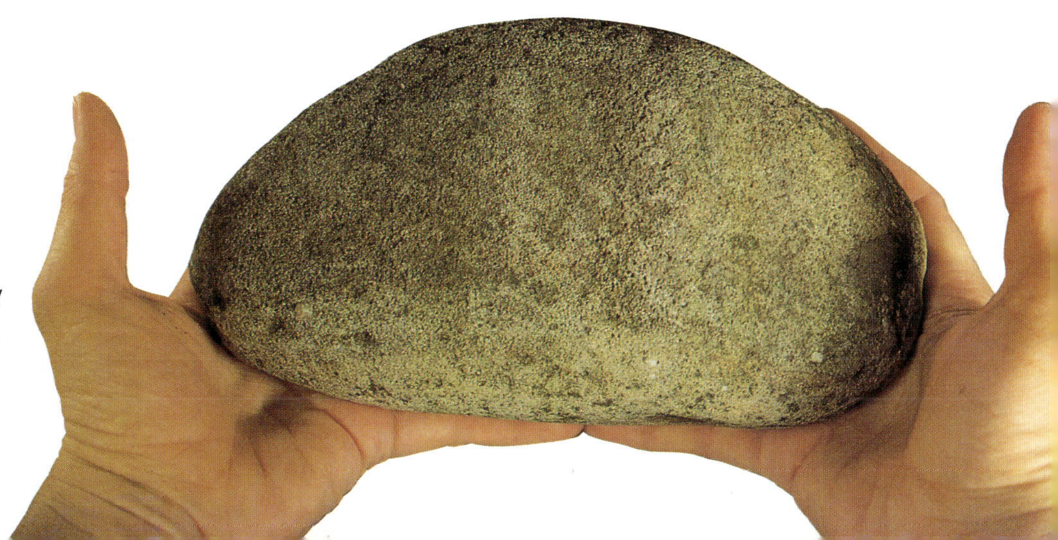

A good-sized fawn stone. This shape and size is quite easy to find.

1 | Layout

The length of your fawn's head (from between the ears to the tip of the nose) should be approximately half of the stone's overall length. The length of the ears often dictates the placement of the head. That means that on my 33cm (13in) stone, the head measures 16.5cm (6½in), so the ears should be a shade over 11.5cm (4½in). Remember that none of these measurements is 'carved in stone'. They are included only to help you get the fawn's features in proportion with one another.

A. Start by bisecting your stone lengthways. On the side you have designated for the head, follow this line to where it is just about to curve around the edge of the stone; this point marks the tip of the outer ear.

B. Move your pencil back down the line the length of one ear and mark that spot; this point is where the base of the ear joins the top of the head.

C. From there, measure off the length of the head at a 45º angle from the midline. If you are not sure how to determine a 45º angle, lightly sketch in a square, using the point on the midline where the ear begins as the upper corner. Cut across the square diagonally from that point to the opposite corner to establish a 45º angle.

D. Next, from the nose end of the head line you just made, move your pencil back up a little way and cross it with a short perpendicular line. This line should be equal to one quarter of the length of the head. On my stone that makes it a little over 4cm (1½in). Now go back to the point that marks the top of the head. Make a second perpendicular line (like the top of a capital T).

E. Connect the ends of the two perpendicular lines. You should end up with a four-sided shape that resembles a wedge.

F. Lop off the two top corners at 45º angles to round the top of the head.

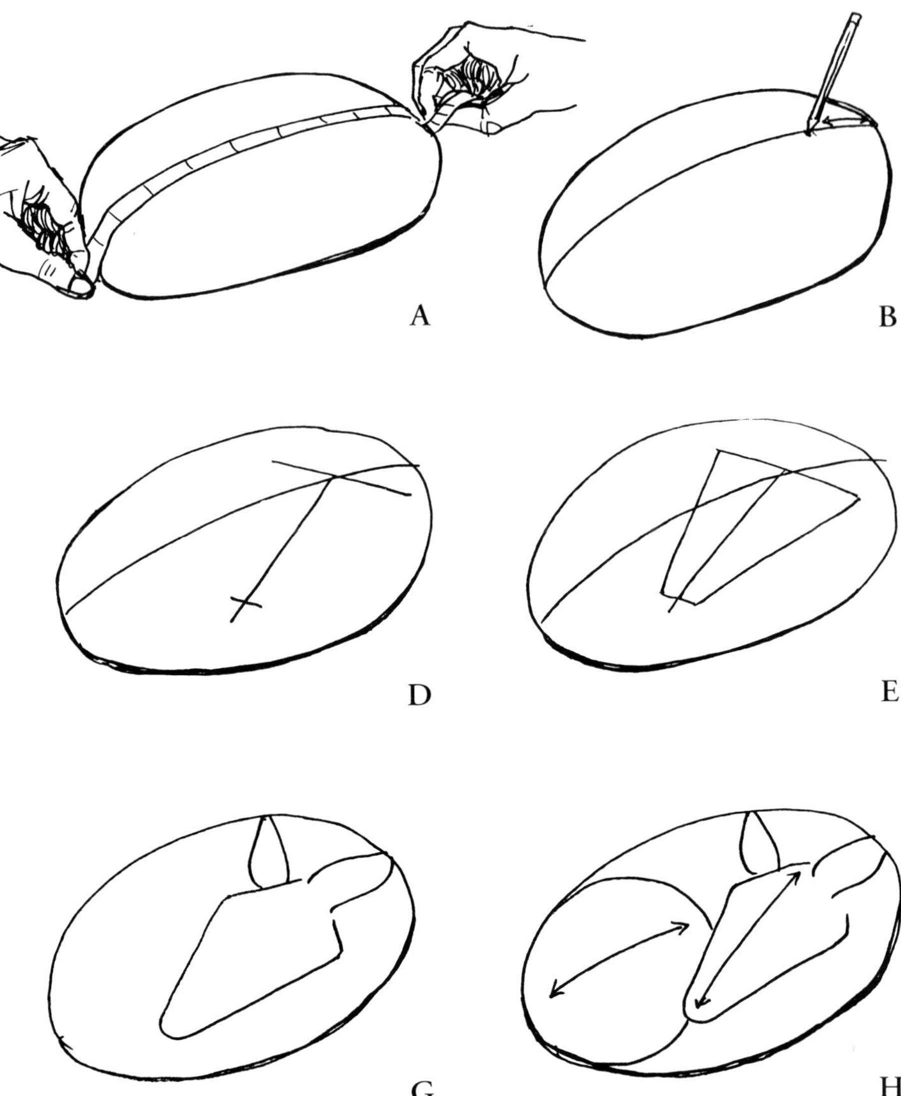

At the nose end, draw a half-circle to form a muzzle.

G. Draw in the ears (see also next page). Here I have centred one ear in the upper angle at the top of the head. Both ears should be about the same length, but the inside one has a curving front side and a straight back edge.

H. Before refining the head shape further, sketch in an oval haunch. Its length along the stone's midline is equal to the length of the head. Depending on the shape of your stone, the fawn's nose may touch or even overlap the haunch.

I. The hind leg forms an L-shape along the bottom edge of the stone. If your stone has a distinct curve along this edge, you will have to keep the hind leg from looking like it bows out. Sketch the leg at an upward-tilting angle cutting straight across the stone. You can minimize this curve later by blacking out the area directly below the leg. The end of the leg has another small downward crook for an ankle, and the hoof is similar to a small rectangle that has been split. The tips of the hooves should tilt slightly upward.

The space between the jawline and hind leg will vary depending on the

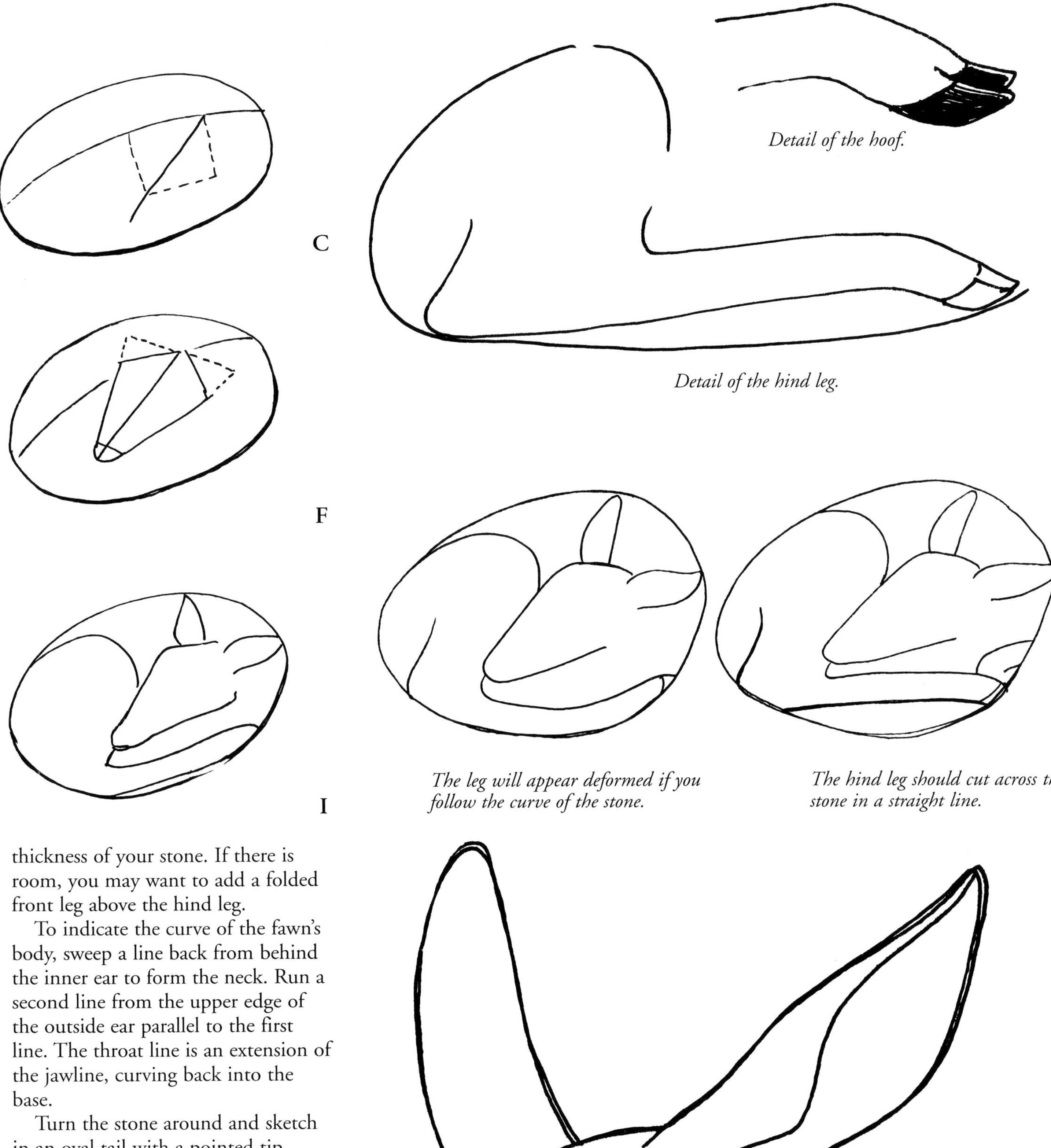

C

F

I

Detail of the hoof.

Detail of the hind leg.

The leg will appear deformed if you follow the curve of the stone.

The hind leg should cut across the stone in a straight line.

Detail of the ears.

thickness of your stone. If there is room, you may want to add a folded front leg above the hind leg.

To indicate the curve of the fawn's body, sweep a line back from behind the inner ear to form the neck. Run a second line from the upper edge of the outside ear parallel to the first line. The throat line is an extension of the jawline, curving back into the base.

Turn the stone around and sketch in an oval tail with a pointed tip.

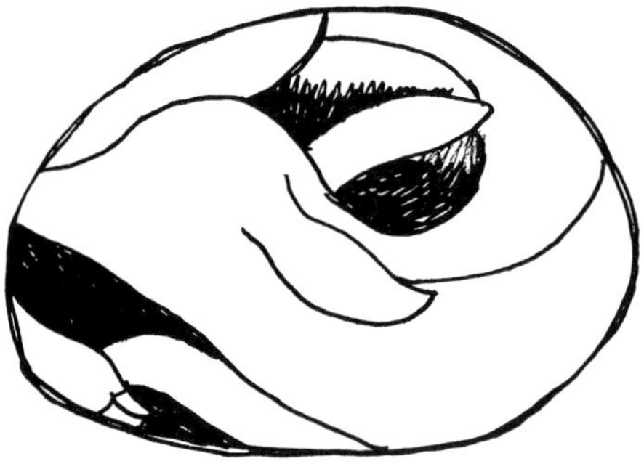

Front view of layout.

Side view of layout.

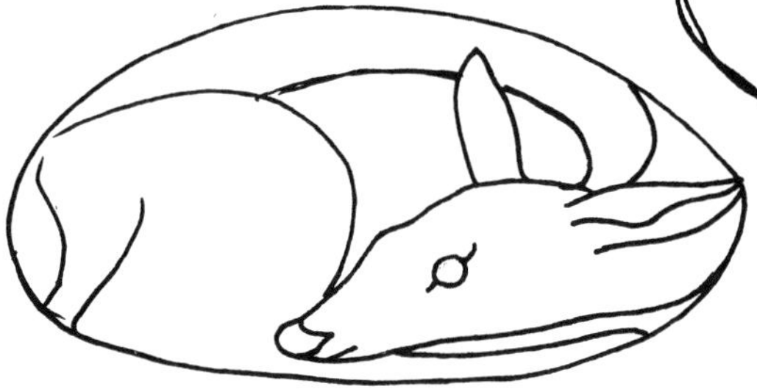

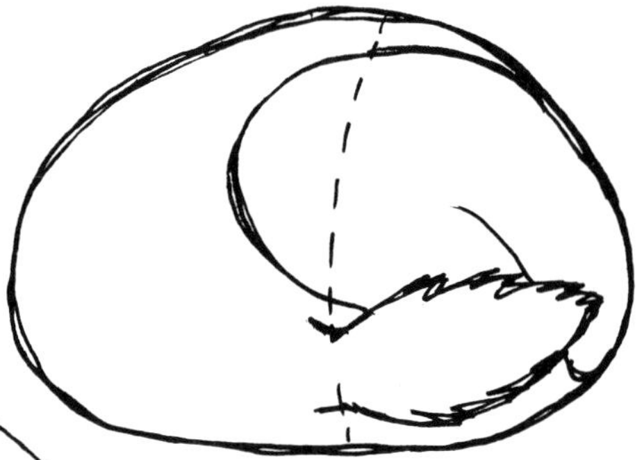

Rear view of layout.

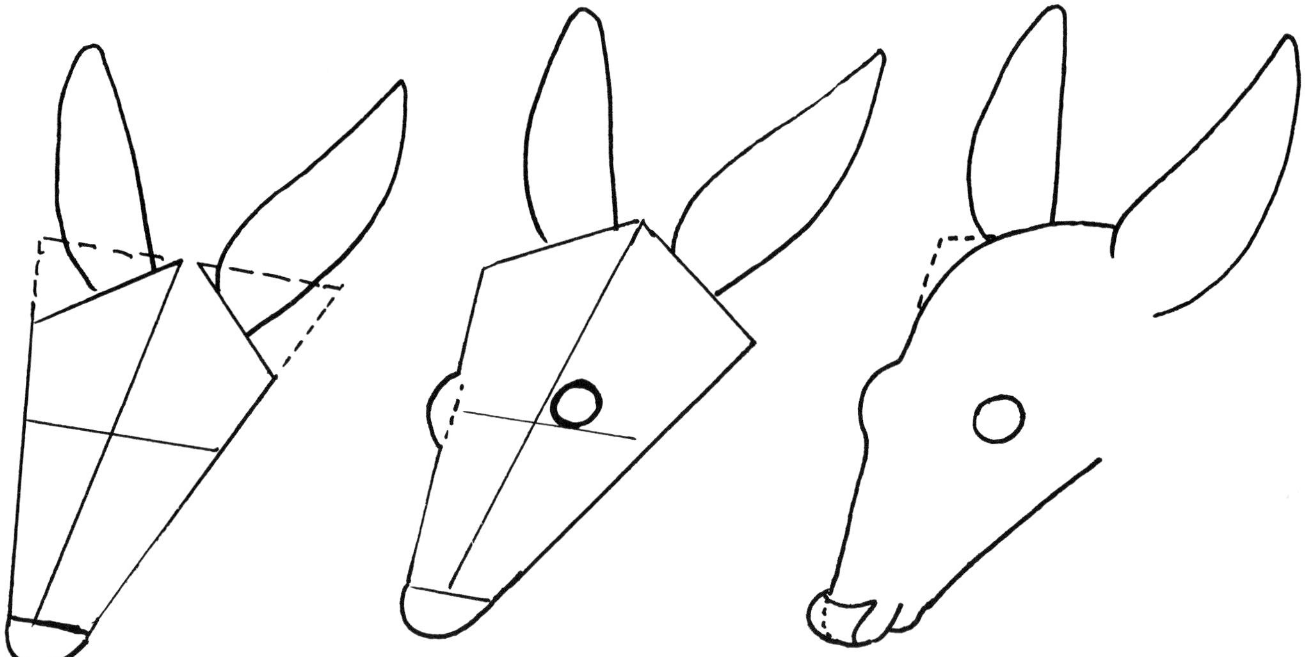

Sketching the facial features.

Since the head is at an angle, only one eye will actually show, but the other eye forms a visible bulge. The eyes should fall halfway between the ears and nose. Draw a perpendicular guideline for reference.

A fawn's eyes are large and expressive. Using the line you just made as your guide, tuck an eye circle into the upper right quadrant of your intersecting lines. On my fawn, the eye is between 2 and 2.5cm ($^3/_8$ and $^3/_4$in) across. Shape the eye by extending the inside lower corner downward and slanting the opposite outside corner upward. Indicate the other eye by sketching in a corresponding bulge along the left side of the head. Just below the eye, narrow the width of the muzzle so the nose tapers slightly. Draw in the nose and mouth as shown. Now you are ready to paint.

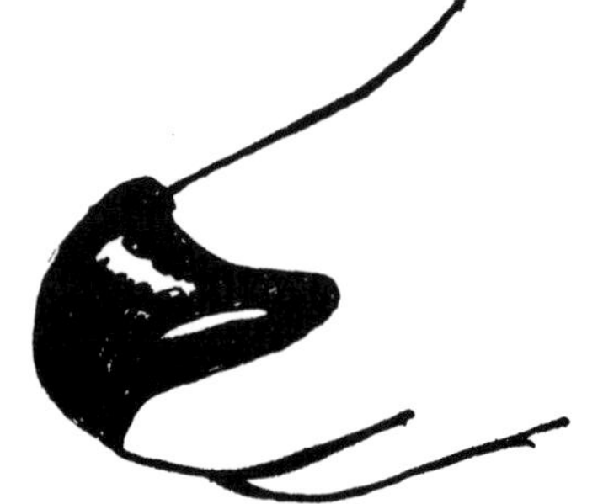

Detail of the nose.

44

2 Painting the Shadows

With a large or medium brush and black paint, fill in the shadows between the haunch and the inside ear, and behind the ear inside the curving line of the spine. Feather out the shadows as you move away from these features. Outline the ears, the upper haunch, and the space between the chin and hind leg. Also black out any portion showing below the crooked hind leg. This is especially important if your stone has a convex front side that you want to minimize. Use a small or medium brush to outline the head and the eye, and to fill in the nose and hoof. Paint the tail in black, feathering out your strokes along the edges.

3 Base Coat

Pour two good-sized pools of burnt sienna and golden yellow into your palette. Use a large or medium brush to mix the two colours in the centre, leaving some unmixed pigment at either side. Fill in the haunch and the entire hind leg. Also fill in the head, being careful not to paint over any black outlines. Dip the tip of your brush into the yellow side of your paint and stroke highlights along the top edge of the forehead and the top of the outside ear. A little neat golden yellow along the upper curve of the haunch will bring out its shape as well. Clean your brush and dip it into burnt sienna. Stroke this colour in a curve, beginning at the nape of the neck and moving back along the spine, all the way around to the base of the tail. Feather a few horizontal strokes here and there in the black area between the haunch and the inside ear to soften the shadows. Use burnt sienna all along the lower edge of the hind leg to give it more volume. Leave the chest area unpainted for now.

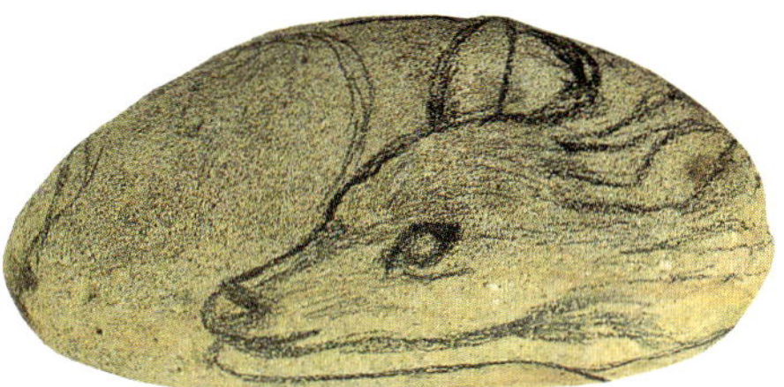

Sketch the layout carefully on to the stone before you begin painting.

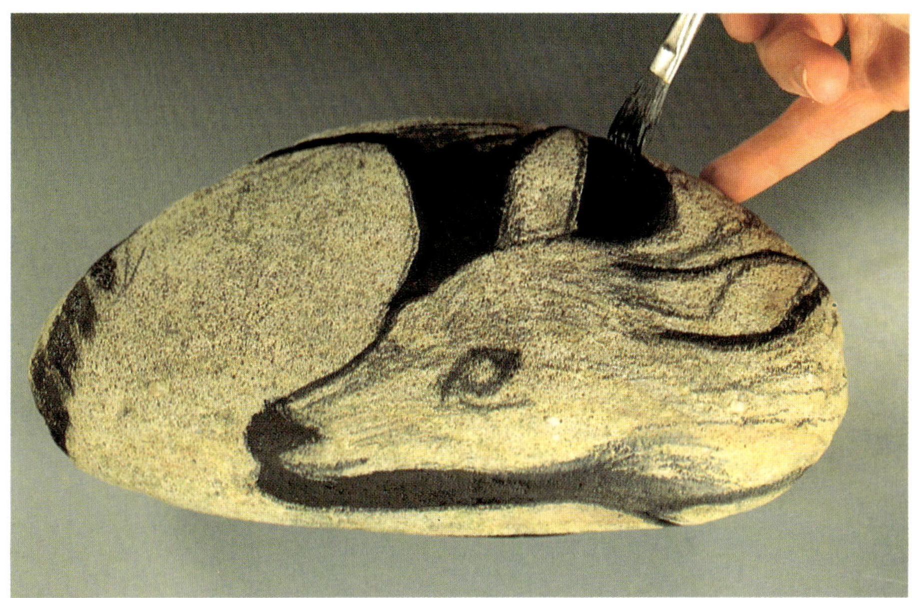

Fill in the shadows using black paint.

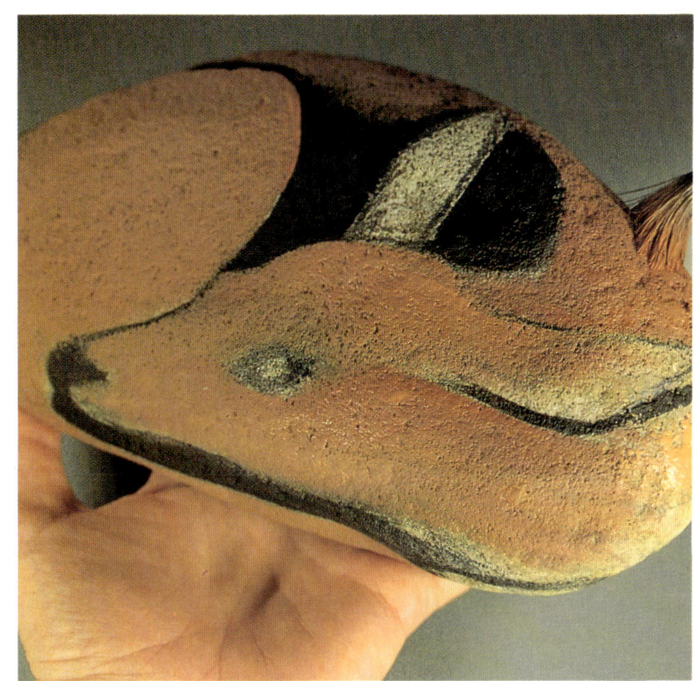

Use burnt sienna as a base coat.

4 Adding Details

Colour the inner portion of the outside ear next. Use a small or medium brush to mix white and red paint to get a medium pink, then add just enough golden yellow to soften it to a salmon colour. The portion of the ear nearest the base should be the most vivid. As you reach the outside edges, add white and a small amount of black to the salmon colour to dull it down to a warm greyish shade. Fill in the other ear with this grey colour as well.

Use a small brush and burnt sienna to fill in the eye circle, then clean your brush and change to white paint to highlight the eye by encircling it as shown.

Use the same brush to make your fawn's spots. I like to start with the spots that show just behind the head. These are small and slightly fan-shaped, running in two parallel rows along the fawn's spine to the tail. Feather the edges of the tail with long strokes.

The spots on the haunch need not be uniform in size or shape, but should conform to the direction the fur would naturally grow – refer to the fur directional guides opposite. Add spots to the shadowed areas as well.

Use white paint to outline both ears. Stroke in a line of white fur along the upper edge of the pink inner ear, longer at the base and growing shorter as you move back towards the tip.

Prop up your stone at an angle, to paint the fawn's white chest. The fur on the chest should be delicate and fluffy.

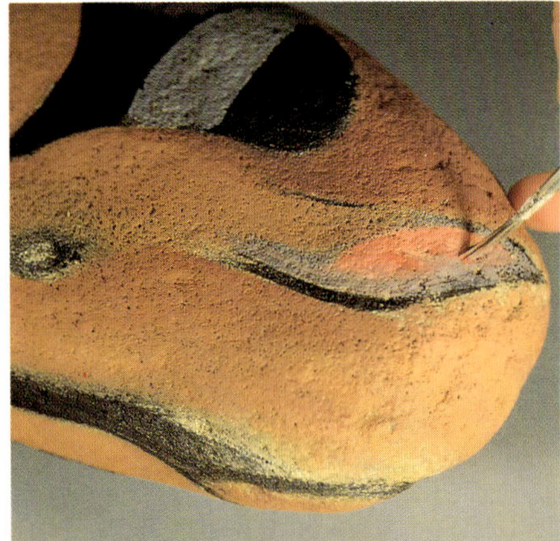

Use pink to fill in the insides of the ears.

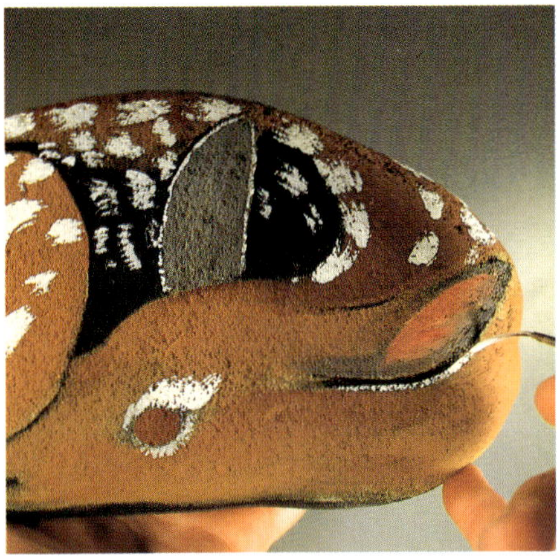

Outline the ears with white.

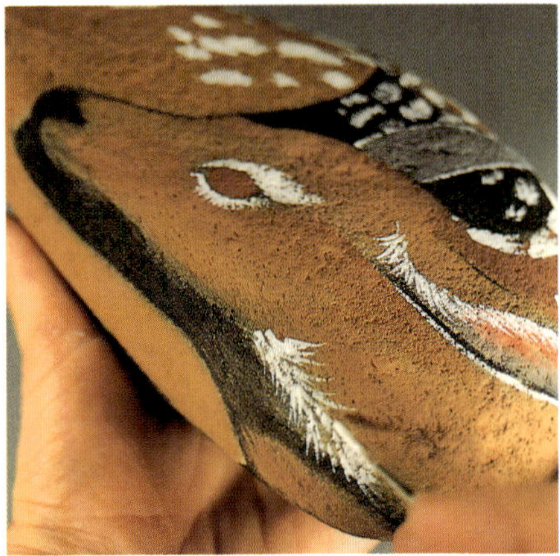

Paint tiny white strokes around the ears.

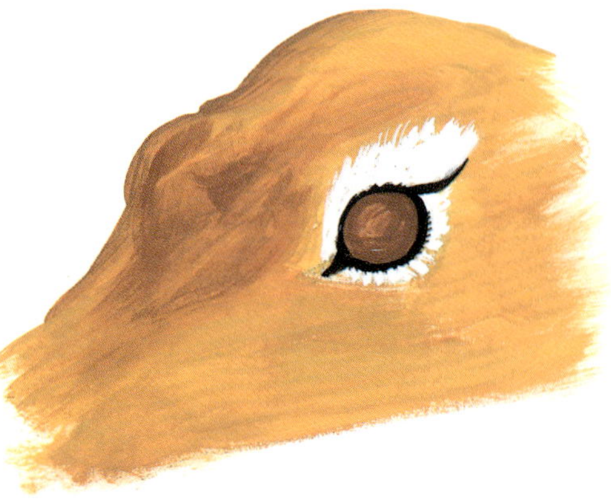

Outline the eyes with blended white lines.

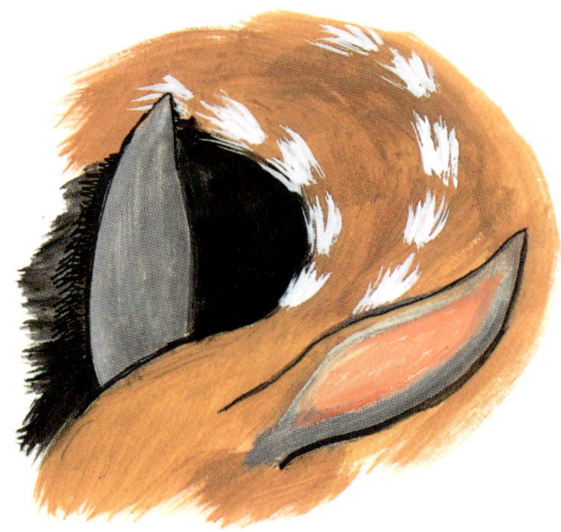

Paint parallel rows of white fur spots. Start with the spots just behind the head.

5 Fur Texture

Now you are ready to give your stone animal its realistically furry texture. Mix white and golden yellow to get a pale straw colour and begin along the muzzle. Leave the central portion of the face (between the eyes and down the muzzle) brown, but angle a row of tiny, straw-coloured fur lines just past the nose and around the bulge of the eye. Allow your strokes to grow longer as you move back along the curve of the forehead. Work in several sets of fur lines on the lower side of the muzzle, filling in that portion of the face down to the jawline and all the way back to the white fur at the chest. Fan a set of strokes back from behind the eye as well. Give your fawn more expression by stroking in two sets of eyebrow lines, angling them down and inward.

Use white paint to create the tuft of fur around the base of the outer ear, then add highlights to the upper edge of that ear. Consult the fur directional guides as you fill in the head and throat.

Next, fill the entire haunch with overlapping fur lines, varying the length and direction of your strokes. At the point where the hind leg crooks, detail the lower leg with short, prickly lines. If you have a front leg showing, detail it in the same manner.

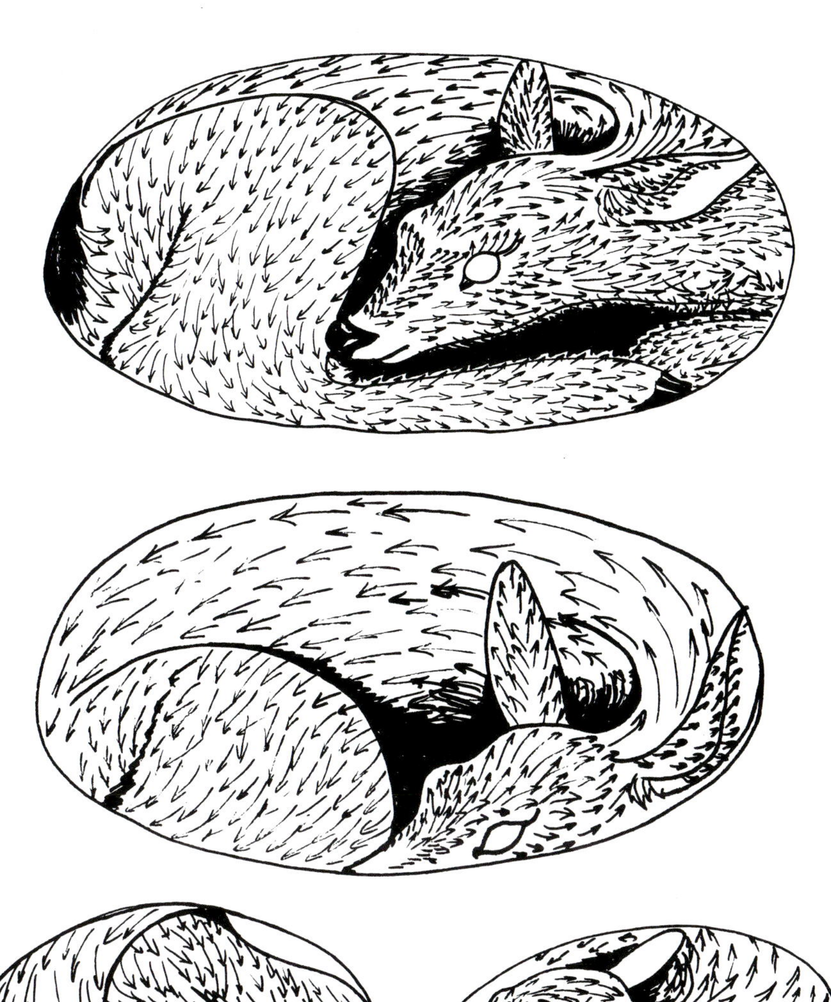

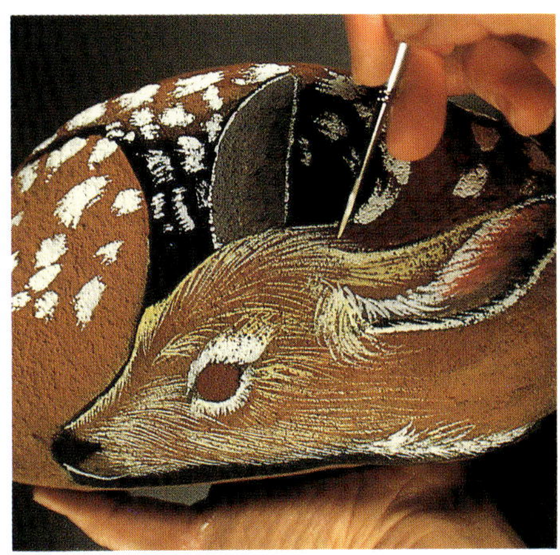

Texture the fur with rows of delicate lines.

Follow these guides to create realistic fur.

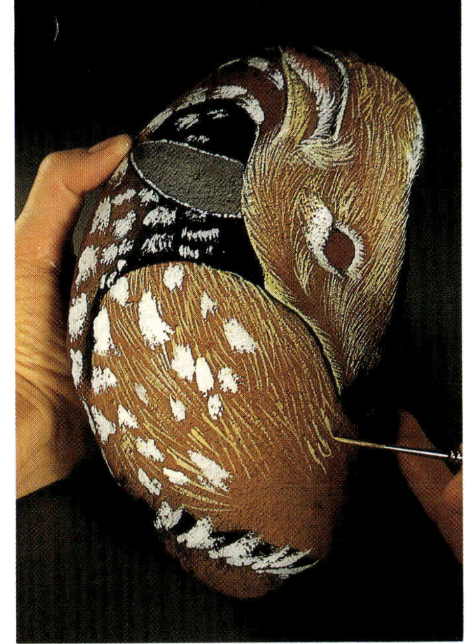

Add texture to haunch fur using overlapping lines.

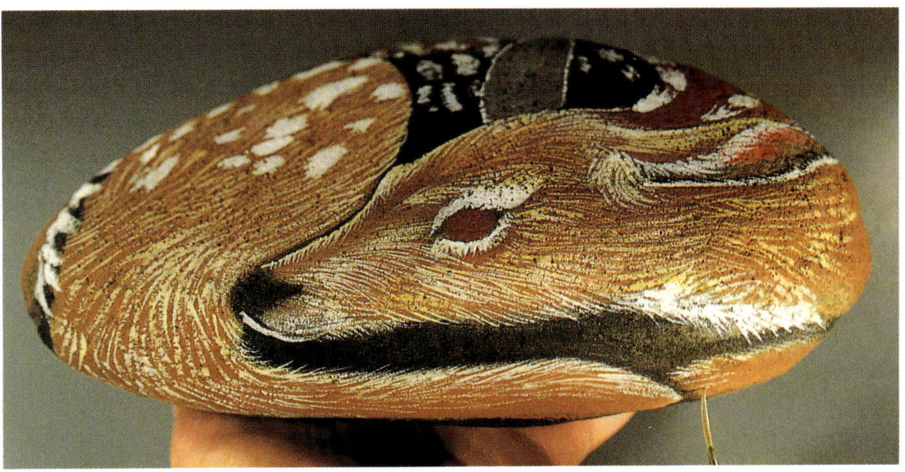

Add detail to the front leg with thin strokes.

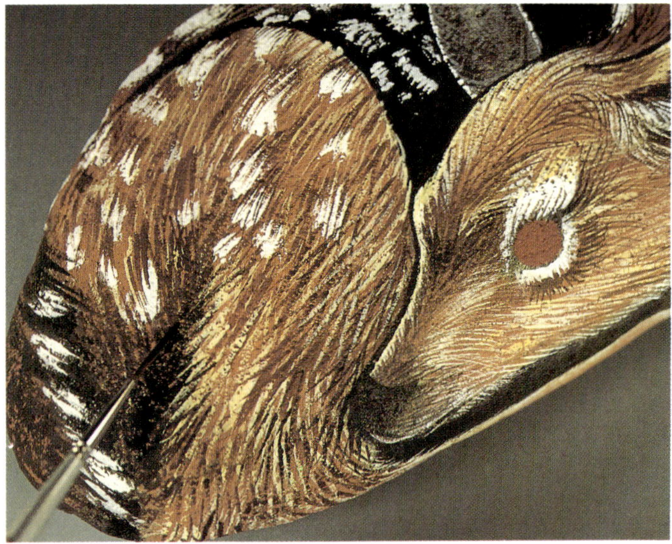

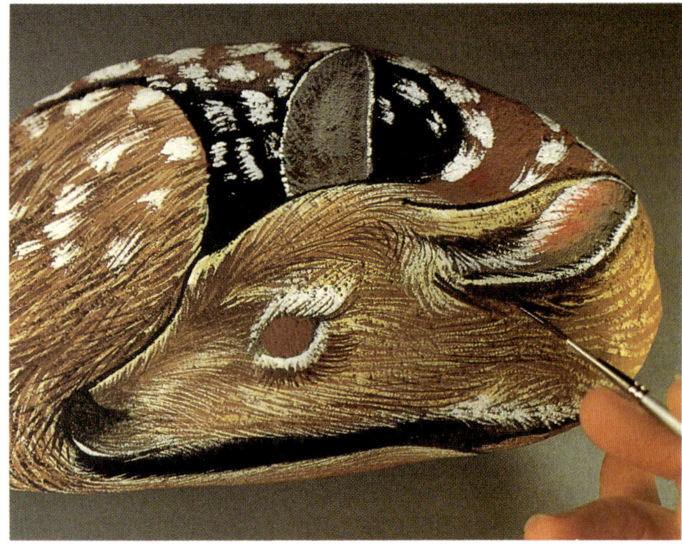

Emphasize the crook of the leg by intensifying the shadows.

Accentuate the ear by darkening the shadow underneath it.

6 Maximizing Contrast

Mix a deep brown from black and burnt sienna. Add depth and enrich the texture of your fawn's fur by using this colour to enhance the areas you just painted. Try to vary the length and direction of your strokes, but be sure to follow the same general fur direction. Emphasize the crook of the leg by darkening a V-shaped area between the tail and the middle of the haunch.

This darker colour can also be used to detail shadowed areas such as the centre of the muzzle between the eyes. Run a series of short lines along the outside ear and just below the white highlighted area of the eye to add dimension.

To define each individual spot, stroke a series of short, dark lines around it. Darken the area directly below the nose and give the jawline added dimension by running a row of short, fine strokes along the bottom. Scatter darker fur lines along the hind leg, making your strokes denser towards the lower edge of the leg.

Do not neglect the spots along the back and in the midsection; they, too, will stand out better with the addition of dark fur lines around their edges. Turn your fawn around and stroke a series of flowing lines along the curve of the spine. Finally, use this dark brown colour to deepen the eye colour, leaving only a narrow half-circle of lighter brown around the bottom.

With black paint and your smallest brush, outline the eye, then place an elongated oval-shaped iris horizontally in the upper centre. Flick the tip of

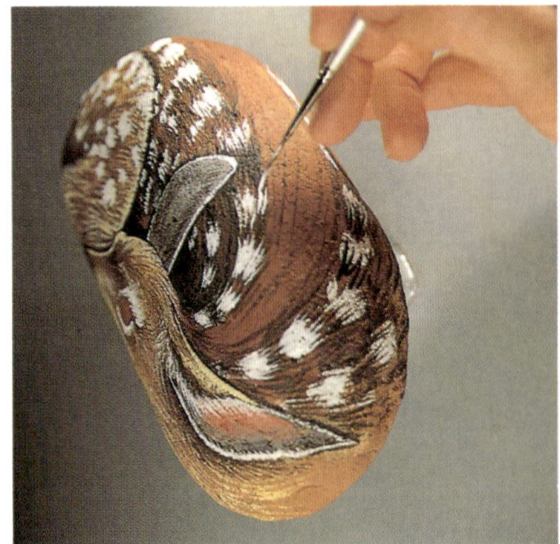

Accentuate the spots with dark outlines.

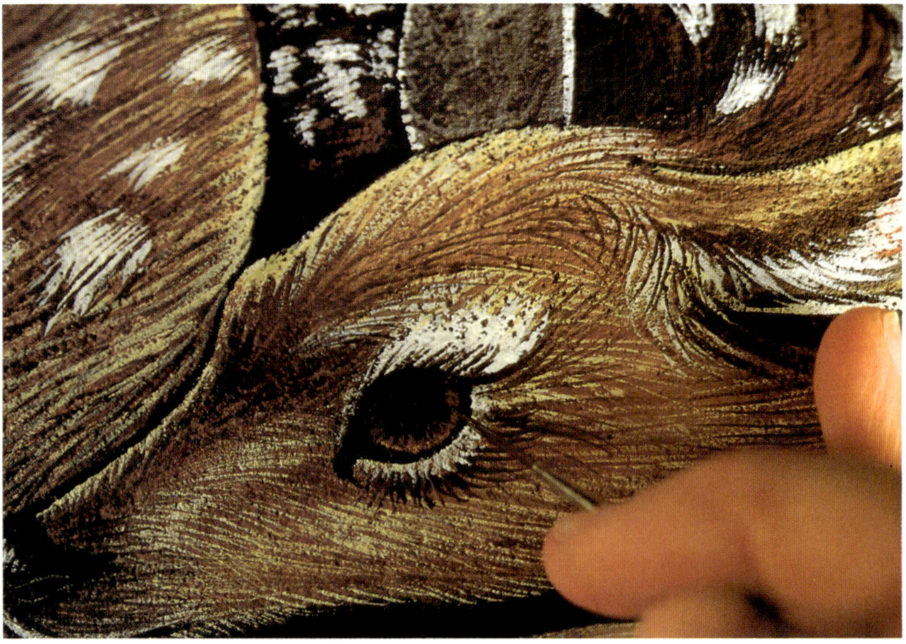

This picture shows a detail of the eye.

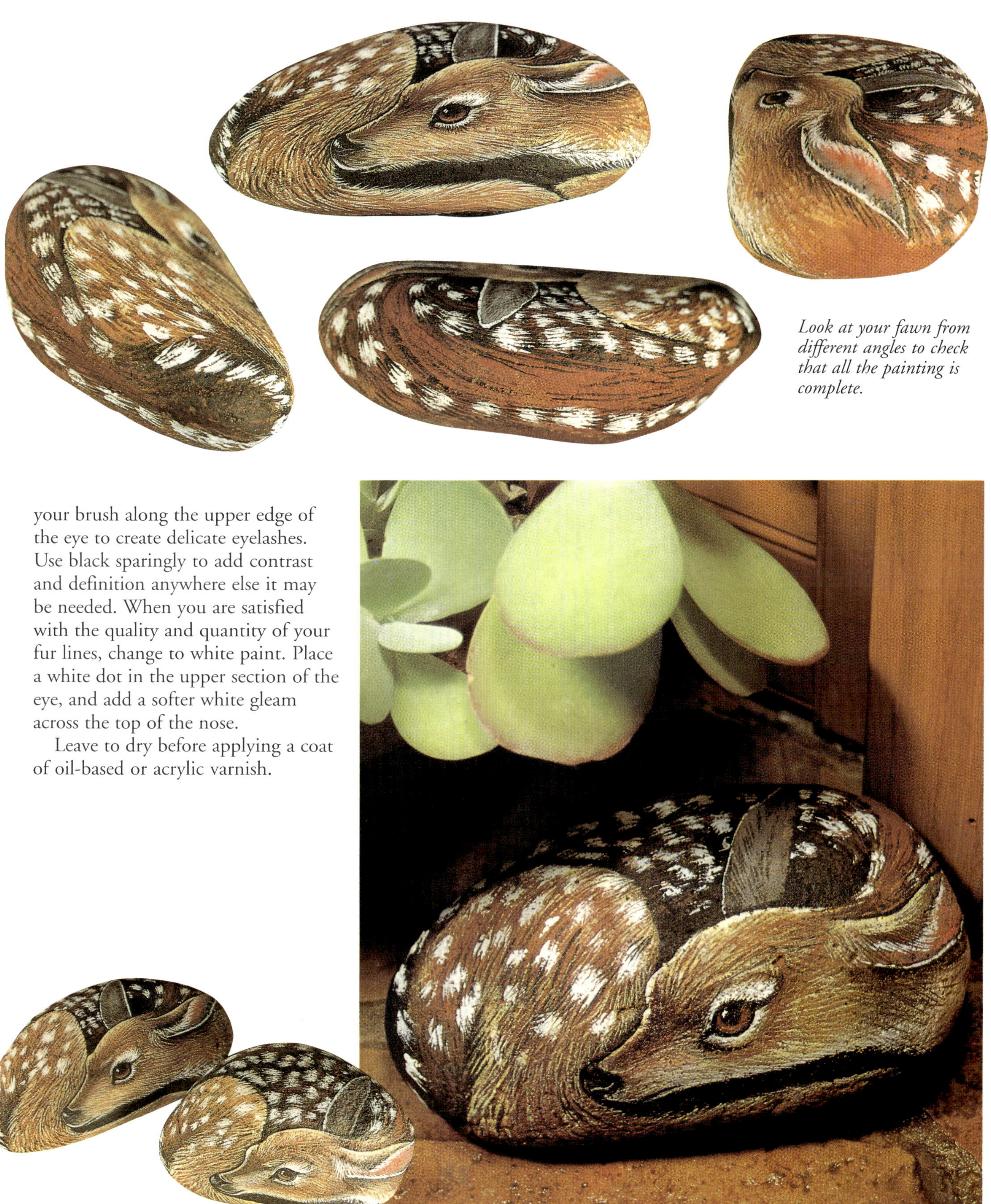

your brush along the upper edge of
the eye to create delicate eyelashes.
Use black sparingly to add contrast
and definition anywhere else it may
be needed. When you are satisfied
with the quality and quantity of your
fur lines, change to white paint. Place
a white dot in the upper section of the
eye, and add a softer white gleam
across the top of the nose.

Leave to dry before applying a coat
of oil-based or acrylic varnish.

*Try tucking your finished creation among potted houseplants, or let
it peer out from underneath a coffee table.*

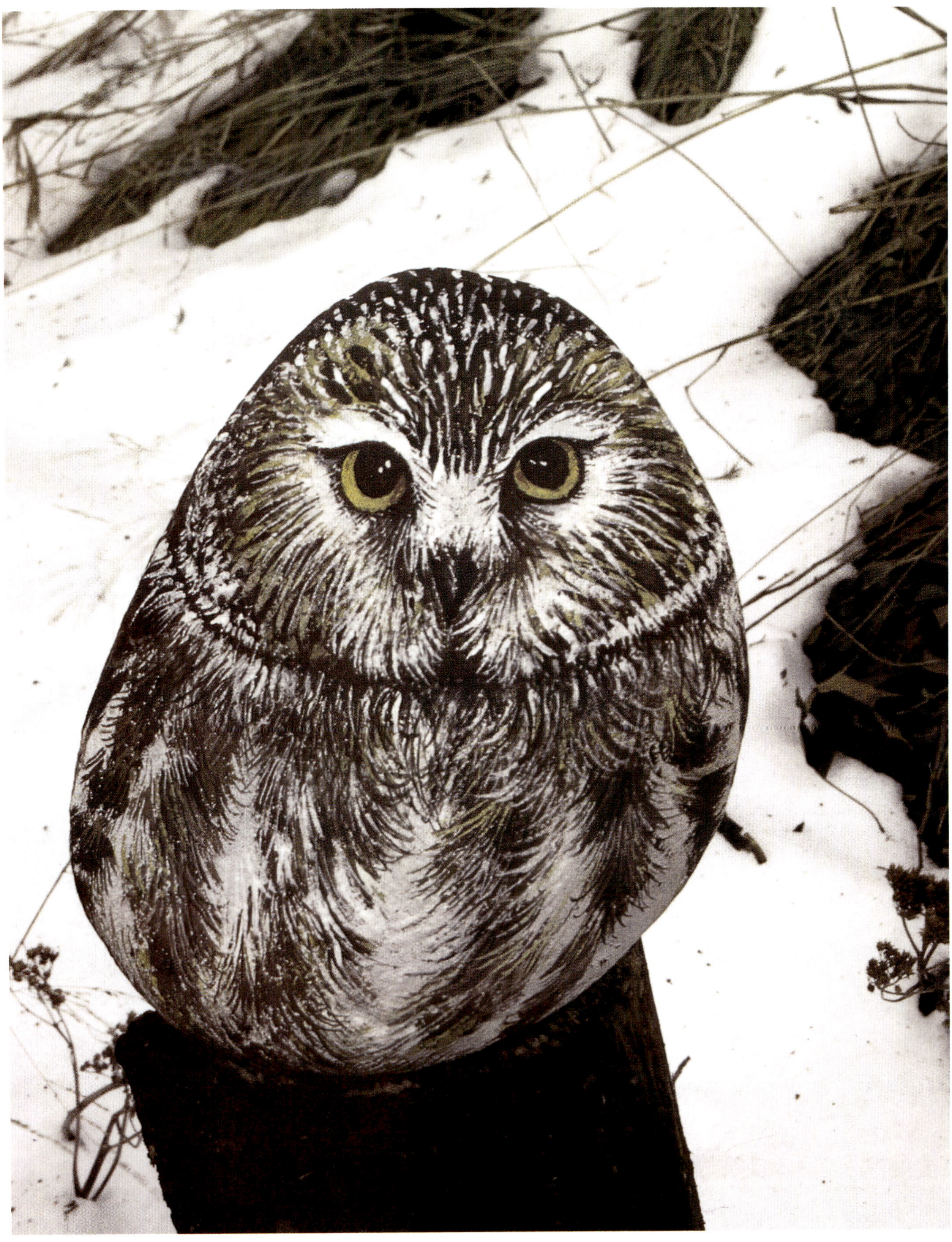

OWL

Birds present a completely different kind of challenge for the stone painter. Fluffy down and smooth overlapping feathers replace fine fur lines. As a rule, there is little or no contouring involved. Not all birds are good subjects – many are not compact enough to fit neatly on to common stone shapes. Owls, however, are particularly well-suited for stone painting. Their bodies are basic, uncomplicated forms that adapt easily to many different stone shapes. There are many species of owl; some are dramatically patterned, some have more subtle colouring.

In your search for a possible owl stone, look for a flat-bottomed, wide-based, upright stone. It should taper gently to a rounded top. Your owl could stand up quite tall, or it could be lower and wider, as though hunched down. An owl stone could be symmetrical, it could tilt to one side, or it could even lean forward – it does not matter, as long as it will sit without tipping over.

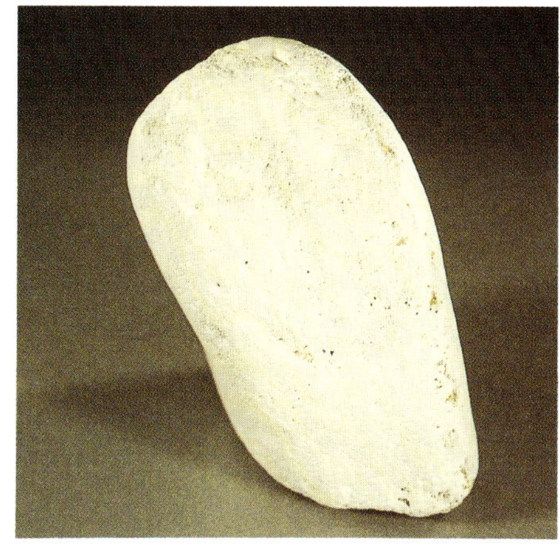

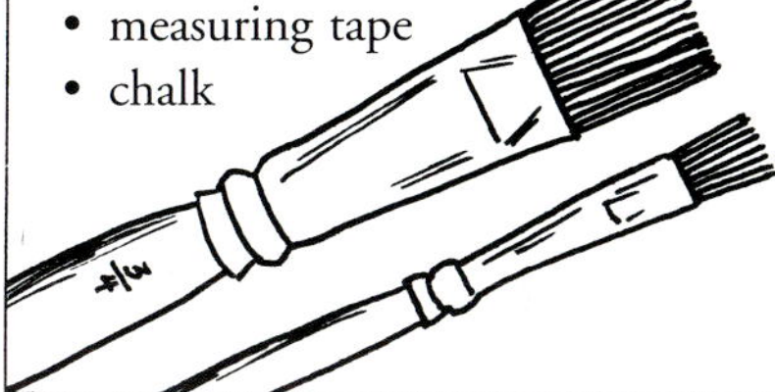

You Will Need
- Acrylic paint: white, black, yellow, golden yellow and burnt sienna
- oil-based or acrylic clear varnish
- assorted brushes
- pencil
- measuring tape
- chalk

Tilted stones work well for owls, provided they do not tip over easily.

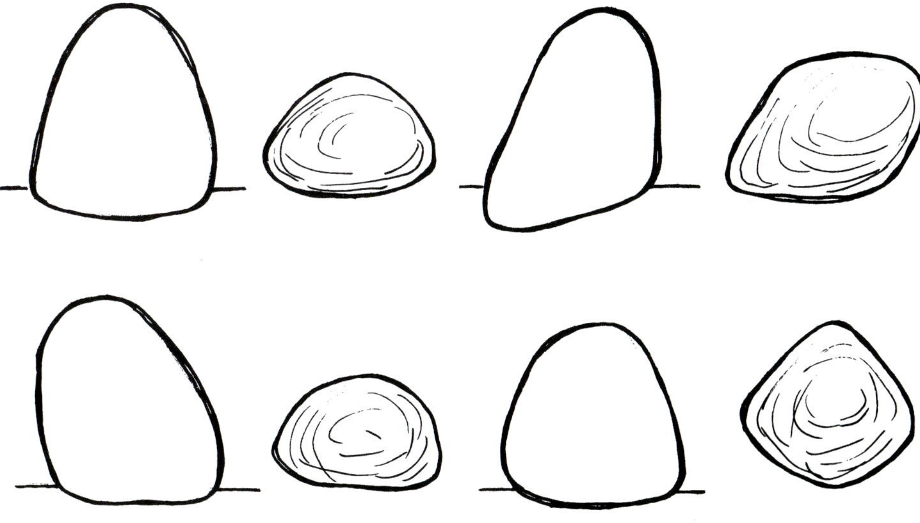

Suitable stone shapes for an owl.

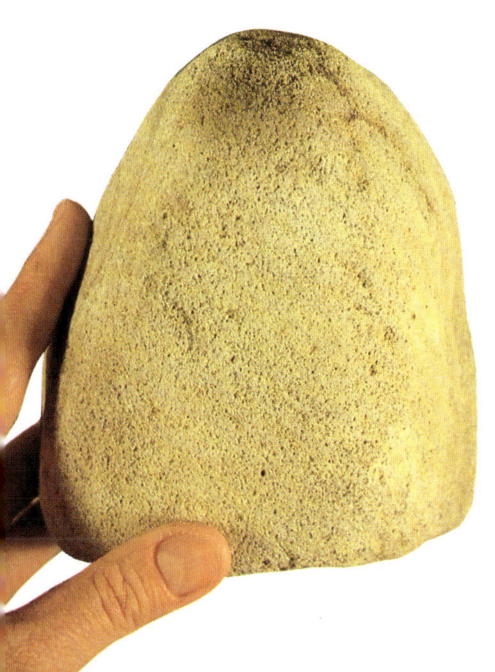

A perfect owl stone.

Choosing a suitable site for the face is the most important layout factor for your owl. The face area should be a relatively wide, flat plane. If the stone has an outward curve, the widest point should form the vertical midpoint of the face. After you have selected the site for the face, determine the best place for the tail. Unlike most animals, owls can turn their heads in nearly any direction, so the tail need not be directly behind or to one side of the head. If the stone you have chosen has a bump at the base, this would be the logical spot for the tail, regardless of where it is in relation to the face. In fact, some of the most successful owl stones are those where the owl is peering back over its shoulder.

Once you have a stone you think will work, clean it well. When dry, use your largest brush to cover all exposed surfaces with white paint. Leave to dry.

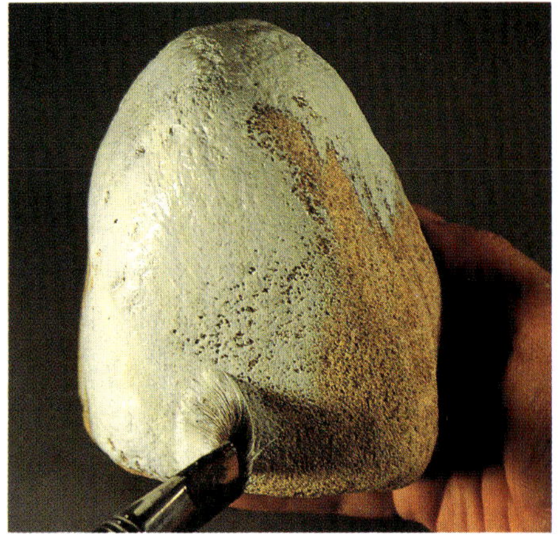

Apply a snowy white base coat to the stone before marking on the layout.

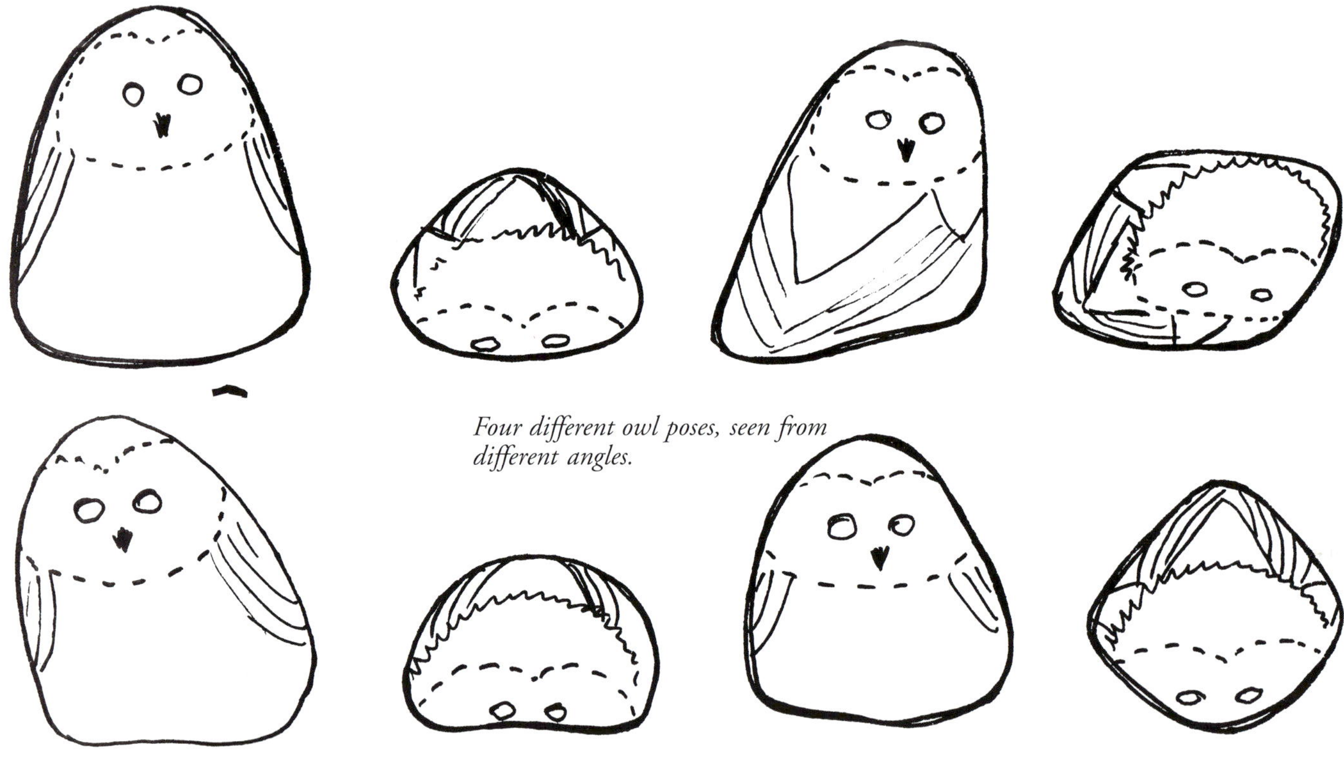

Four different owl poses, seen from different angles.

1 Layout

Measure the stone's height. This measurement will help you determine the dimensions for the face. For stones 20cm (8in) or taller, the face may go halfway down the stone and nearly all the way across. On smaller stones, though, the owl will look best if the face is slightly shorter. To illustrate these proportions, I measured a number of my stone owls, and came up with the following figures, which you may find helpful.

Owl 1
Overall height: 18cm (7in)
Vertical face measurement: 7.5cm (3in)
Horizontal face measurement: 11.5cm (4^1/$_2$in)

Owl 2
Overall height: 15cm (6in)
Vertical face measurement: 6.5cm (2^1/$_2$in)
Horizontal face measurement: 10cm (4in)

Owl 3
Overall height: 14cm (5^1/$_2$in)
Vertical face measurement: 5cm (2in)
Horizontal face measurement: 8cm (3^1/$_4$in)

You do not have to find a stone that adheres exactly to these measurements, but it is safe to say your basic layout will not be too far off if you bear these relationships in mind. Use a pencil to measure off the proportions for your face oval.

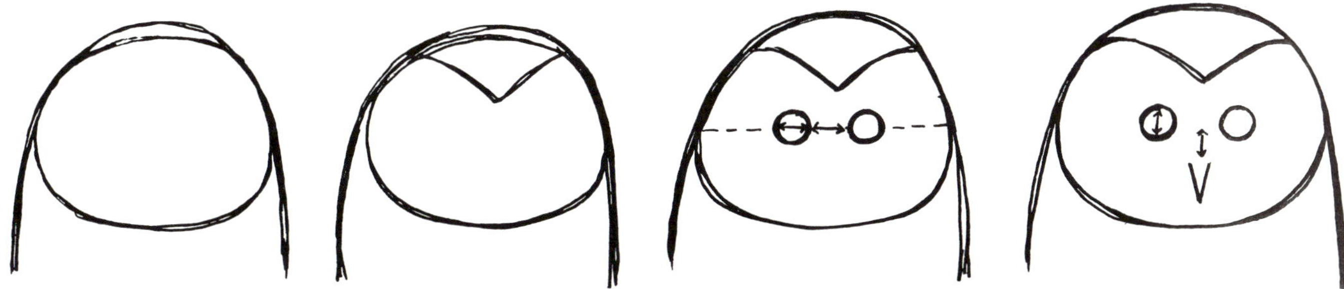

This sequence shows the steps for face layout.

After the face oval is in place, modify it by creating a V-shape in the middle of the forehead. Bisect the oval horizontally and use the midline as a guide for the eyes. Owls have dramatically large, round eyes but eye diameter will vary with the size of your stone. On the three owls I measured previously, the size of the eyes were:

Owl 1

Eye diameter: 1.25cm ($^1/_2$in)

Owl 2

Eye diameter: just over 1cm ($^3/_8$in)

Owl 3

Eye diameter: just under 1cm ($^3/_8$in)

Use the height of your own stone to determine the size of the eyes, then centre them on the midline one eye space apart. To determine beak placement, measure one eye-width down from between the eyes on the midline. Mark that as the top of the beak. The beak itself should be a narrow triangle whose point does not quite reach to the bottom of the face.

Now turn your stone and draw a neck line around the back of the head. Indicate the tail with a wide V-shape at the base. The sides of this V-shape should bow gently outward around the curving sides of your stone and touch the perimeters of the face oval in front. If you look at your stone sideways, the wing lines should cut diagonally from the face to the tail. The remaining portion of the body will be the breast.

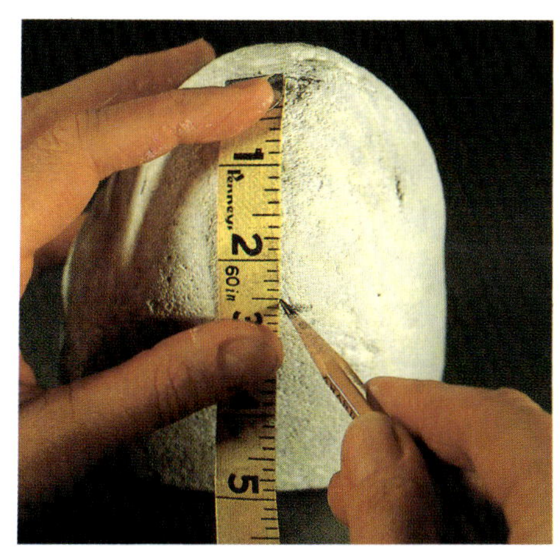

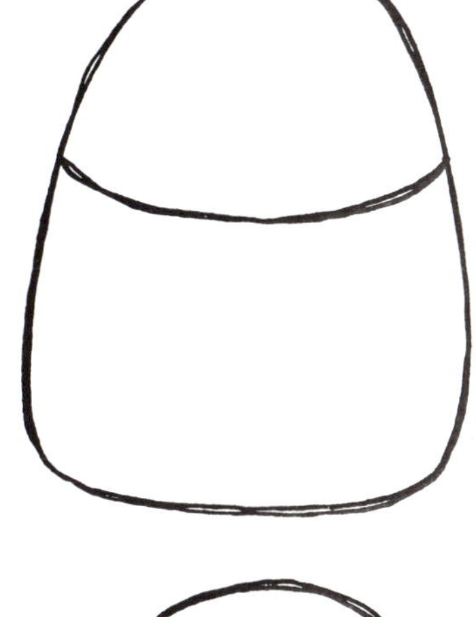

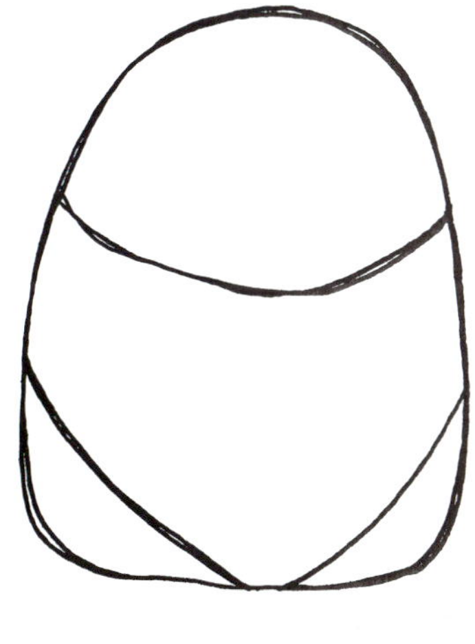

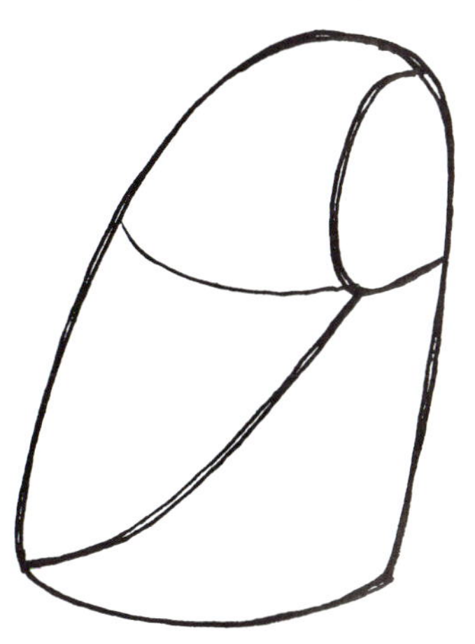

This sequence shows the layout of the neck, tail and wing relative to the face.

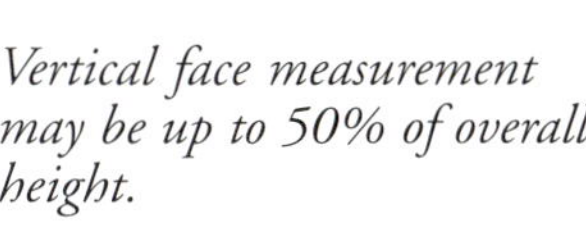

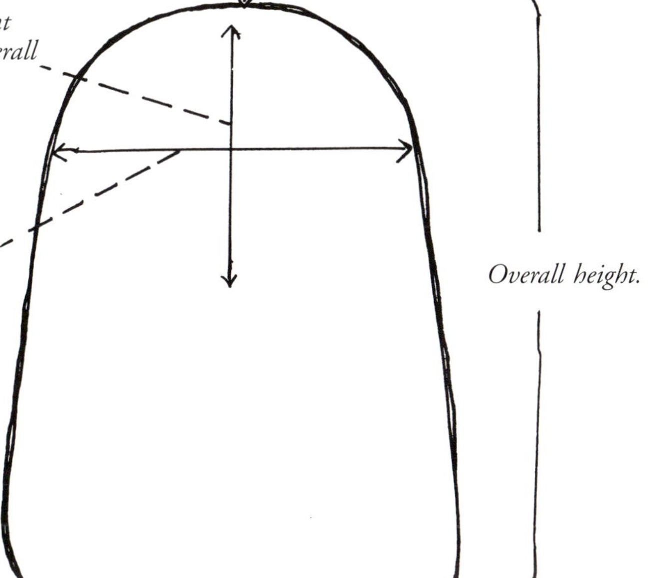

Vertical face measurement may be up to 50% of overall height.

Horizontal face measurement may be up to 75% of overall height.

Overall height.

2 Face and Head Details

Use a liner brush to outline the eye circles in black. Paint the beak next, making the point sharp and well-defined. The wide upper end should be ragged-looking to create the illusion of small overlapping feathers. Next, use a medium flat brush to encircle the face with short, dense strokes. Create feathery points along the bottom of the face.

Fill in the rest of the head shape with solid black all the way around. Let the paint dry.

Now take up your smallest brush and change to golden yellow paint softened with a little white. Use this colour to make thin, dense lines like sunrays radiating from the eyes and beak. Leave a border of white encircling the eyes, but allow your brushstrokes to overlap some of the dark areas on the head.

Use golden yellow to fill in the eye circles. The owl's eyes will be the focal point of the piece, so take your time to paint them as neat and round as you can. If you accidentally paint over the black outlines, repaint them with black when the eyes are dry.

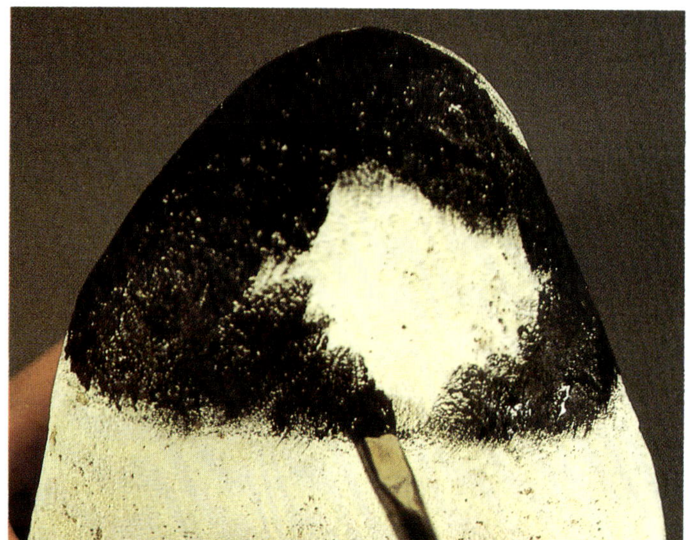

Fill in the back of the head with black.

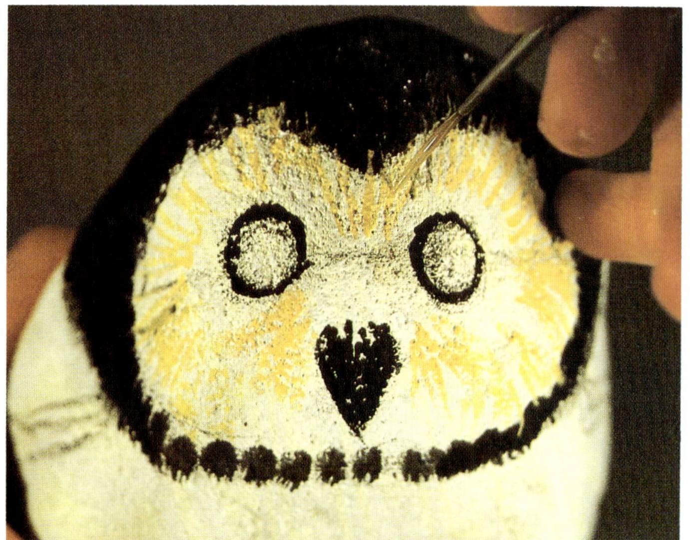

Surround the eyes and beak with subtle golden yellow highlights.

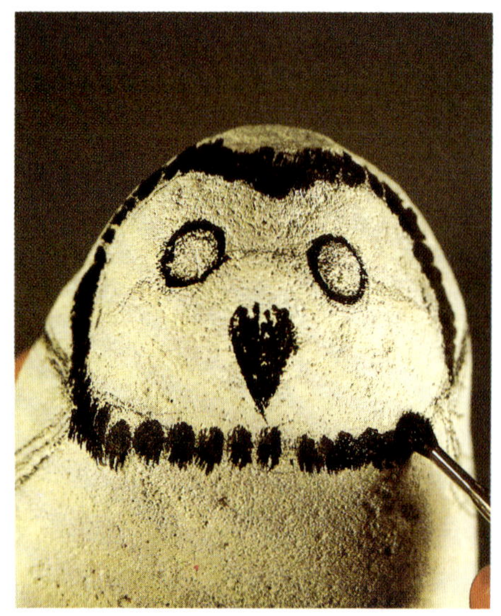

Outline along the bottom of the face.

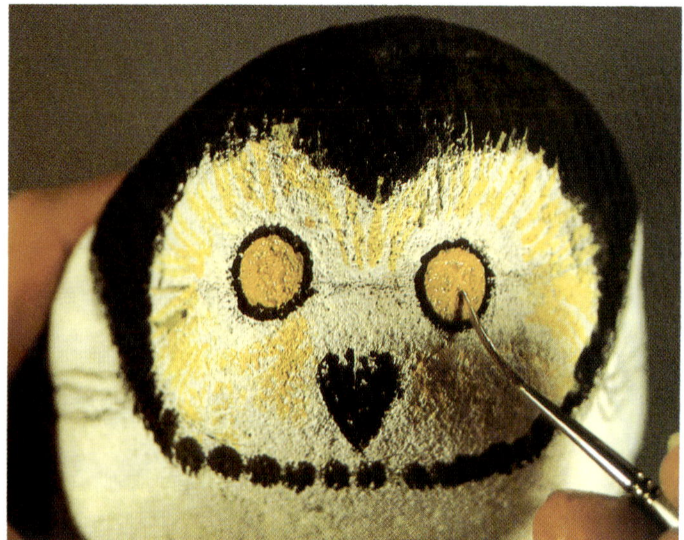

Fill in the eyes with golden yellow.

3 Feather Patterns

Use random brushstrokes to feather the breast. Use a medium round brush and burnt sienna to paint a raggedy-looking row of feathers below the black edging at the neck. Next make several vertical rows of broken strokes down the breast. Allow these strokes to vary in both size and spacing, but curve them slightly inward. Leave plenty of white area showing between these strokes.

Tilt the stone backwards to expose the lower front edge and brush a series of dense, random lines to the bottom portion of the breast. Use a brush that will allow you to taper your strokes.

Next use a large brush to mix black and burnt sienna into a deep brown. Paint in the back and tail feathers. Leave a narrow collar of white showing between the head and shoulders. Leave to dry.

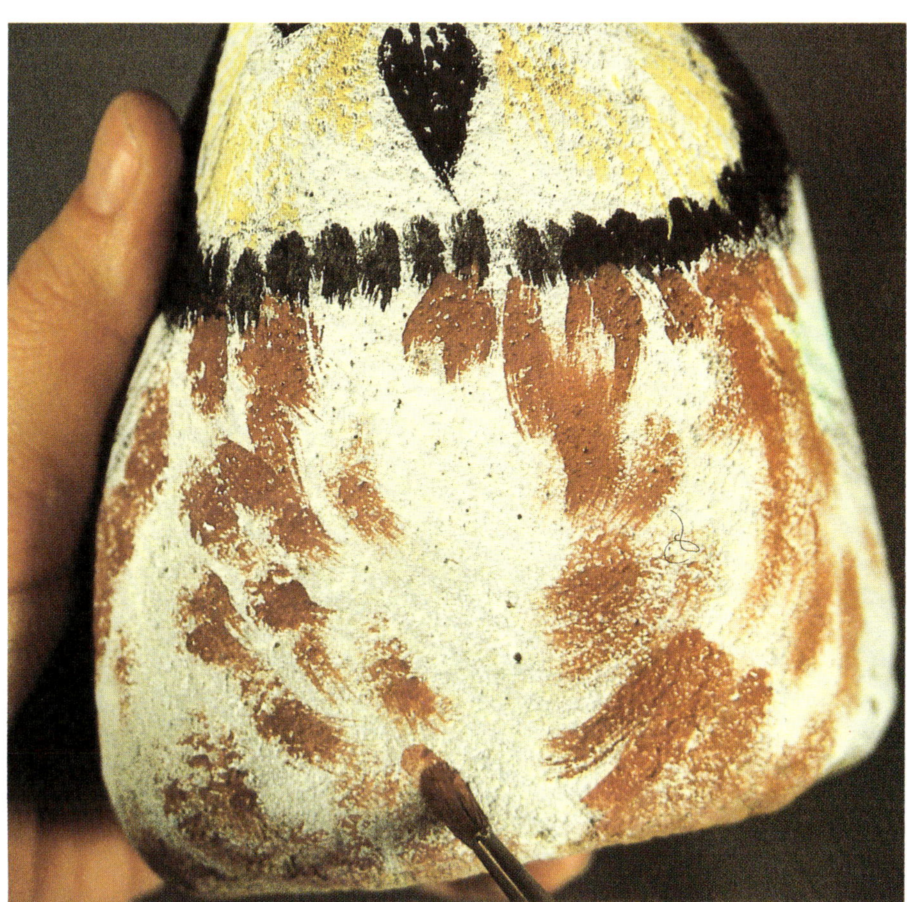

Roughly paint in the breast feathers.

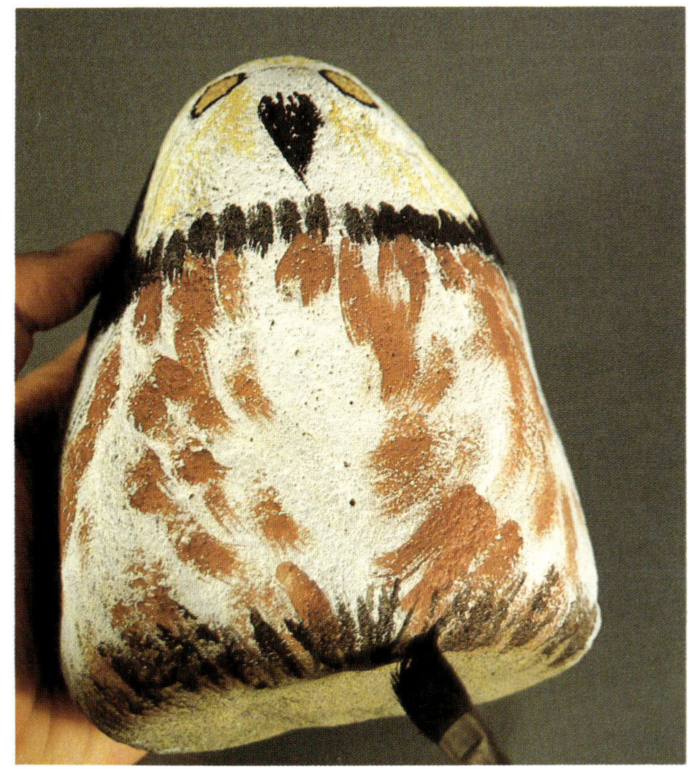

Tilt the stone to paint the feathers at the base of the owl.

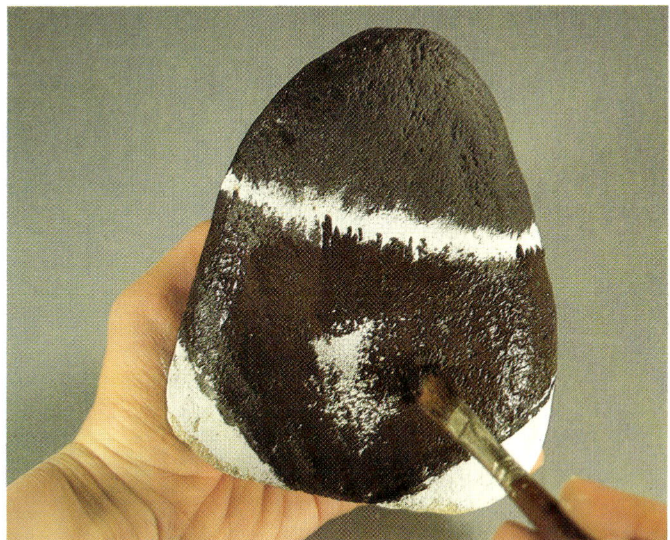

Fill in the back and tail feathers with deep brown.

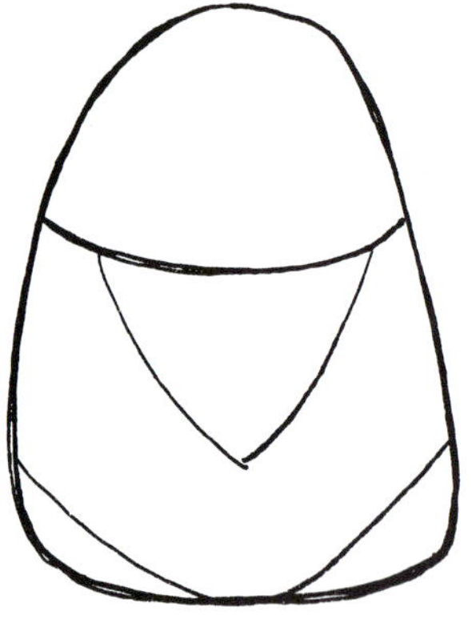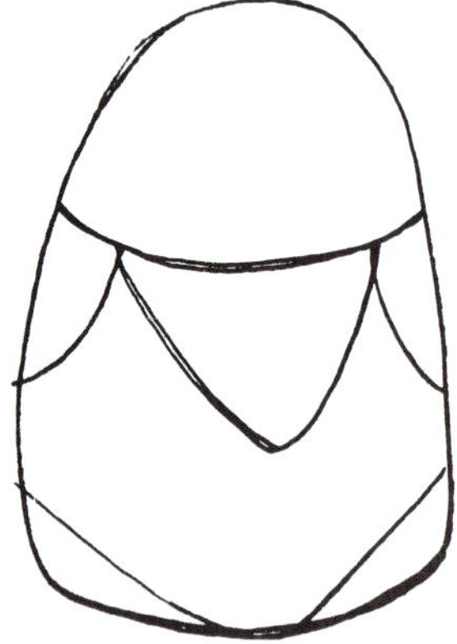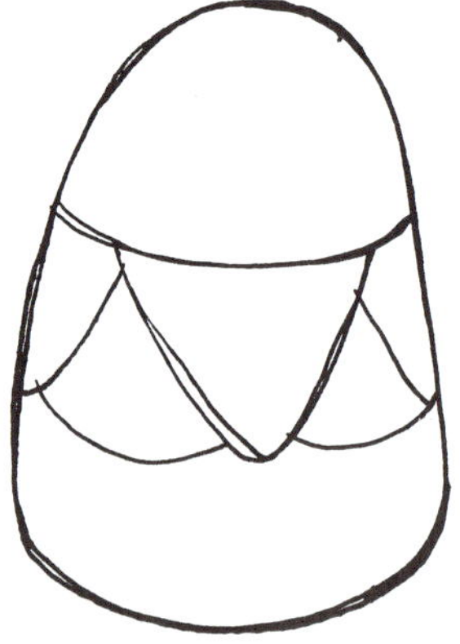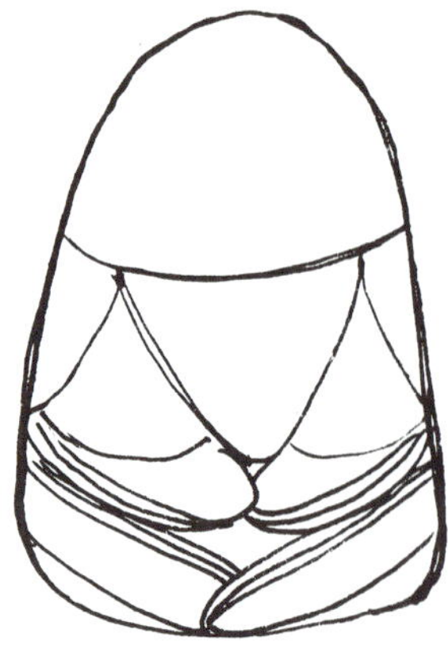

The pattern for the feathers.

4 Wing and Tail Feather Layout

Use chalk to sketch the pattern for the feathers. Begin at the neck and extend a V-shape halfway down the back, mirroring the V-shape of the tail. On each side make narrower V-shapes like epaulettes at the shoulders. Connect the bottom points of these V-shapes with curved lines. Below these curved lines, sketch in two sets of overlapping feather patches as shown. If you are not happy with your layout, rub out the chalk and start again.

5 Painting the Feathers

Add a series of white strokes along the back V-shape with a small or medium brush. Use a liner brush to outline both upper and lower sets of wing feathers, and to make a series of white dots along the two curving lines connecting the shoulders to the back V-shape.

Next, mix burnt sienna and golden yellow paint in equal proportions to get a warm golden brown. Use a liner brush to make a row of connected U-shapes along the white neckline at the back. Do a second row below the first, starting each U-shape in the middle of the one above so that you have an overlapping effect. You should have room for four or more rows, each one shorter than the previous one until there is space for only a single U-shape at the point. Work a similar pattern on the epaulettes at each shoulder.

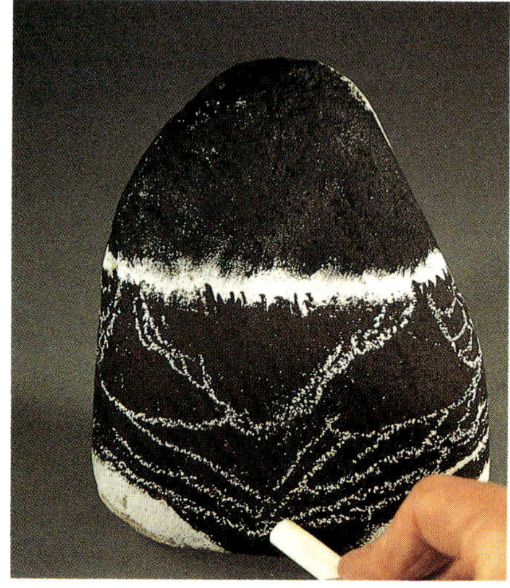

Use chalk to sketch in the feathers.

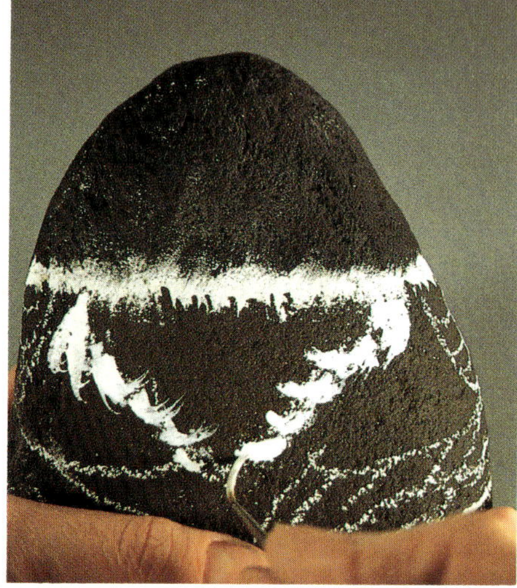

Add white strokes along the back V.

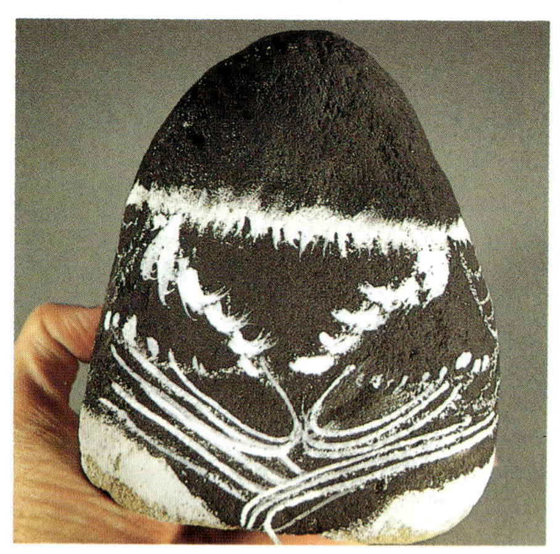

Outline the tail feathers with a liner brush.

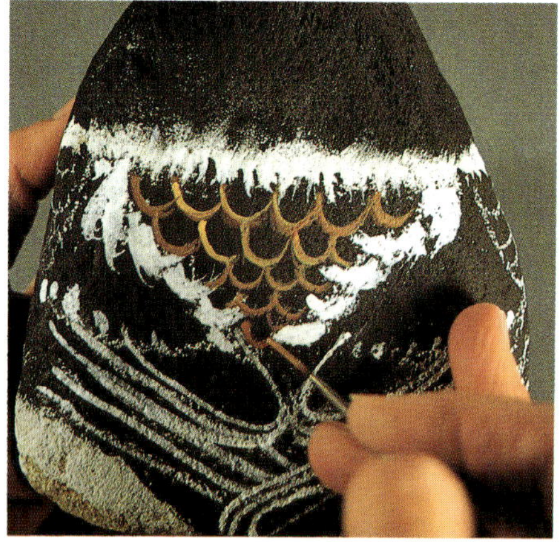

Paint in rows of U-shapes at the neck.

To connect the shoulder pattern and the back pattern, make a series of diagonal feather lines as shown. Add depth and visual interest to the very bottom set of tail feathers by running several thin lines of brown alongside the white outlines.

Add black to the brown colour you have been using and shade the bottom edges of each row of U-shaped feathers. Use this same colour to shade the base with thin, wispy brushstrokes.

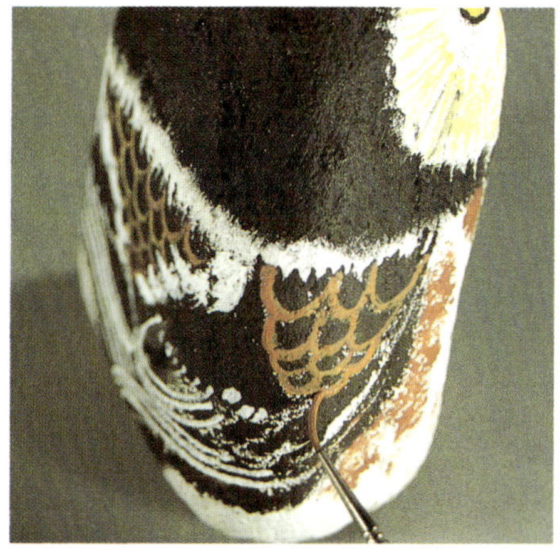

Paint a series of overlapping U-shapes at each shoulder.

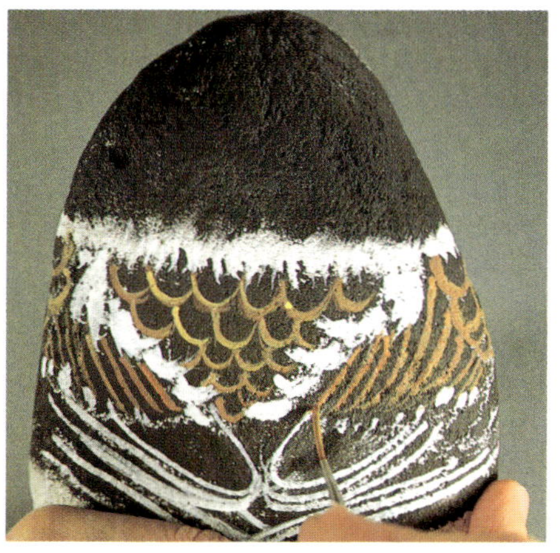

Apply diagonal feather lines to connect the shoulder pattern to the back pattern.

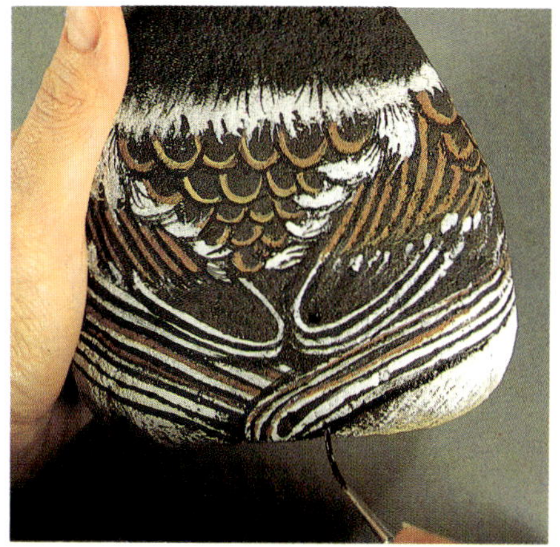

Intersperse a few delicate brown lines with white among the tail feathers.

6 Head Feathers

Use a liner brush and white paint to paint a series of short, crooked, broken lines along the top border of the face and into the black area of the head. Allow your strokes to become more uniform as you work around the sides of the head. The strokes should radiate out like short spokes. Add consecutive layers of similar strokes to cover the back and sides of the head.

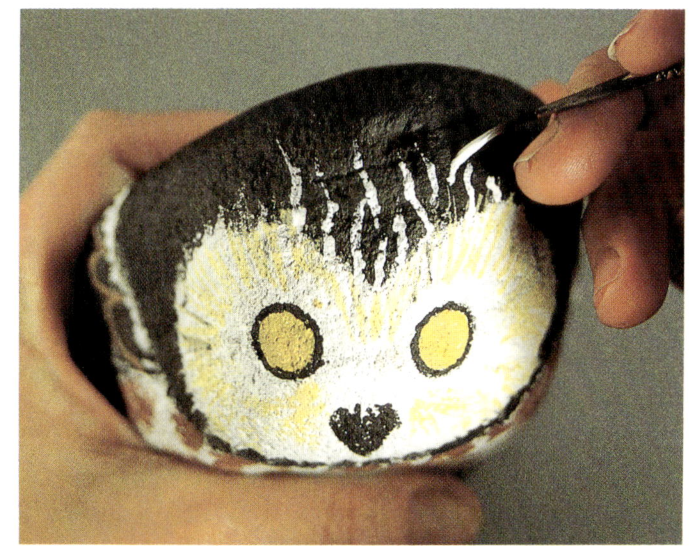

Radiate short, crooked, broken lines from the top of the head.

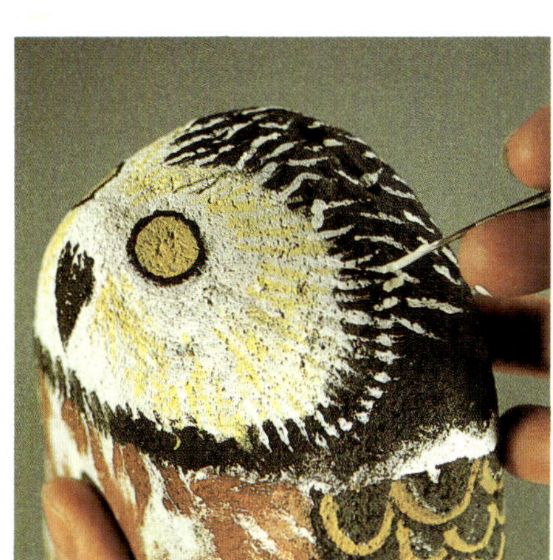

Add more white lines around the sides of the head.

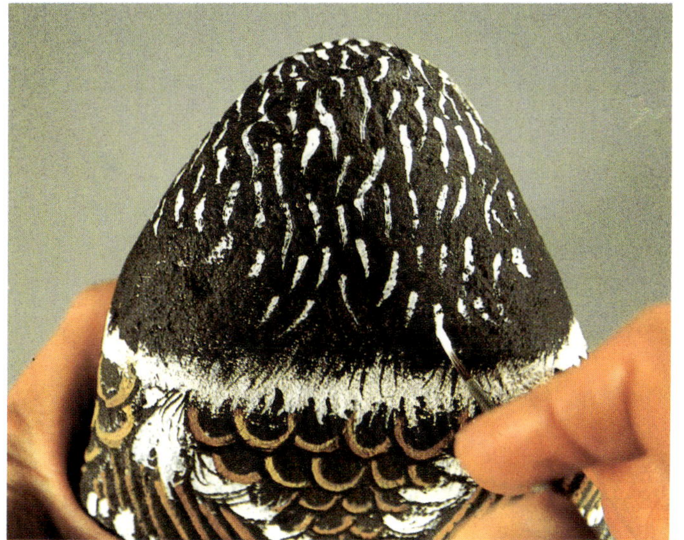

Layer the white lines down the back of the head.

7 Feather Details

Change back to the deep brown shade and add crisp details to the lighter brown feathers at the breast. Paint a row of dense, random strokes just below the neckline, then scatter more of these lines in clustered sets among the breast feathers.

8 Finishing Touches

Refer to the directional guide for feather placement. Surround the eyes with delicate lash-like strokes. At the inside lower corner of each eye, elongate the strokes and fan them out to look particularly dense and heavy. Allow a few strokes to reach over the top of the beak and a few more to stretch horizontally above the beak from either side until they almost touch.

Fan another set of strokes below each eye – a few should even overlap the top of the beak, while others should curve away in the opposite direction.

Brush in a set of short lines just inside the face oval from either side of the V-shape. Follow the curve of the face.

Paint a black, oval iris in each eye (see opposite). Each iris should be slightly skewed towards the centre of the eye circle. Darken each upper portion with burnt sienna to add depth, then highlight by stroking a narrow half-circle of bright yellow around the lower half of each eye.

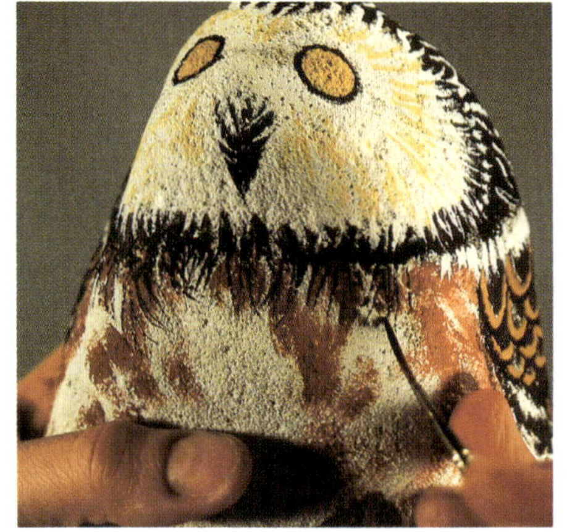

Paint dense strokes along the neckline.

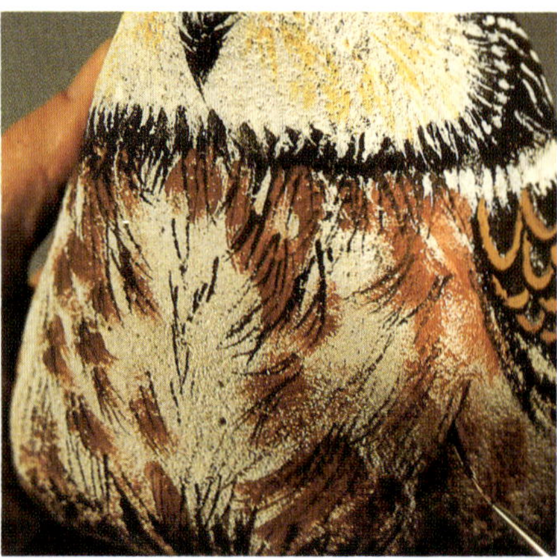

Scatter fine lines among the breast feathers.

Refer to this directional guide when adding the facial feathers.

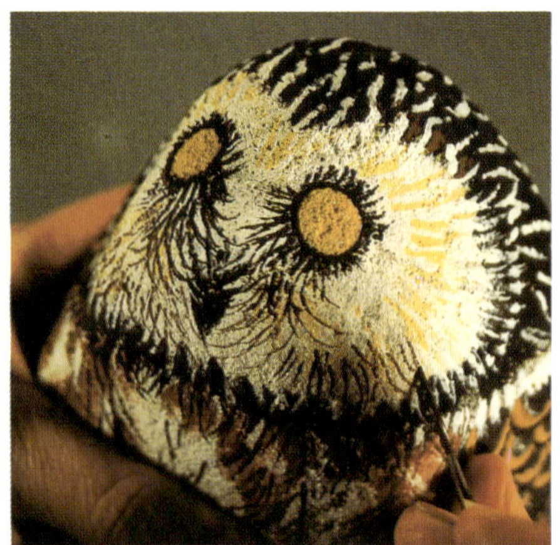

Brush short lines just inside the face oval.

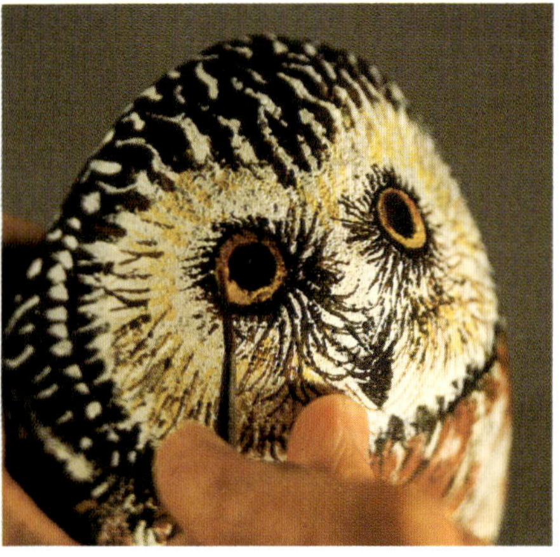

Darken the upper portion of each eye.

Finally, change to white paint and use your liner brush to define any light areas that may require more detail. Pay particular attention to the outer edges of the wings on either side of the breast – these feathers should look fluffy.

Add some white strokes to the breast, overlapping with brown streaks here and there. Finish by placing two small dots in the inside upper quadrant of each eye for a lifelike sparkle.

Leave to dry before applying a coat of varnish.

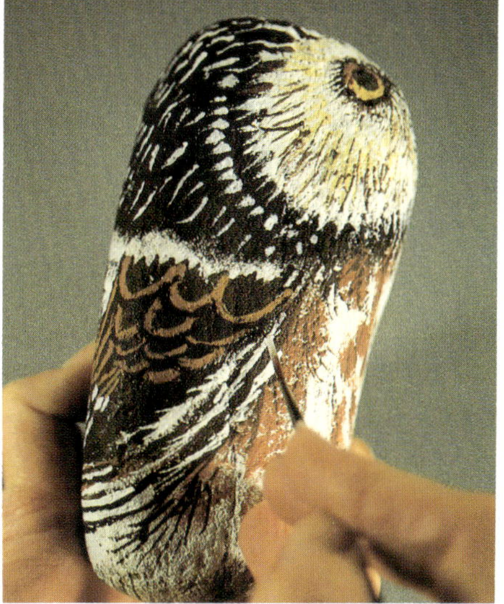

Touch up the wing edges.

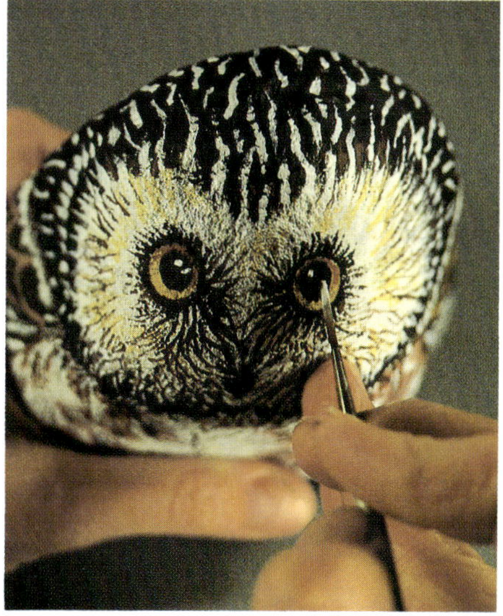

Add a dot of white to each eye.

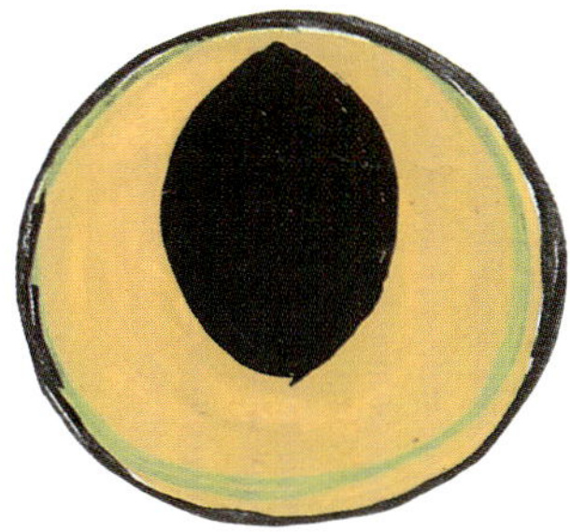
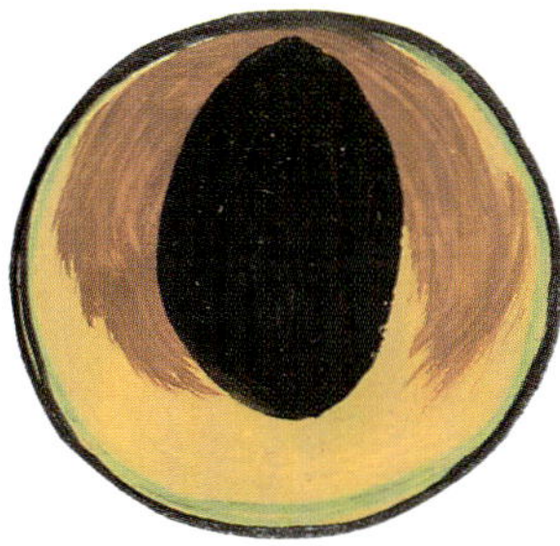
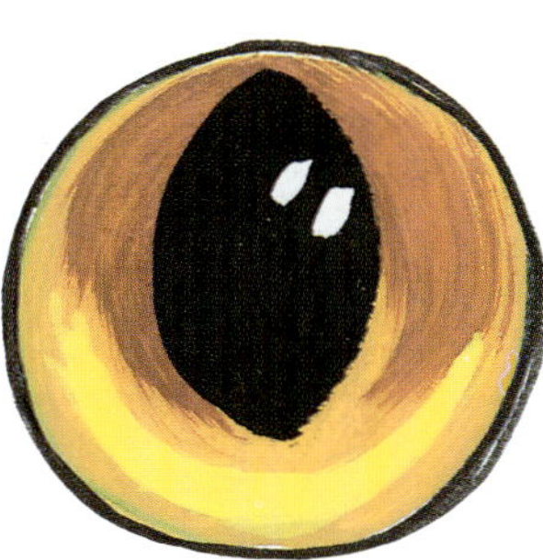

Steps for painting the eyes.

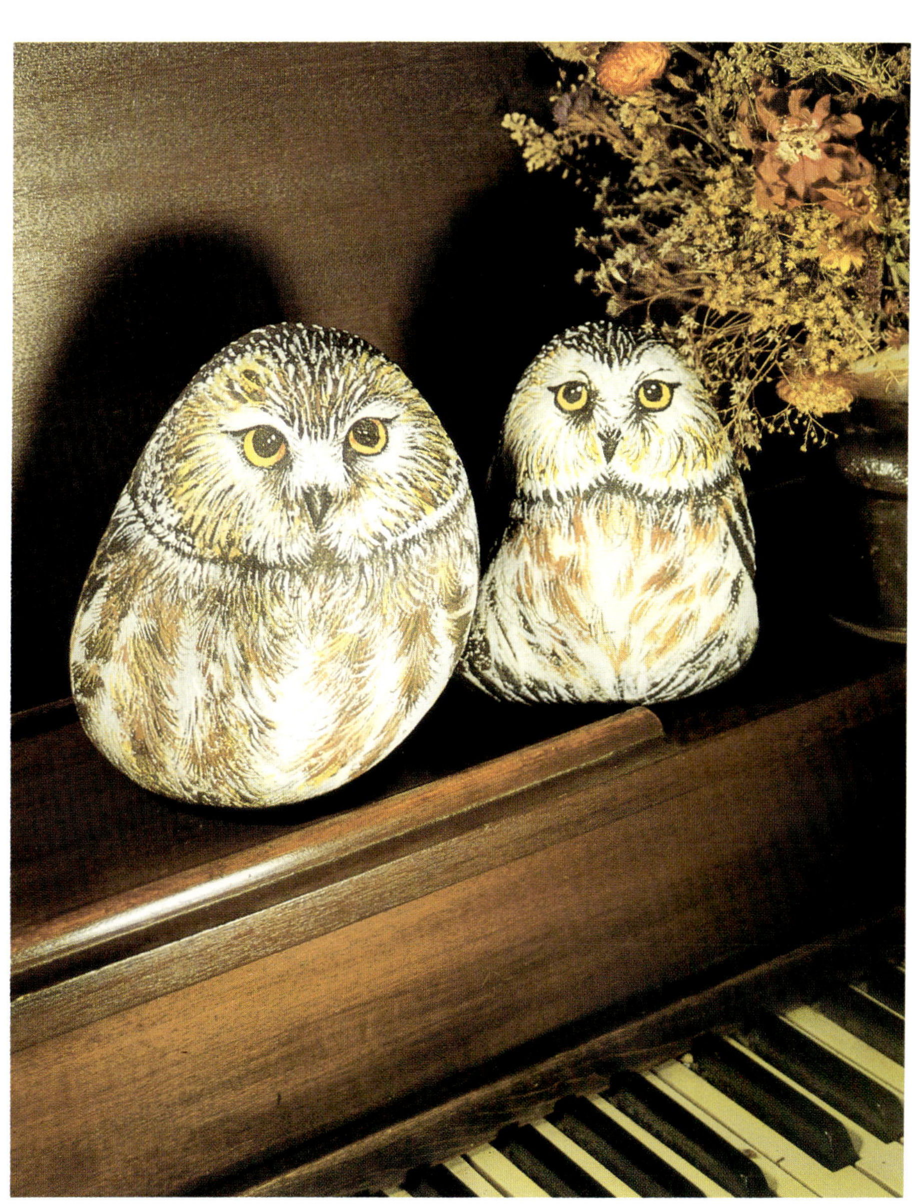

Owls are quite ornamental and will add an exciting touch to any decor. Try perching one or two on a wooden surface to create an impact.

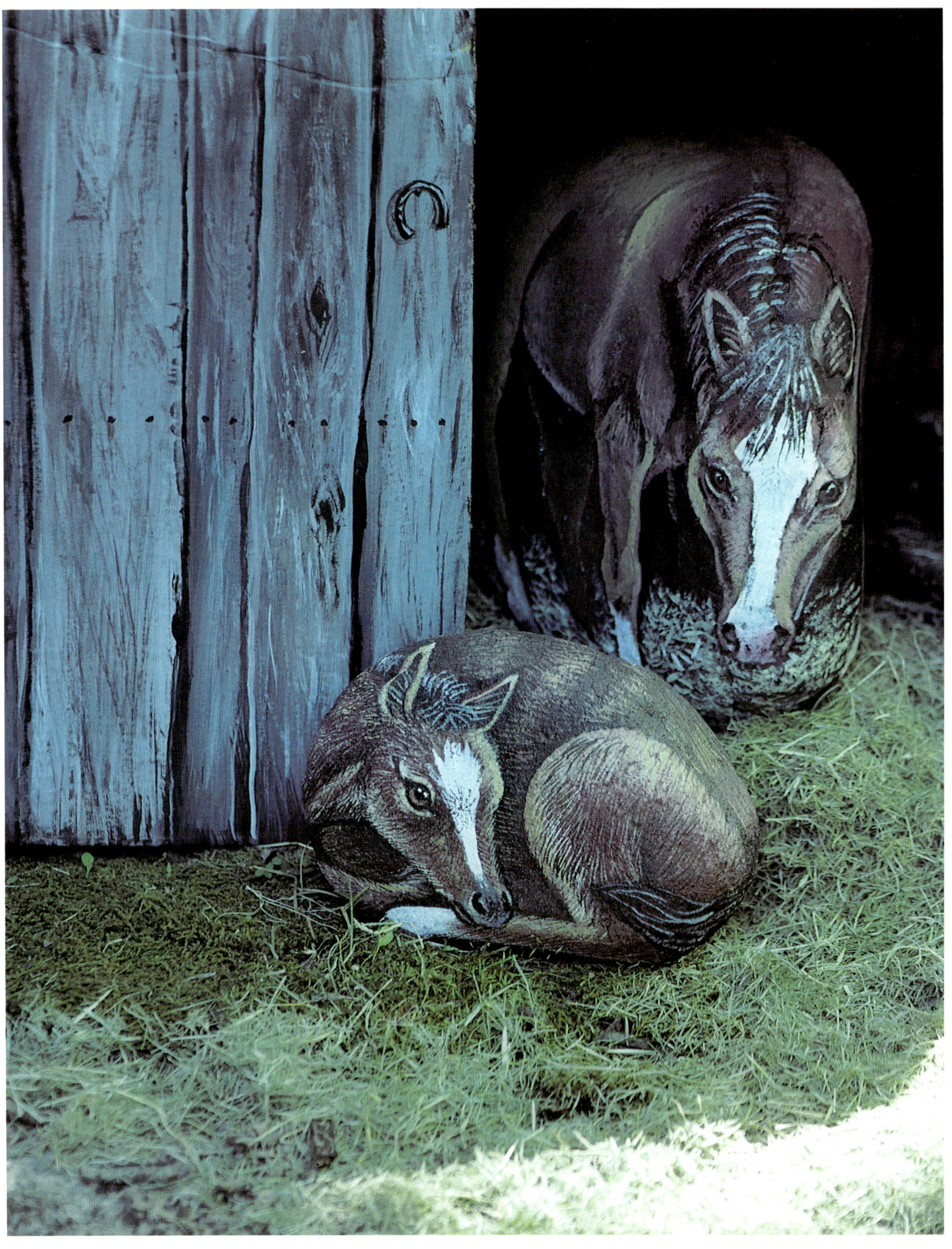

How to Paint a
FOAL

A newborn foal makes a wonderful addition to any menagerie of stone animals. It is a great gift for horse lovers, too. Best of all, foals are surprisingly simple to paint. Good foal stones come in a variety of easy-to-find shapes. They can be painted on plain, plump oval stones or ones whose tapering ends suggest the sharp crook of a folded rear leg. Foal stones can also be semicircular and can sit up on their flat end like the stone I have picked to demonstrate this project. Once you have decided on a stone to use, clean it thoroughly then leave it to dry.

<table>
<tr><td>

You Will Need
- acrylic paint: black, white, burnt sienna and yellow ochre
- pencil or marker
- assorted brushes
- oil-based or acrylic clear varnish

</td></tr>
</table>

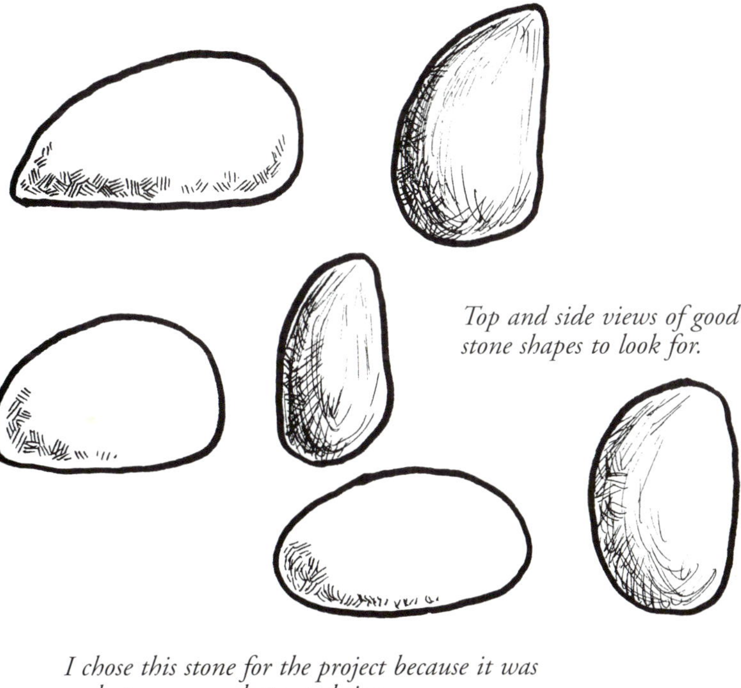

Top and side views of good stone shapes to look for.

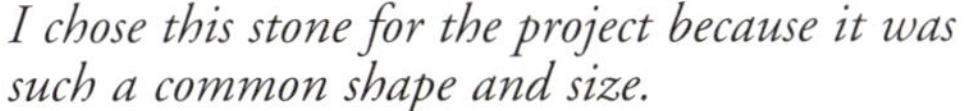

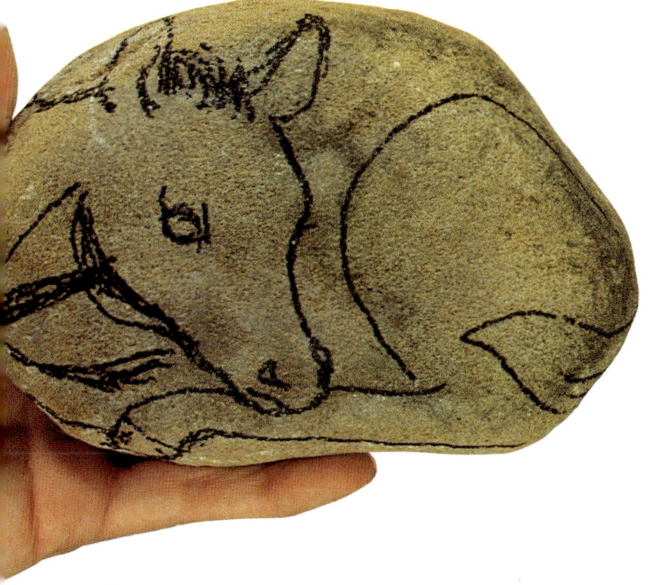

I chose this stone for the project because it was such a common shape and size.

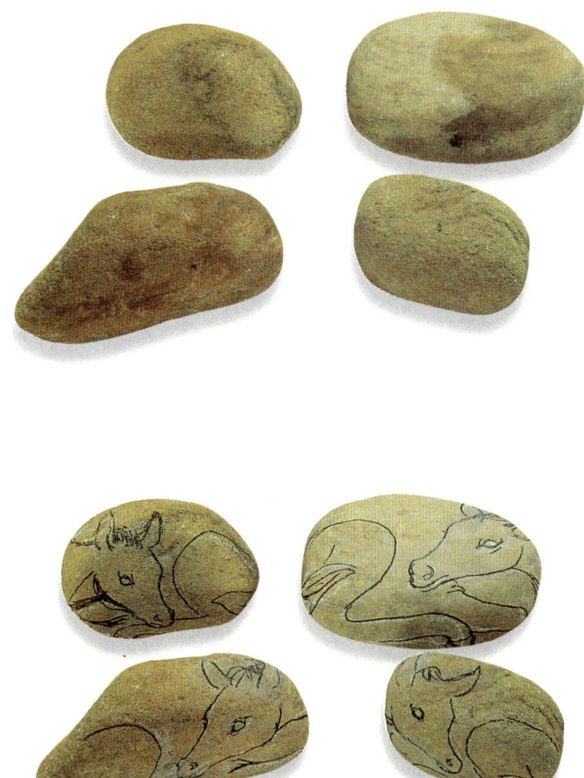

This selection of foal stones, shown with and without layout sketches on, illustrates the wide variety of shapes that will work for a foal.

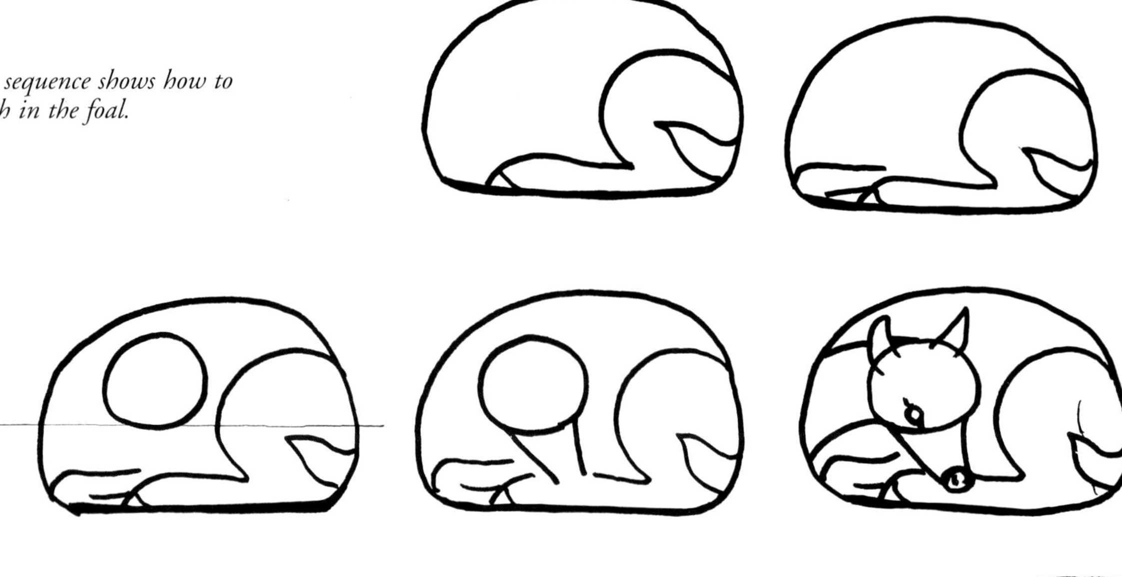

1 Layout

To determine the best layout for your particular stone, decide where the hind leg would look best. On my stone, one side was quite rounded, but the other side looked irregular and it had no definite crook. Sweeping the tail in just above a tightly-folded rear leg helps disguise the lack of a distinctive angle.

Next, curve a rounded haunch into place above the tail, taking up a little less than half the front surface of the stone. Extend the lower part of the leg along the bottom of the stone, ending it with a curving hoof.

The suggestion of a folded front leg is achieved by sketching in a rounded knee at the base of the head end, then running the leg line back towards the middle.

A horse's head can be broken down into three basic shapes. First, make a circle that is slightly smaller in diameter than the top curve of the haunch. Position this circle so that its bottom edge is halfway above the base of the stone.

Taper two straight lines off the head circle, with the outside line touching the curve of the head circle, and the inside line slightly indented. These two lines should measure no more than the diameter of the head circle, and they should ease towards each other until they are half as far apart as when they began.

Join them with a semicircular muzzle. It may take you more than one attempt to get the proportions just right, so be patient. Next, sketch two pointed ears, one on either side above the head circle and with about an ear width between their bases. Add two nostrils to the muzzle and place the eye at the bottom edge of the head circle as shown. Another important feature is the broad, arching neck. Curve a line back from the top centre point of the head to the edge of the stone, then swing it back in a C-shape following the imagined spine of your foal. The lower neck line should curve around the end of the stone and stop just past where you placed the front knee.

On the other side of the stone, sketch a second knee and leg. If it is an upright stone, indicate a second haunch on the back side with a tucked-in rear leg and hoof. Finally, add a few spiky lines between the ears and along the neck to indicate a short mane.

Compare your layout to mine and make any adjustments if necessary.

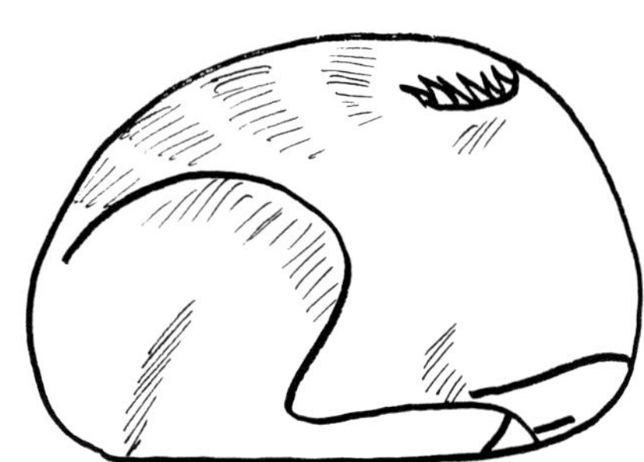

Rear view

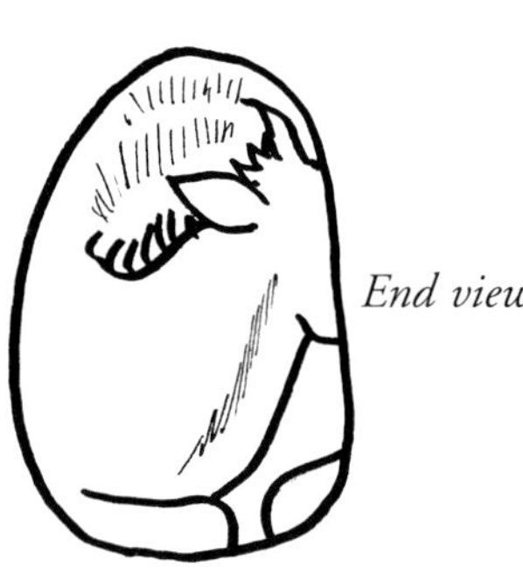

End views

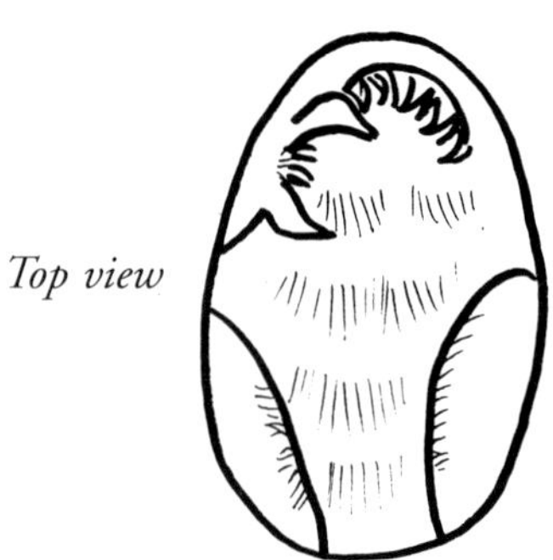

Top view

2 Base Coat

Use a medium-sized brush and black paint to outline all the features you just sketched. Darken the area between the head and haunch, and shade the area directly below the head, along the bottom edge of the neck. Turn the stone around and outline the back features, too. Do not forget to outline the bottom edges of the legs to help define them.

Next, mix burnt sienna and black paint to get a deep brown. You can use the same brush you used for the outlines, or switch to a bigger one. Blend this deep brown into the edges of your black shadows, then use it to completely cover the top of the foal and around the back, leaving the head, neck, haunches and legs unpainted.

Rinse your brush or change to a slightly smaller one and use burnt sienna to paint the head, neck, haunches and legs. Leave a blaze-shaped area on the face unpainted.

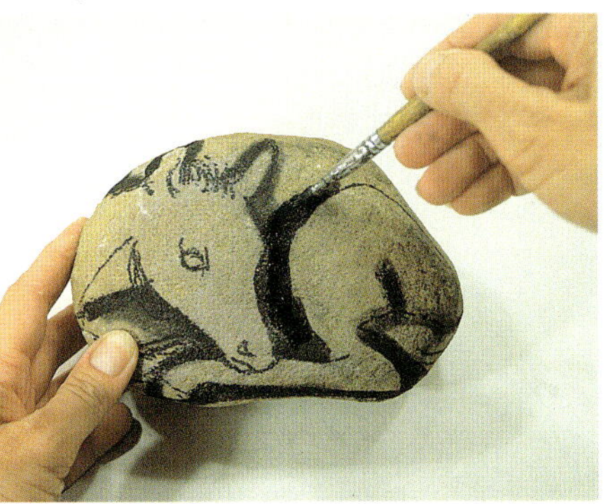
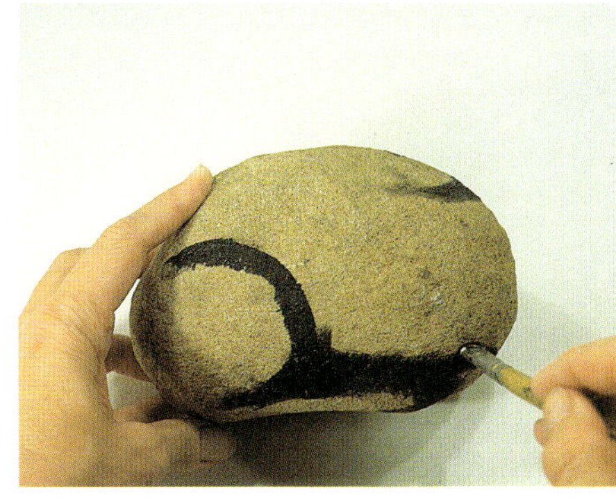

Bold black outlines suggest the illusion of contours.

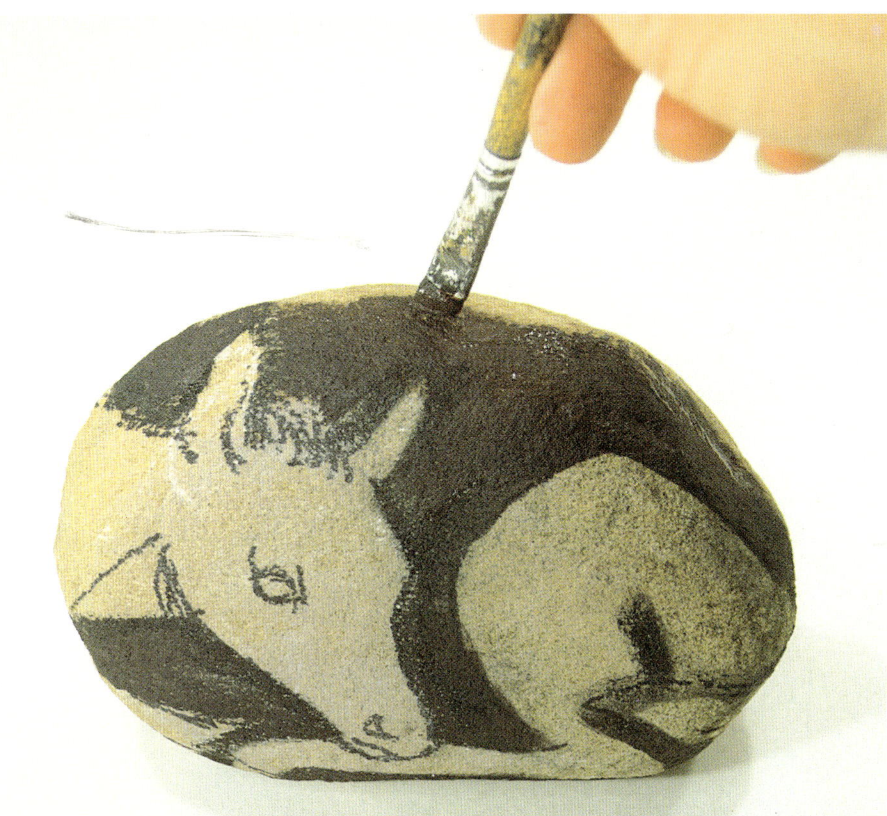

This deep brown background helps the head and haunches stand out.

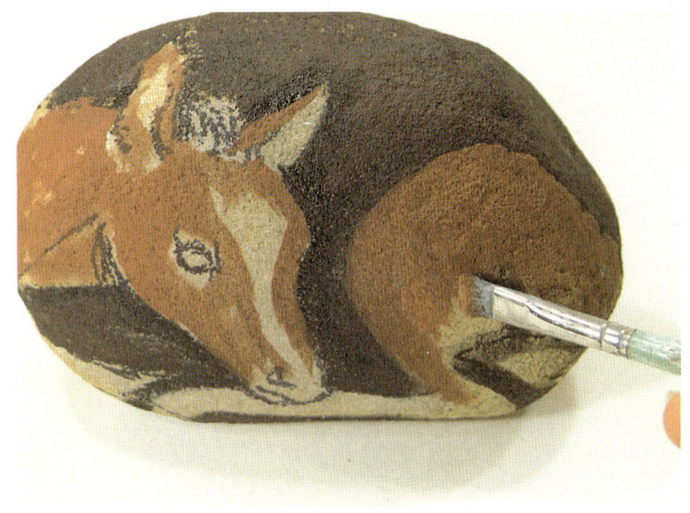

Use a warm reddish-brown colour to pull the head and haunch forward.

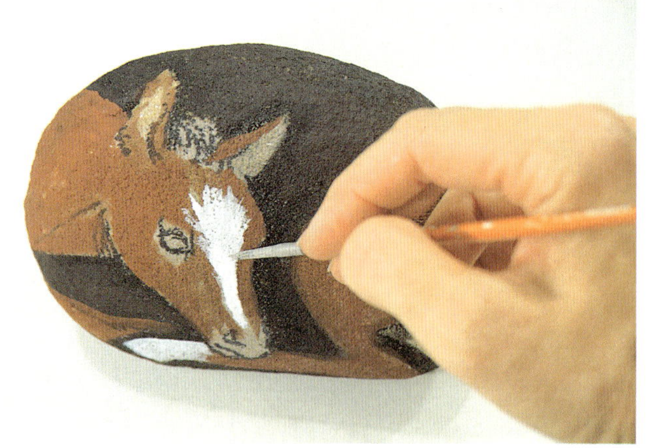

Add a white blaze on the face and one white sock to the leg.

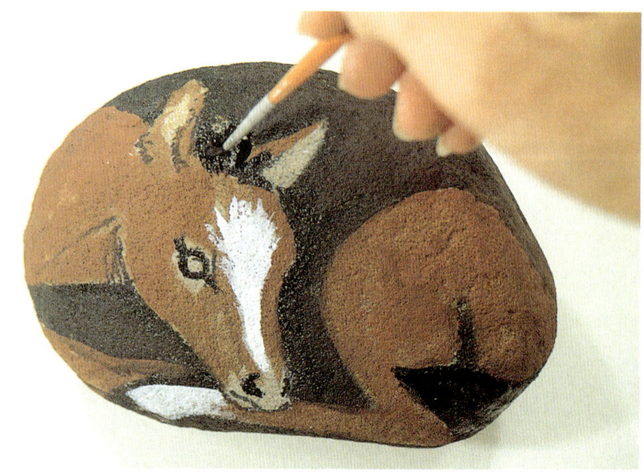

Use black to emphasize the eyes, nostrils, mouth and mane.

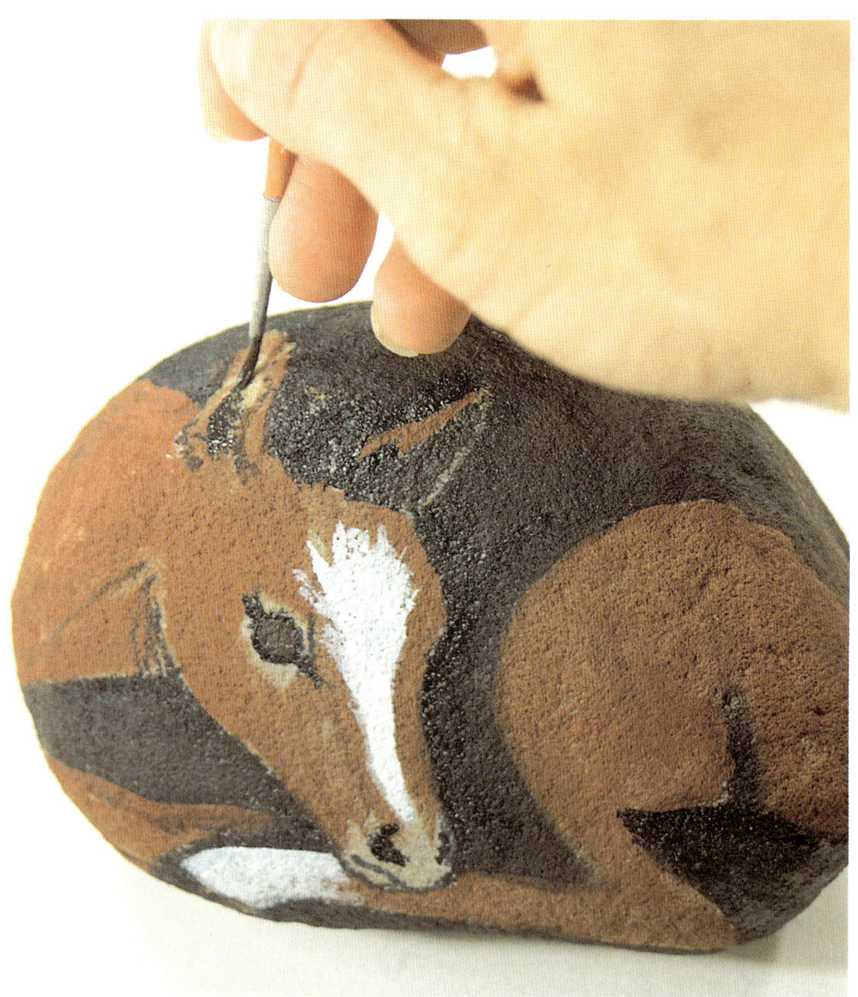

Fill in the eye and the centres of the ears with dark brown.

With a small brush, add a crisp white blaze and one white sock. Change to black paint to outline the shape of the eye and fill in the nostrils. Indicate the mouth with a simple straight line. Colour in the tail and create a tuft of mane between the ears.

Mix a little more deep brown paint to fill in the eye circle and darken the insides of the ears.

3 Contours

To add to the illusion of contour and to give the foal's coat a sheen, use a stubby round brush (one of those worn out brushes you were about to throw away is perfect). Mix yellow ochre with just a touch of white and use this to highlight the sides of the foal's face, the entire top and inside edge of the haunch all the way down to the rear leg, and along the top of the leg. Use small, more distinct strokes on the underside of the head to add emphasis. Continue past the line of the neck to highlight the semicircular curve of the jaw line. Add a simple line from the top of that curve down towards where the neck joins the chest, indicating a prominent muscle there. Highlight the top of the front leg then turn the stone around and add the same highlighting touches to the rear side.

Outline the pointed ears using a small brush and a slightly paler shade of golden yellow. Highlight the bump indicating the unseen eye, then encircle the outside eye with light golden yellow. Note that the bottom of this eye highlighting is a simple half circle, while the upper half sweeps up in the direction of the ear.

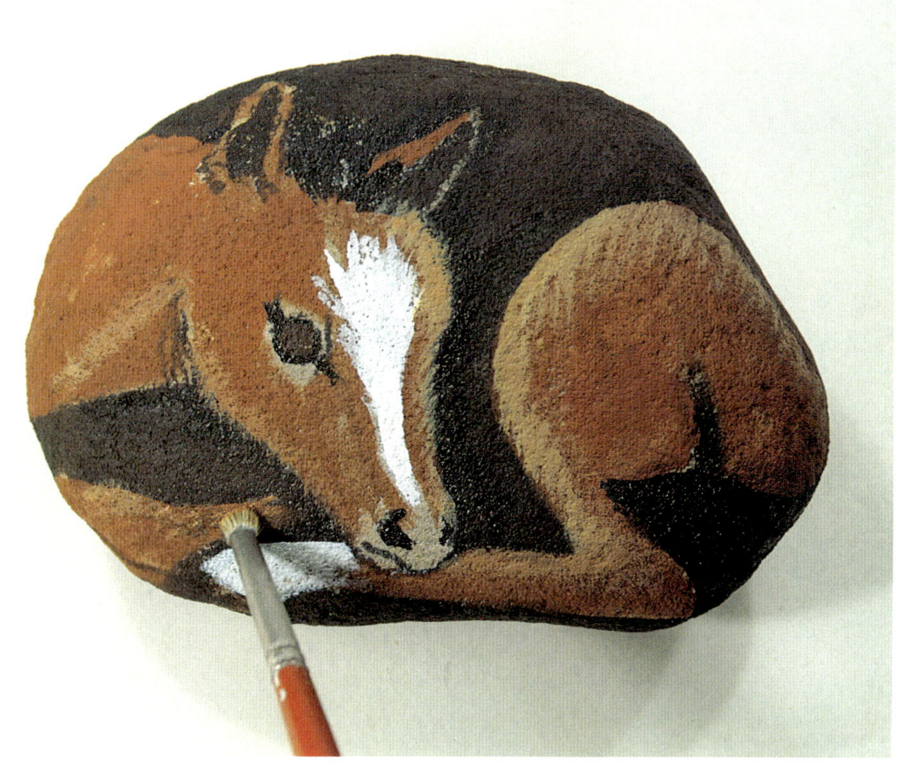

Scrub in touches of golden yellow to add a lifelike sheen to the foal's coat. Make the colour denser along the haunch and leg, more subtle on the head and neck.

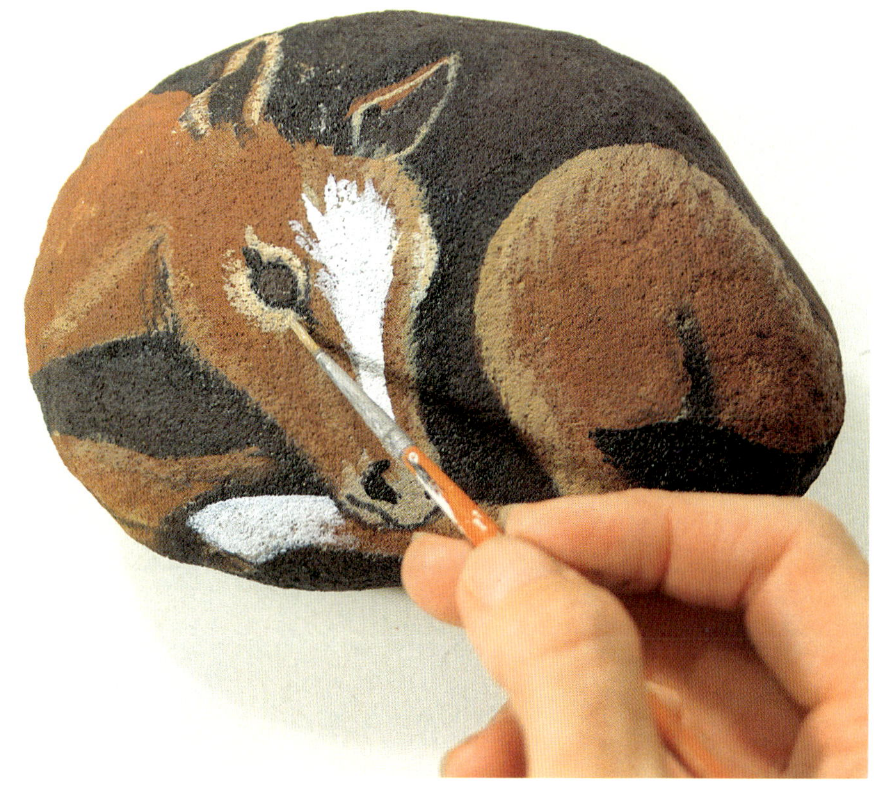

Use a small brush and lighter golden yellow to frame the eye.

4 Finishing Touches

Mix a little deep grey paint then use a liner brush to highlight the tuft of mane between the ears and to add a few sweeping lines to the tail. Carefully fill in the muzzle around the nostrils and the mouth.

Turn the stone around and add a row of short, spiky lines to the mane along the arch of the neck. Add an outline of grey to the shape of the hoof to define it.

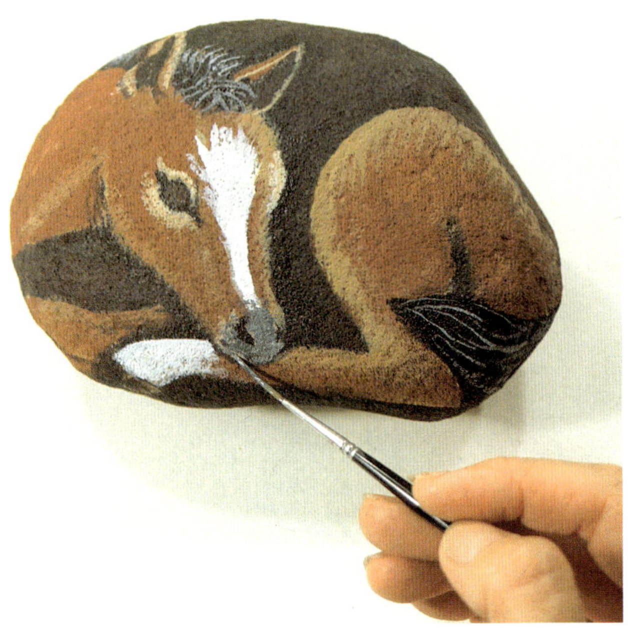

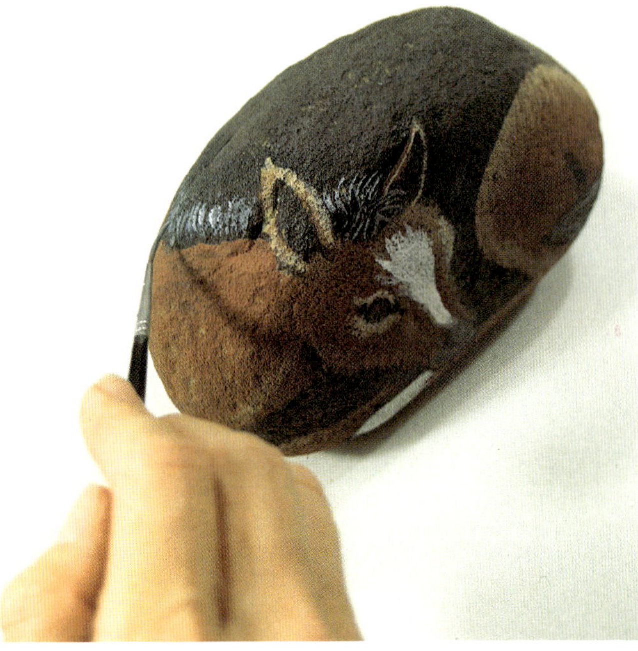

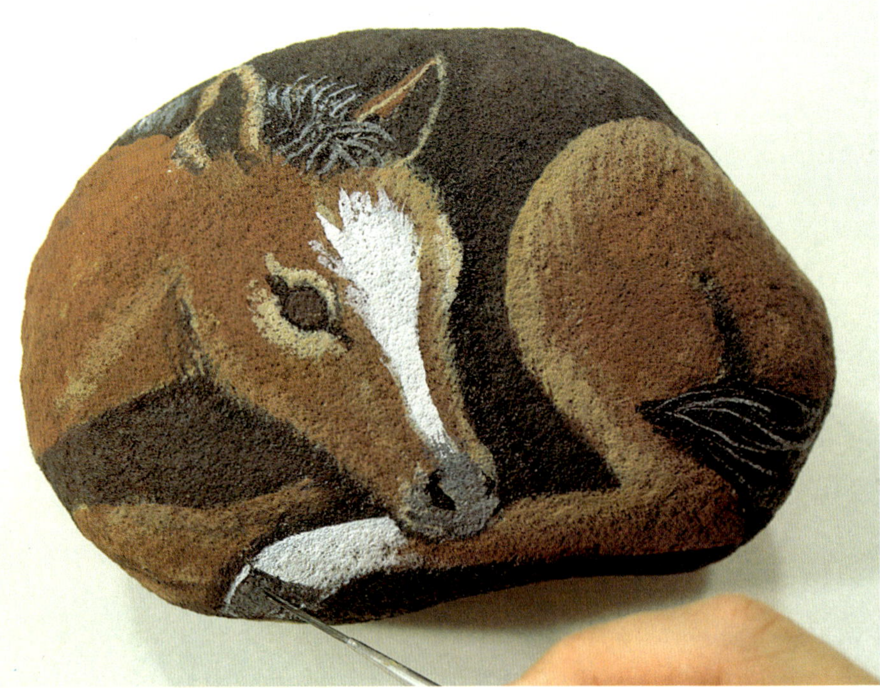

Grey paint covers the end of the muzzle and creates contrast when stroked on as a highlight along the mane and tail. Turn your stone if necessary to highlight the mane along the arch of the neck. Use grey to define the shape of the hoof.

Rinse out the liner brush and place small pools of white, yellow ochre and burnt sienna on your palette. Pick up a touch of white on your brush tip, then a touch of yellow ochre. Mix them and check the consistency with a test stroke to see if you will need to add water so your strokes will go on cleanly. Use the fur directional guide to add numerous small fur lines to the face, neck, haunch and legs. Add a few lines to the insides of the ears, too. As you scatter these fur lines around, vary the combination of colours to achieve a subtle, random look.

Use a darker blend of burnt sienna to add detail to the upper portion of the neck and the darker areas of the back and sides. Add touches of golden yellow here and there. Fur lines can be less dense in the darker areas. Along the back and in the shaded side areas, use a dry brush and straight burnt sienna to indicate less distinct sets of lines.

Clean your brush and change to black paint to add an iris to the eye that is visible. Darken the centre between the nostrils, then surround them with lighter outlines to accentuate them.

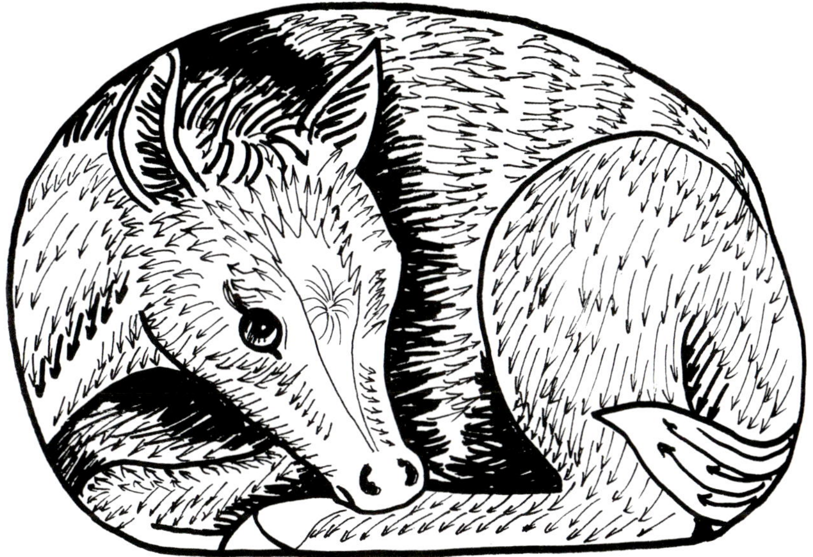

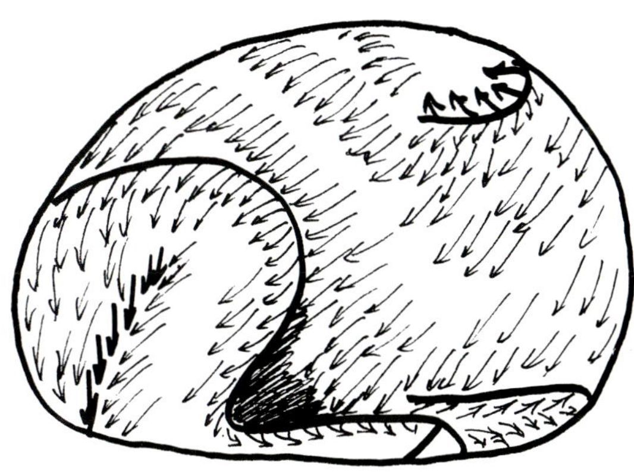

Use these fur directional guides to help determine your detailing strokes.

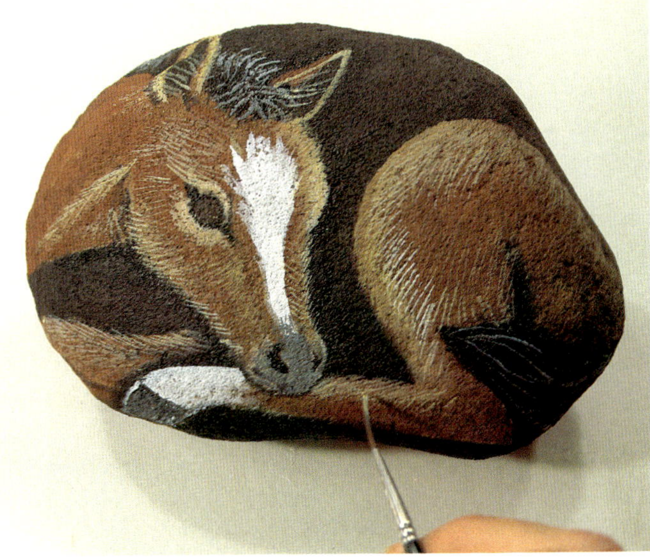

Golden yellow fur lines should be densest near the edges of the haunch. Use sparser streaks around the face and along the tops of the legs.

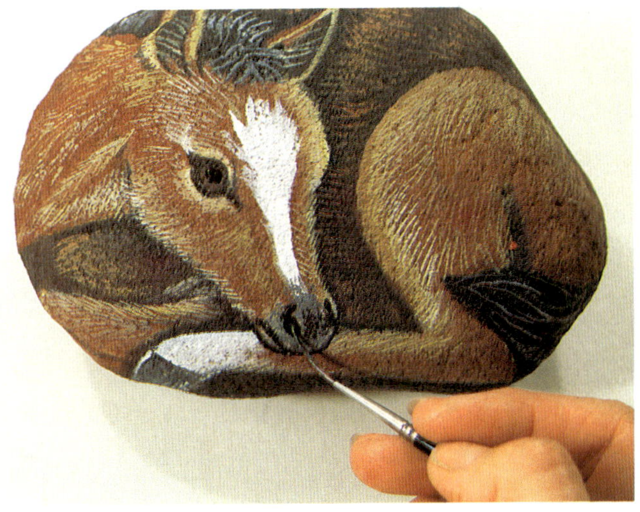

Use burnt sienna to add a set of dry brushed lines to the chest area below the neck. Move on to dry brush more of these diffused lines along the top, back and sides. Small black details such as the iris, more clearly defined nostril shapes and a sharp mouth line are also important additions.

To give the eye more depth, encircle the outermost edge with a narrow line of lighter brown.

Add more fur lines in dark brown as necessary. Pay particular attention to the neck just above the muscle line, the area around the base of the outside ear, the eye area below the golden yellow highlighting and the areas along both sides of the blaze. Add darker fur lines to the haunch, slightly in from the outside edge and curving to suggest the substantial nature of that muscled area. Add a row of dark detailing lines to the lower side of the legs to emphasize the shading.

Finally, place one or two tiny dots of white in the upper portion of the eye.

Look carefully at your piece from all angles to make sure you have added enough detail. Pay special attention to the base of the neck and to the base of the tail, both of which can be easily overlooked.

When you are completely happy with your foal, leave to dry and then apply a coat of varnish.

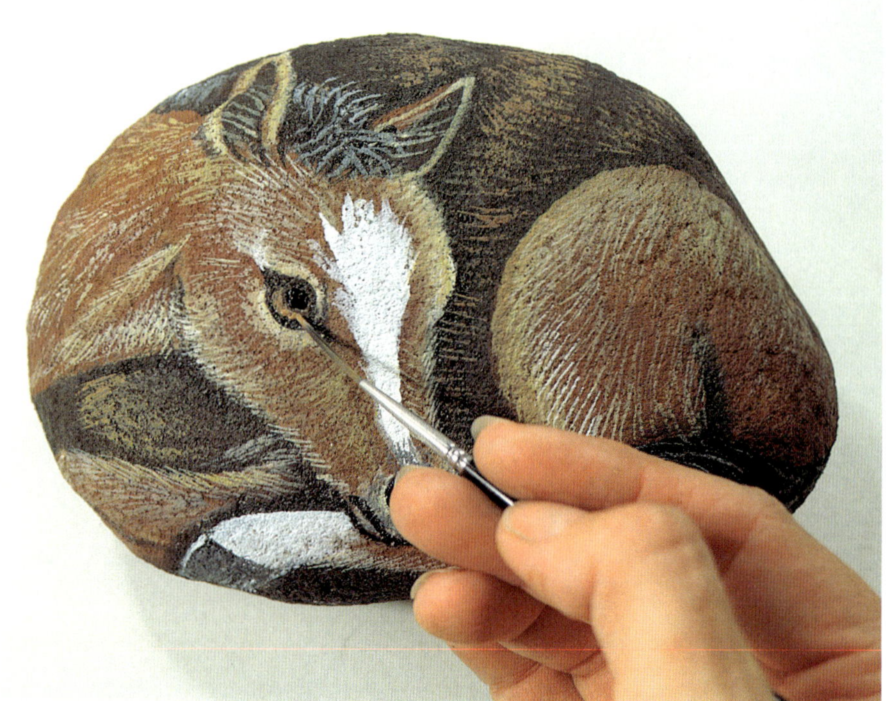

An outside rim of lighter brown gives the eye a warm glow.

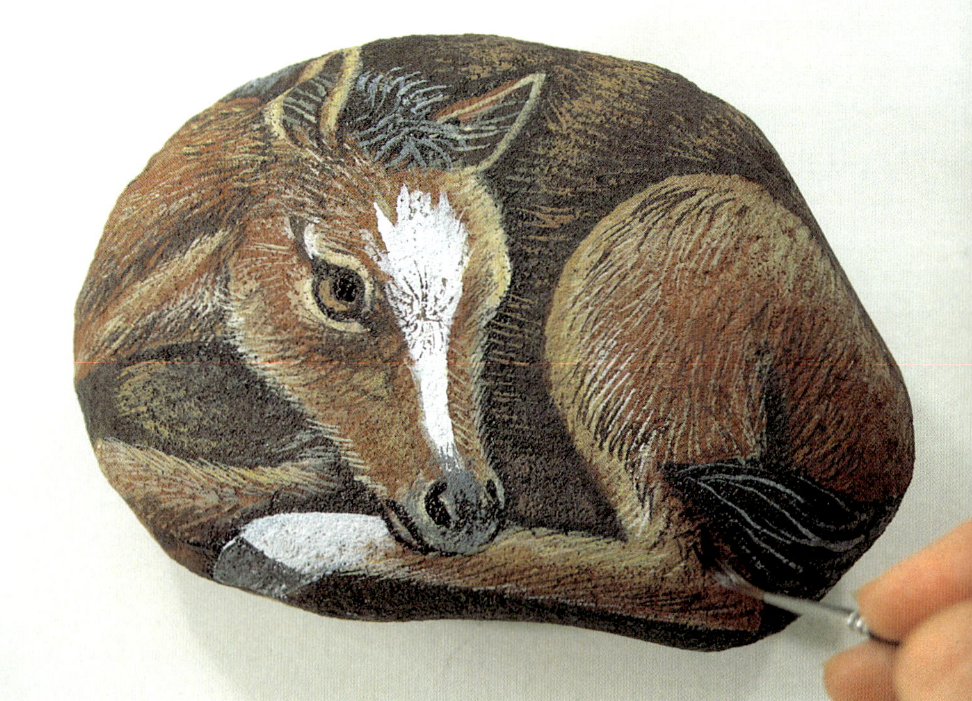

Blend dark fur lines among the lighter ones to give your foal even more texture and contour. Concentrate on the entire lower edge of the rear leg, the lower portion of the folded front leg, the areas under the eye and above the highlighted muscle along the neck. Add some dark lines right behind the ear, too, then move to the haunch to detail the area just above the tail. Scatter a few more dark lines just inside the curve of the haunch to give it bulk. A star-shaped cluster of lines in the centre of the face blaze will create the effect of a whorl.

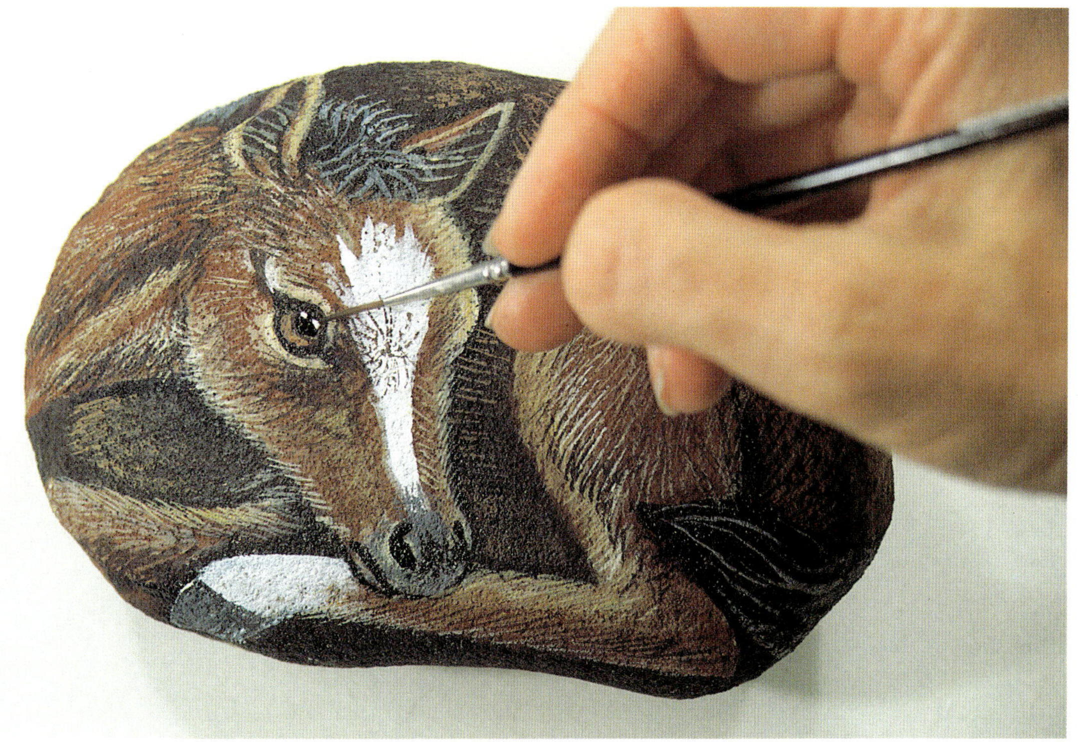

Add a couple of bright gleams in the eye to complete the foal.

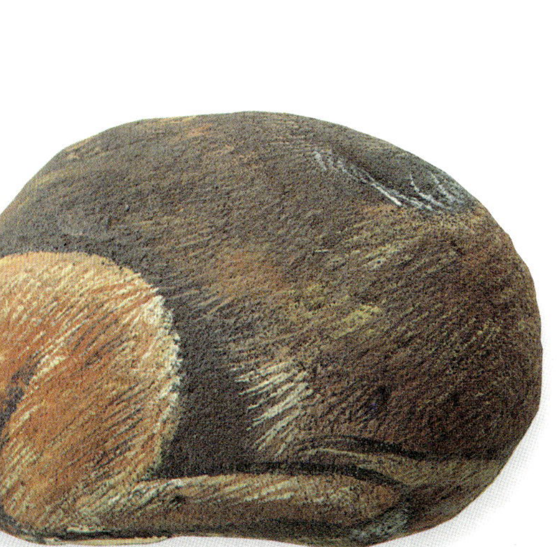

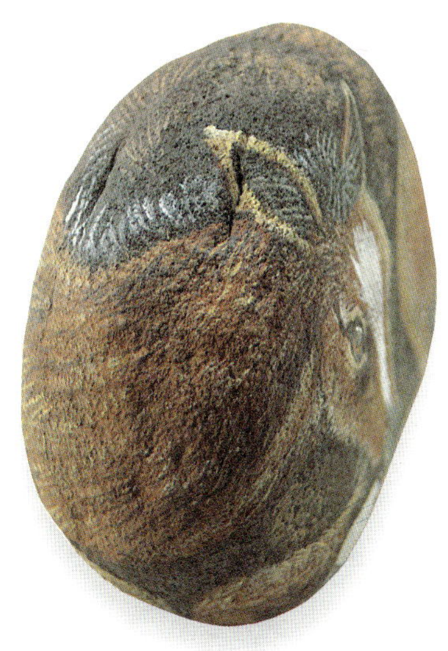

Look carefully at your piece from all angles to make sure you have added enough detail.

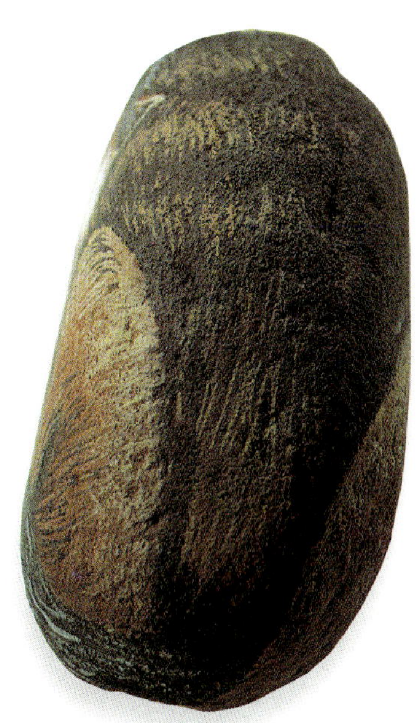

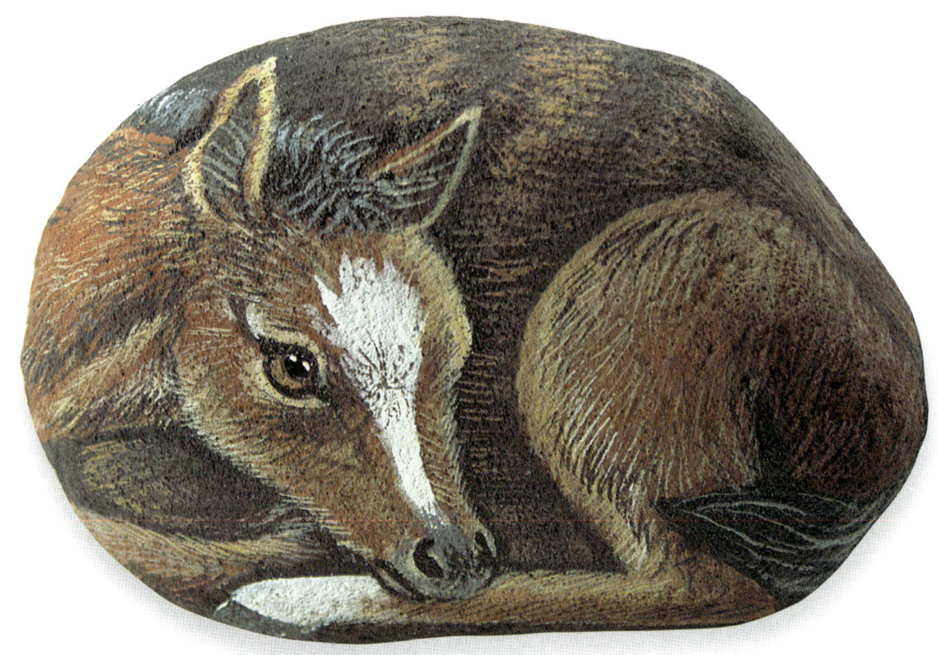

The finished foal.

Foals are particularly appealing posed on a bit of hay or dried grass. Try painting a standing mare to nuzzle your foal (see page 60). Black out the stone to suggest spaces between the mare's legs.

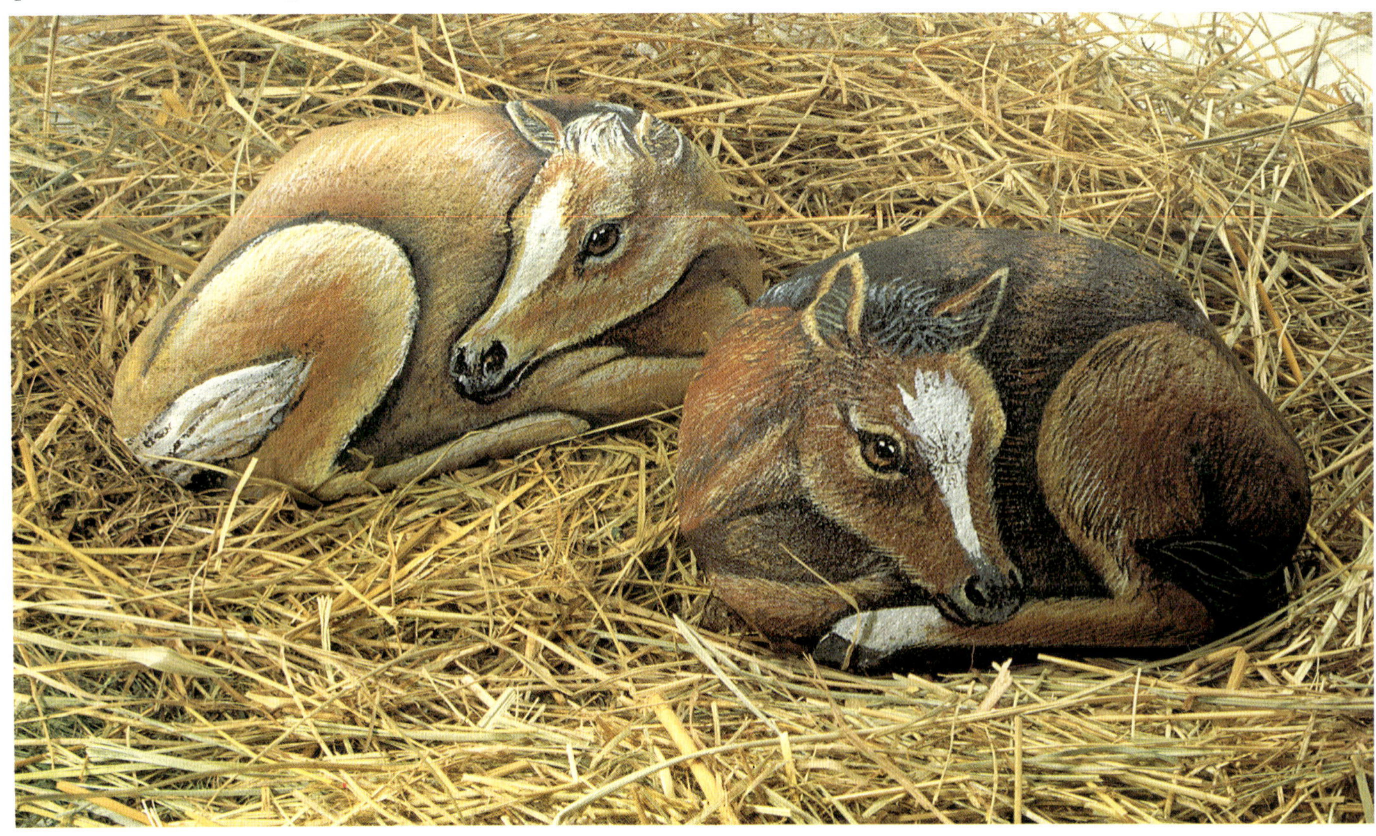

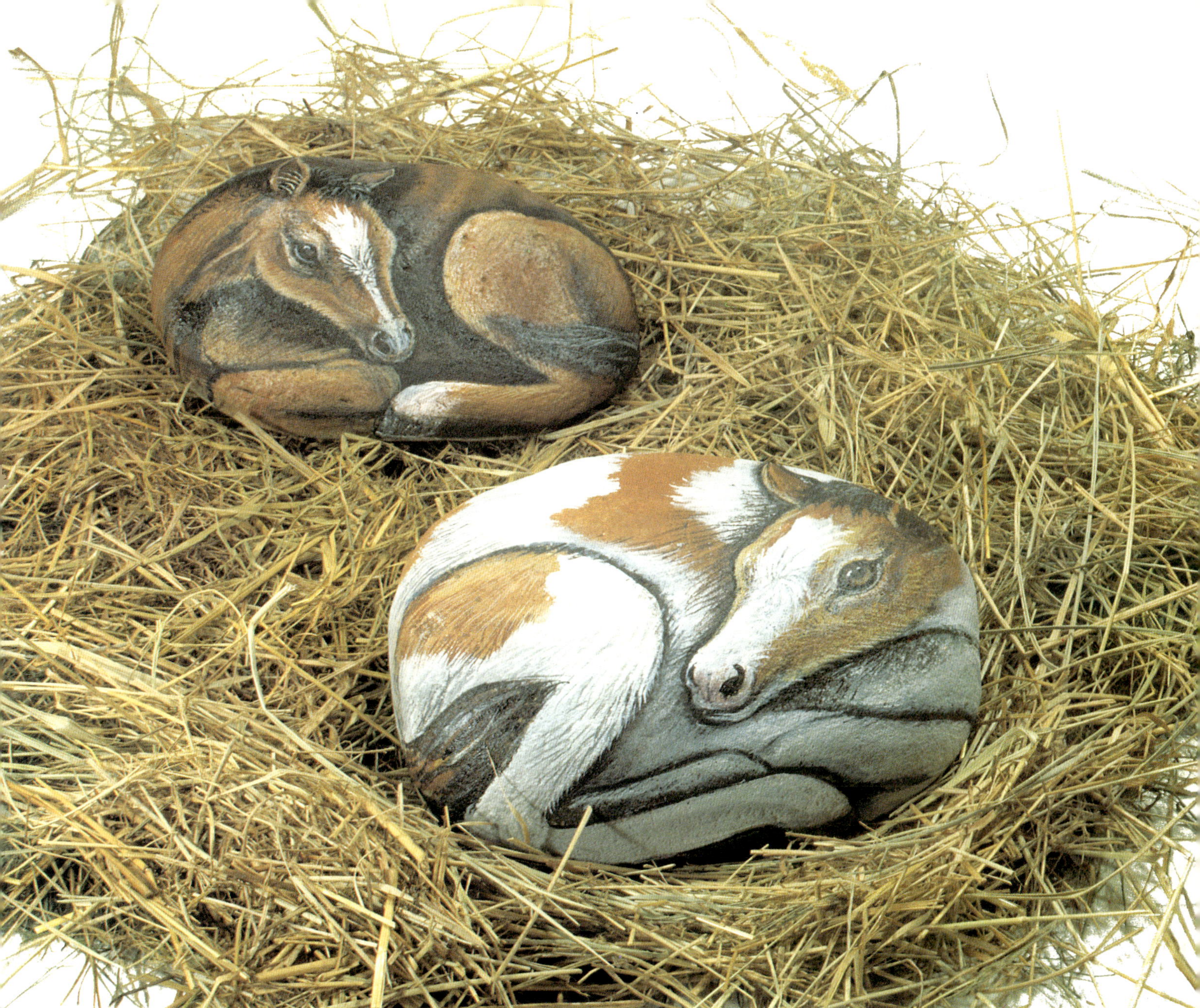

These foals look quite at home in a bed of straw. They are painted using the same technique as shown in the project, with slight variations to the colours.

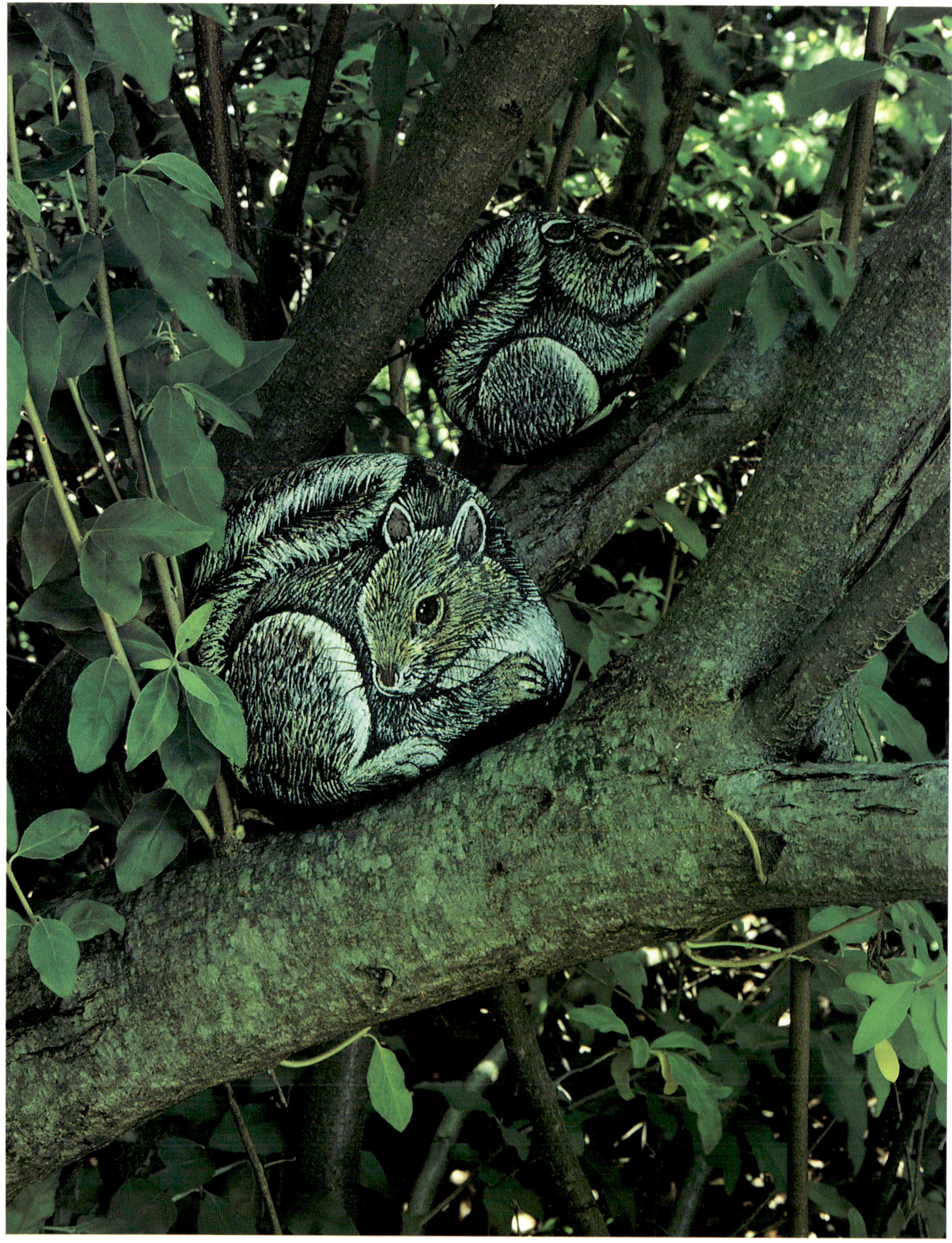

SQUIRREL

If you have ever been entertained by the antics of these cheeky little acrobats, I am sure you will agree that squirrels are great fun to watch – they are also great fun to paint.

When selecting squirrel stones, bear in mind that full, fluffy tails are their hallmark. To be suitable, a stone must have enough height to allow such a tail to curve and bend over the animal's back. The nearly square stone I picked for this project offered plenty of room for the tail, and it was wide enough without being too round.

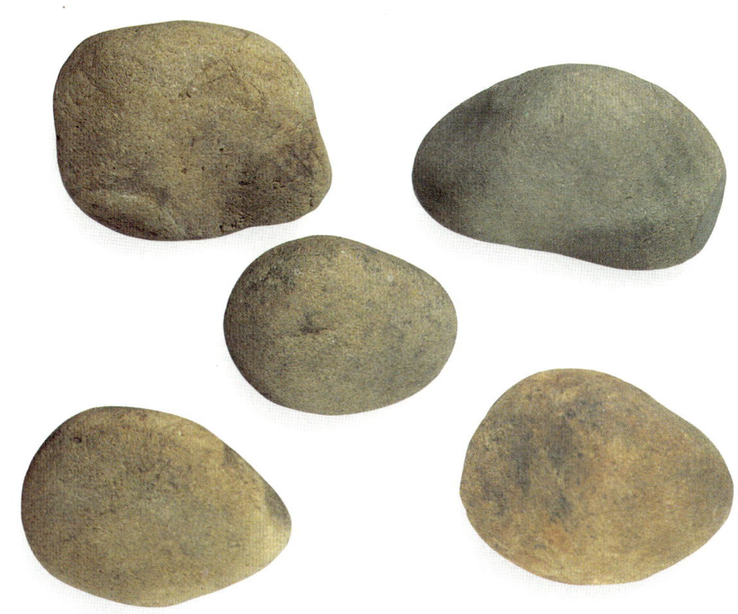

Any of these stones are suitable for a squirrel. Note the nicely rounded tops.

You Will Need
- acrylic paint: black, white, burnt sienna, yellow ochre and red
- chalk or a white-lead pencil
- assorted brushes
- oil-based or acrylic clear varnish

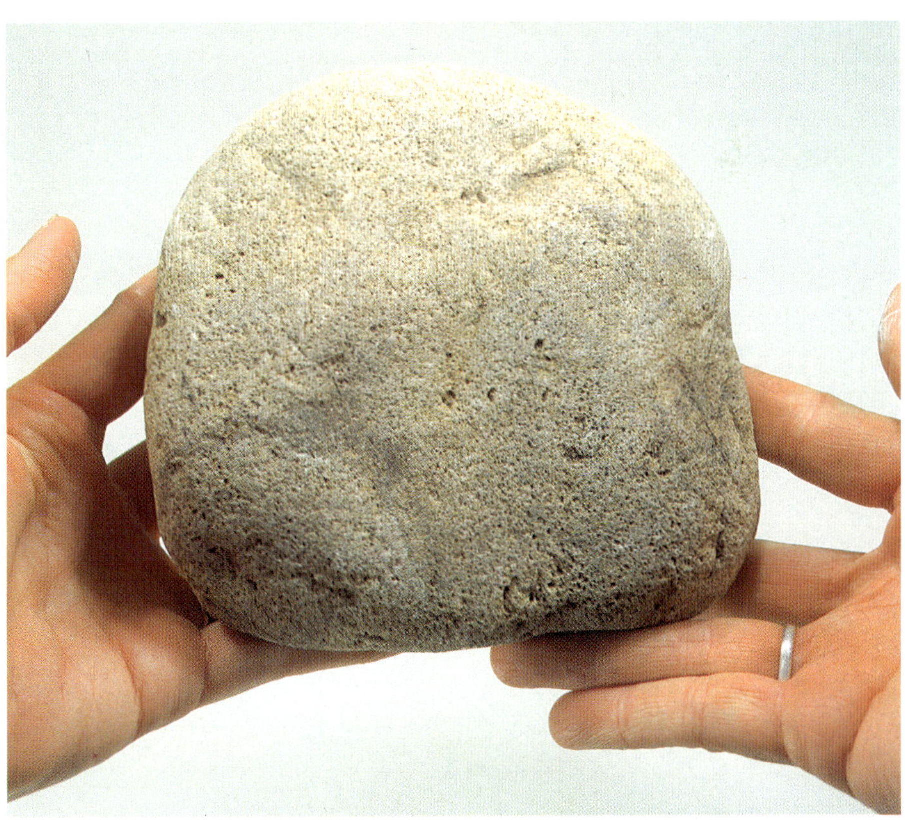

I liked the almost square shape of this stone because it provided ample room for the tail.

1 Base Coat

Once you have chosen your stone, make sure the surface is scrubbed clean. Begin this project by painting the entire surface of the stone black. A large brush will make for quick coverage.

2 Layout

When the paint is dry, use chalk or a white-lead pencil to sketch in the details. Place the head so that the squirrel seems to be looking back over its body. Sometimes it is possible to come across stone shapes that allow the head to be positioned at one end, but stones for the pose I demonstrate here are much more common. Keep the placement of the head fairly low to ensure plenty of room for the tail.

A squirrel's head is basically a tilting egg shape, with the smaller, lower end as the muzzle. Try to keep the size of the head in proportion to the size of the stone. Generally, the head should take up about 25% of the side surface of the stone. Make the head too large and your squirrel will look like a cartoon animal – a smaller head is less distracting.

Divide the head oval in half lengthways (following the degree of tilt you gave it) and set one pointed ear at the top, so that the inside edge of the ear lines up with the dividing line. Centre a large round eye at the midpoint of that line and sketch in a Y-shaped nose at the bottom of the oval. Next, sketch in a slightly larger oval haunch set lengthways across from the head.

Curve the tail up, beginning along the back edge of the haunch and angling it forward over the body in a gentle arc, stopping just above the head. Double the tail back upon itself and taper your line inward to form a folded-over tip. Turn the stone around and copy the curved lines on the other side to complete a flat, flowing tail.

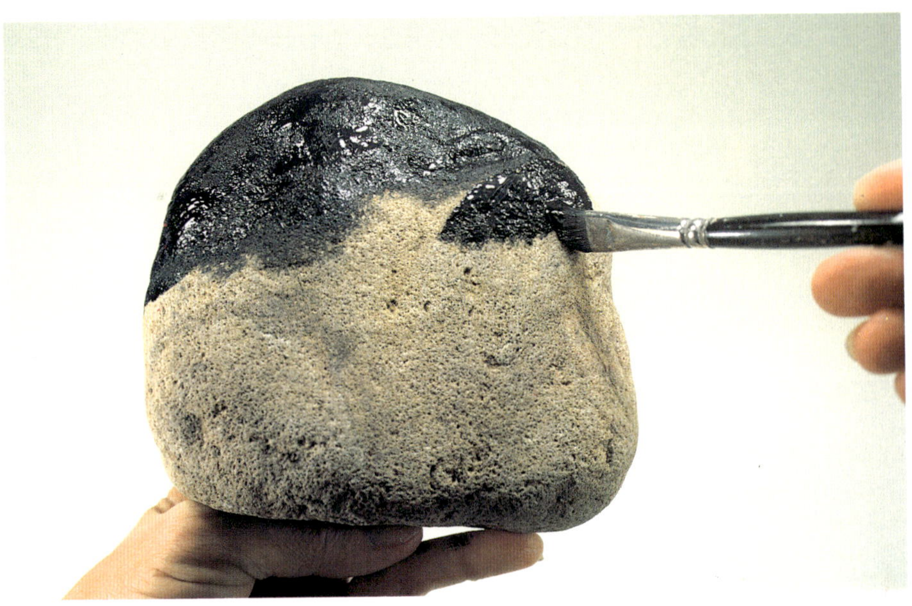

Apply a solid black base coat.

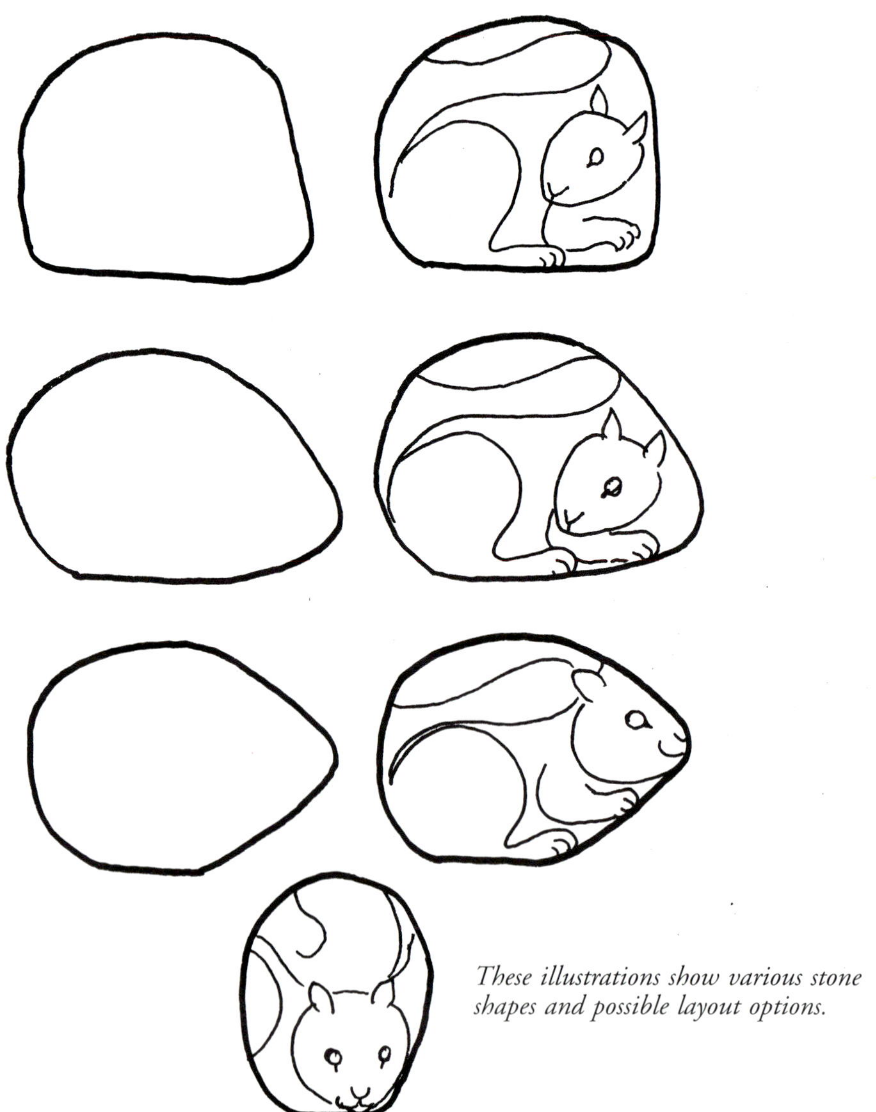

These illustrations show various stone shapes and possible layout options.

Finish your layout by tucking rear
paws at the bottom edge of the stone
where the haunch curves in. Make the
rear feet narrow and elongated, with
simple claws curving down. Extend
the front paws forward below the
head, and draw in shorter, more
rounded paws and the suggestion of
bending elbows.

Turn your stone around and draw
the layout on the other side.

Look at your layout carefully to
make sure the proportions seem
balanced before proceeding to the
next stage. Remember that you can
brush or wash away any marks that do
not look right, then simply try again.

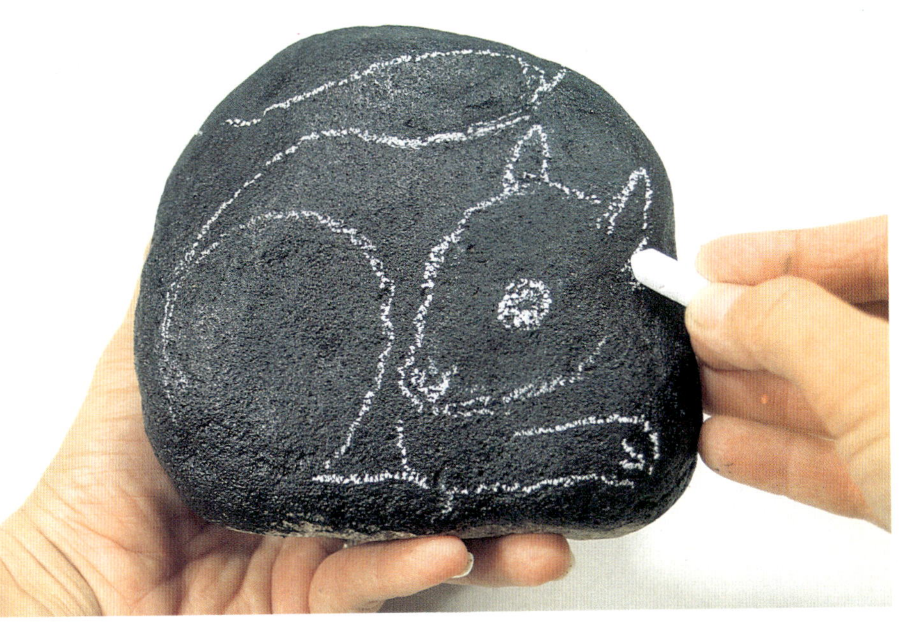

*Your layout may differ slightly to mine,
depending on the stone you chose.
However, the head, haunch, tail and feet
should still be in the correct proportion to
one another.*

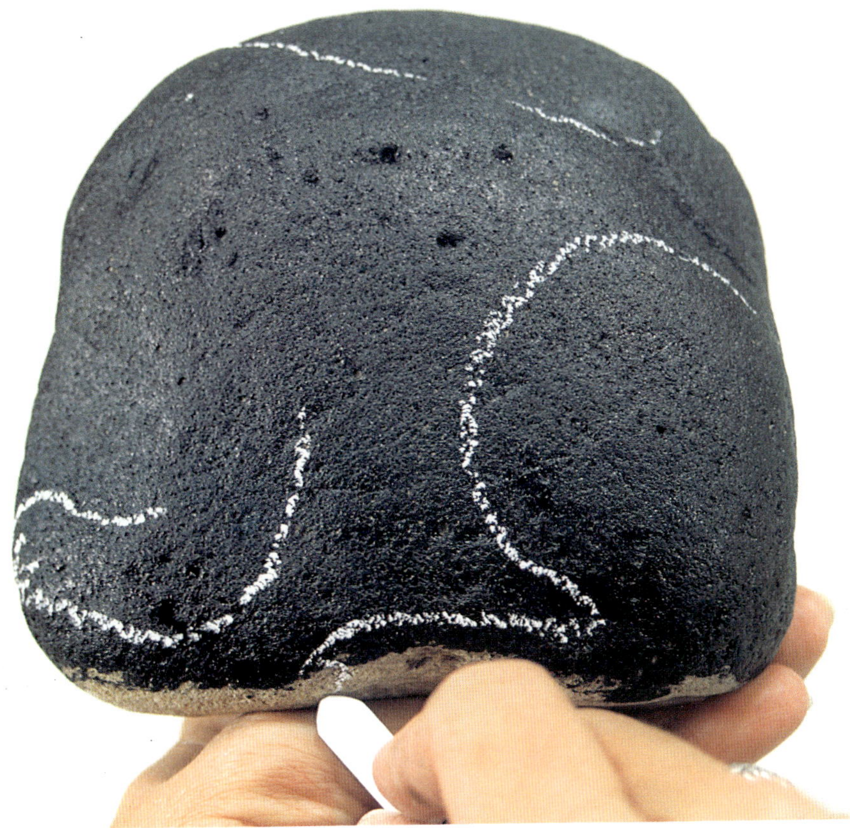

Do not forget to turn your stone around, and drawing in the layout on the other side.

3 Fur

Use a medium round brush to scrub in the white patches that set off the curves of the haunches all the way down to and including the rear feet. Fill in the chest area below the head and between the front paws. If the bristles of your brush are stiff enough for the strokes to suggest individual fur clumps, use it to outline the tail too. If not, change to a liner brush to create the desired fuzzy look with a series of short strokes.

Check the fur directional guide to help determine how your strokes should slant for a natural look. Define the edges of the ears and the curve of the head with short, spiky fur lines.

Now you are ready to cover the entire squirrel with more of these short fur marks that will give the animals its realistic texture. Begin along the top edge of the haunch and layer in successive rows of tiny white strokes; vary both the length and spacing, and allow some strokes to angle or cross others.

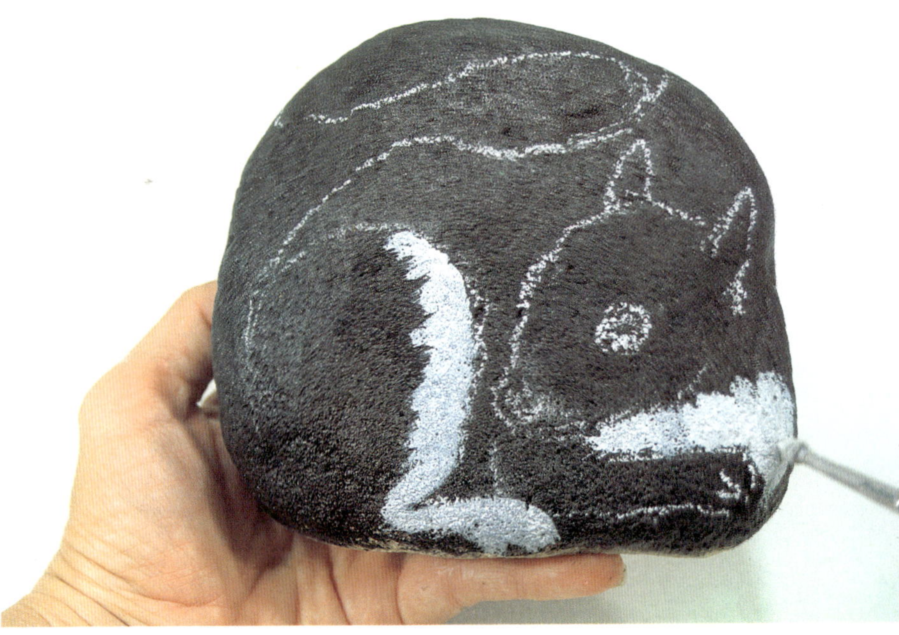

Crisp white patches of fur on the edges of the haunch and on the chest are an important element in the squirrel's design.

When you have filled in the haunch areas on both sides, move to the head. Since the fur grows from the tip of the nose upward, you may want to hold the stone upside down to make it easier to apply the brushstrokes. Pay close attention to the way fur looks around the muzzle and below the eye.

Now move to the side area between the head and the haunch and again follow the fur directional guide when detailing this space. Leave a narrow border of black to outline the head, haunch and tail and to make them stand out. When the front side is complete, move to the area behind the head and work your way around the curve of the stone to the other side. Since the head does not show on this side, the fur lines should continue along the back as well as angling downward to form the upper portion of the other front leg. Outline the rear paw with spiky little strokes too.

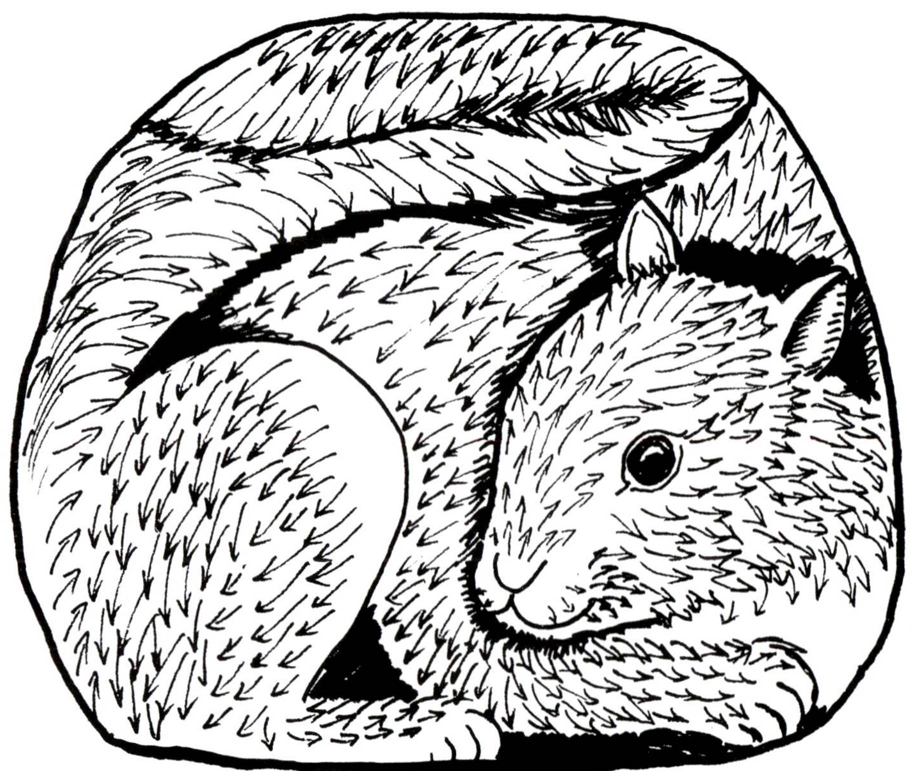

Use this guide to determine the direction the fur grows on the squirrel.

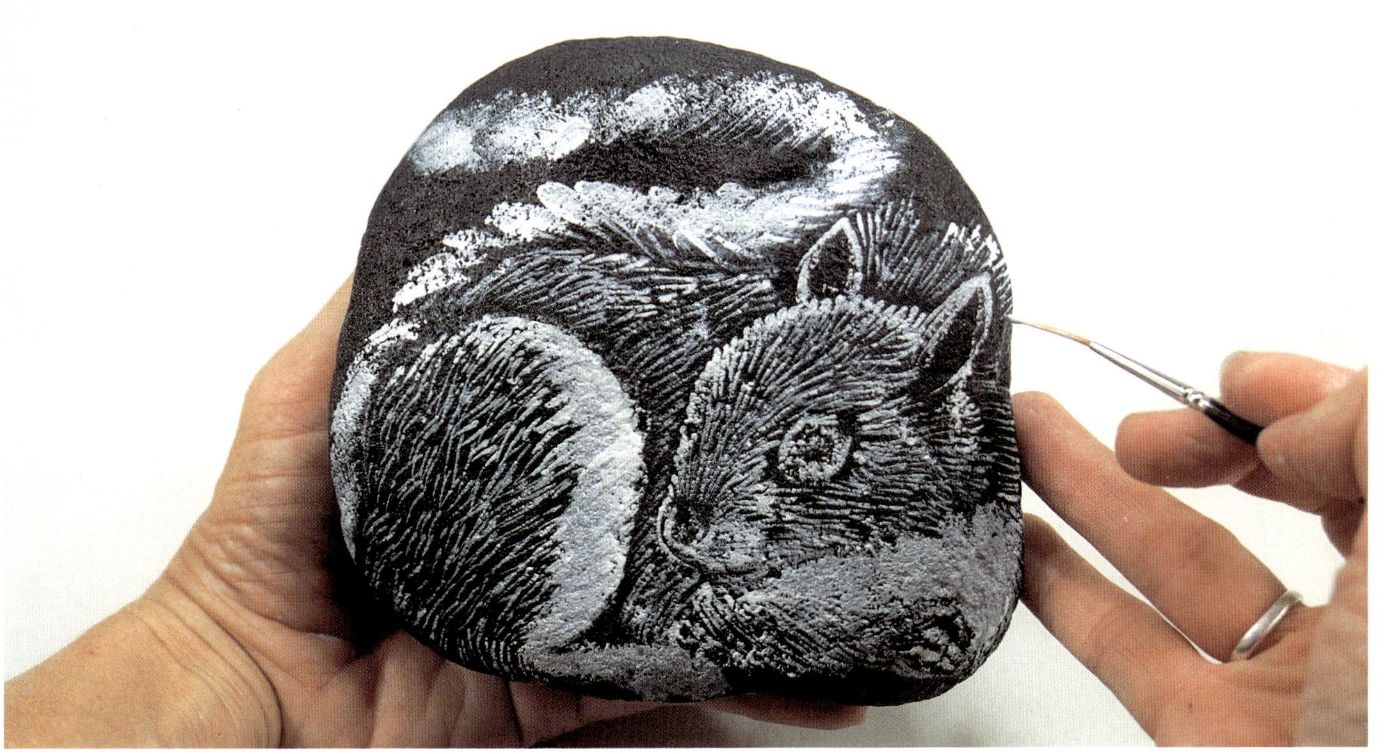

Apply delicate fur lines to give your squirrel a realistic texture. Keep brushstrokes short and fairly dense. When adding fur, always leave dark borders around your main features to make them stand out. Continue fur lines above the head and around to the back side of the stone.

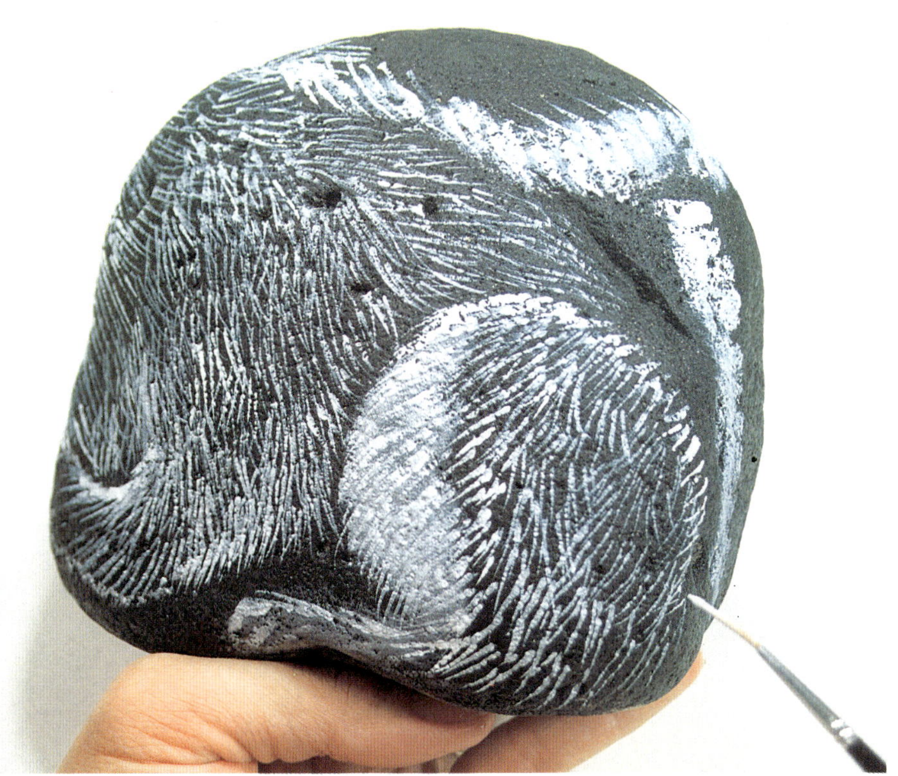

Paint in fur lines along the back. Some fur angles downward to fill in the front leg.

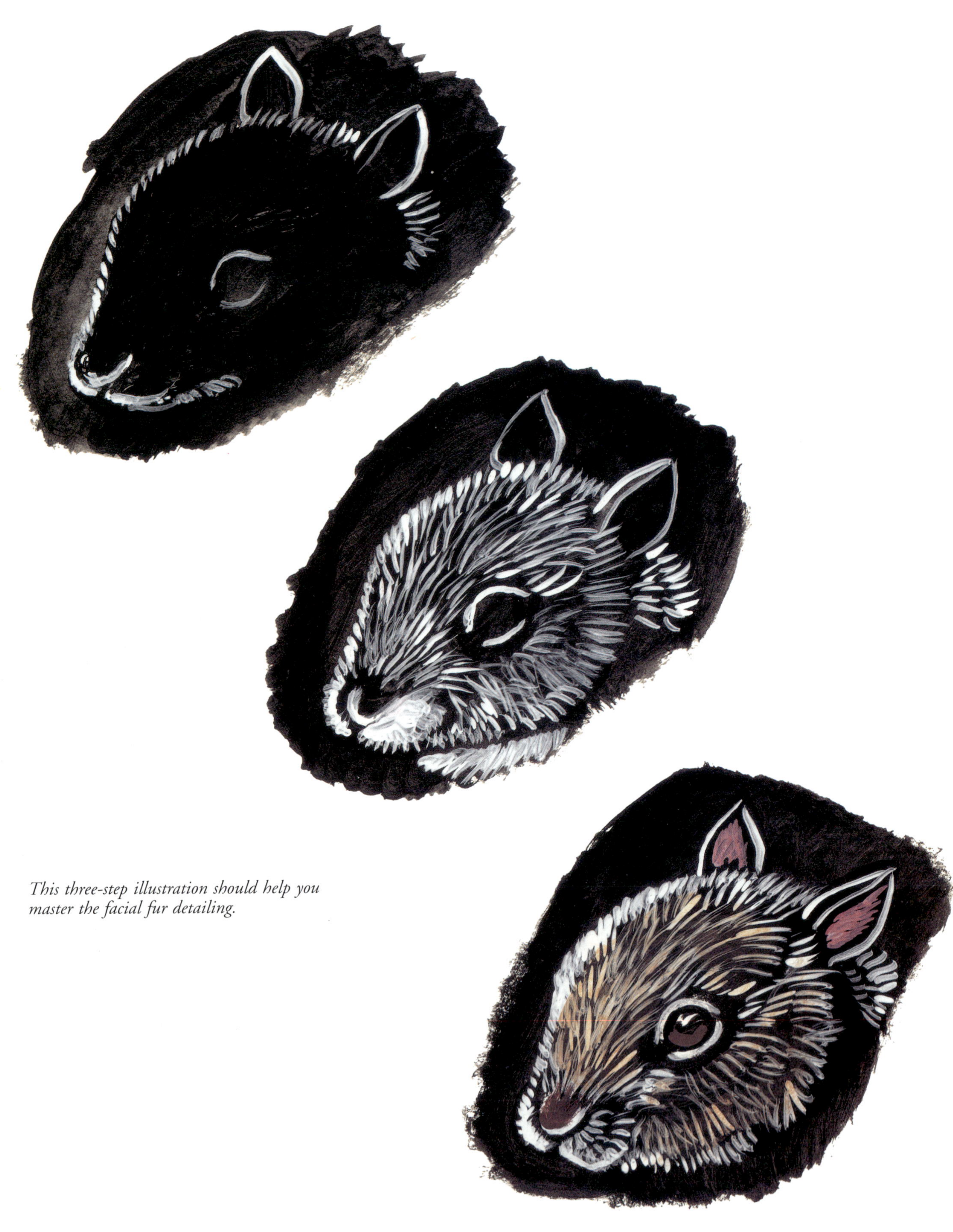

This three-step illustration should help you
master the facial fur detailing.

4 Details

Change to a larger brush and mix equal parts of yellow ochre and burnt sienna. Add enough water to this mixture to create a translucent wash that will tint your white strokes without altering the darker tones. You may want to try a test area to check the effect. If your tint is too strong, it will dull down the black undercoat. If this happens, use absorbent paper to blot it away, then try again with a more diluted mixture. The idea behind tinting the fur is to add visual interest, so use it sparingly here and there. Leave some fur lines white, particularly those along the outside edges of the head and haunch.

Now return to your liner brush and add enough white paint to your golden brown mixture to get a pale golden colour. If the pigment is too watery, you may need to add more yellow ochre. Use this golden yellow to add details to the fluffy tail. Start at the bottom back edge of the stone and angle your strokes upward and outward along the base of the tail, leaving a dark section down the centre. Move to the folded-over tail tip, working upward from the tapering end. Allow your strokes to grow longer and more flowing as they extend along either side of the tail's top.

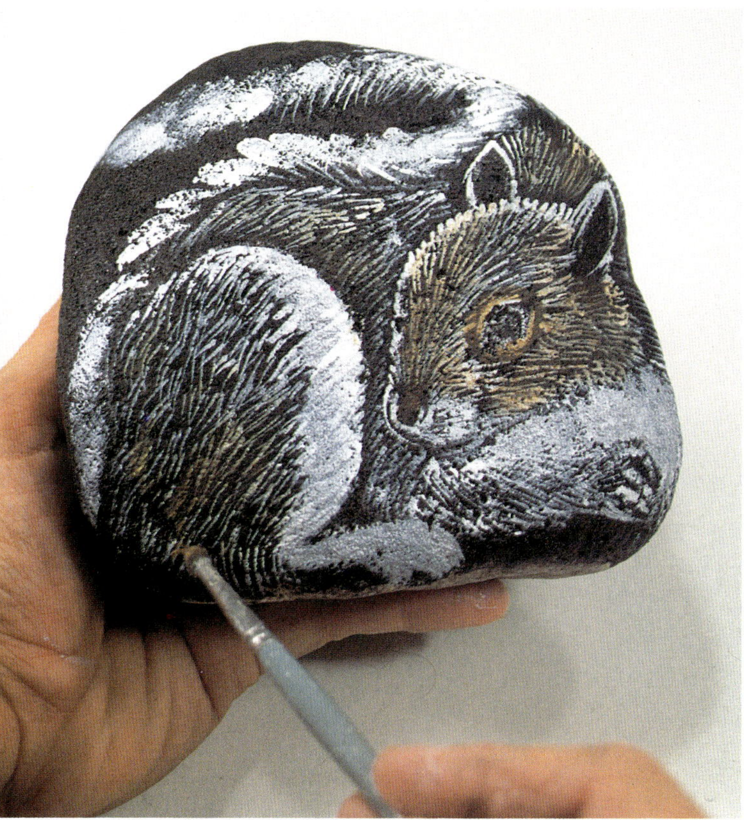

Tint portions of the squirrel's fur with a very diluted mix of yellow ochre and burnt sienna to add natural looking shading. Leave some areas of white, particularly around the edges.

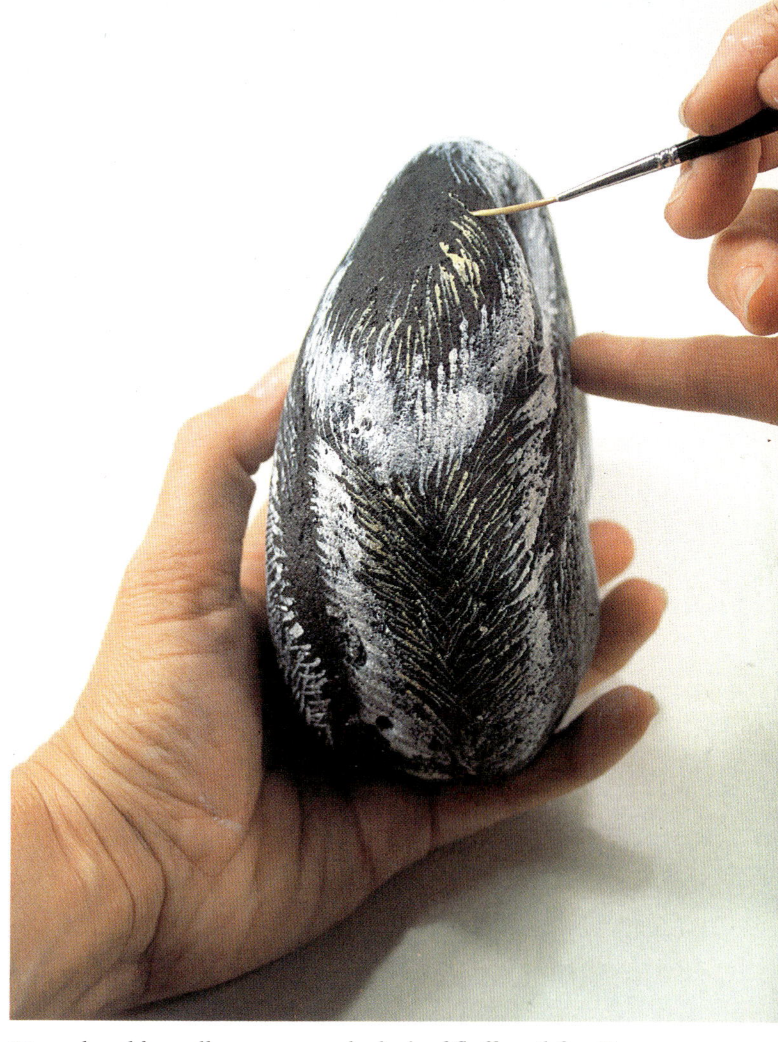

Use pale golden yellow to create the look of fluffy tail fur. Try to leave a dark area down the centre of the tail.

Change to burnt sienna and scatter
some reddish fur lines in among the
golden yellow ones, occasionally
overlapping into the fringe of white
tail fur. Use this same colour to fill in
the small U-shaped nose.

Mix a medium shade of grey, then
add a touch of red paint to create a
dusky pink colour. Use a small round
brush to dab this into the ears, leaving
just a suggestion of darker paint
between it and the white ear outlines.

Next, change to a liner brush and
black paint to fill in the eye circle.

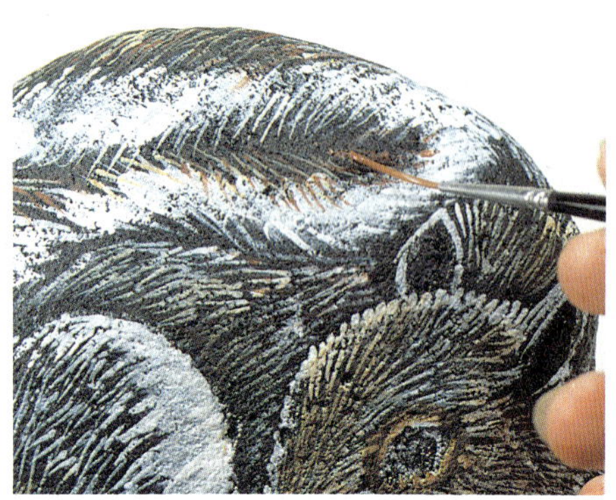

Contrasting strokes of burnt sienna help
define the tail and add a reddish hue.

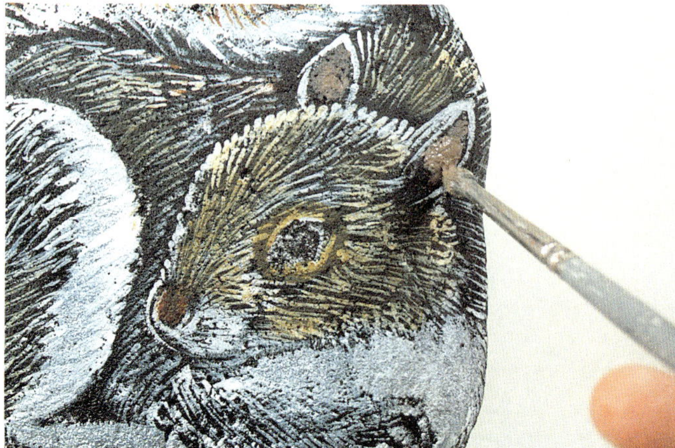

*Use a subtle shade
of pink to fill in the
ears. Leave a dark
border between the
pink centres and the
white outline.*

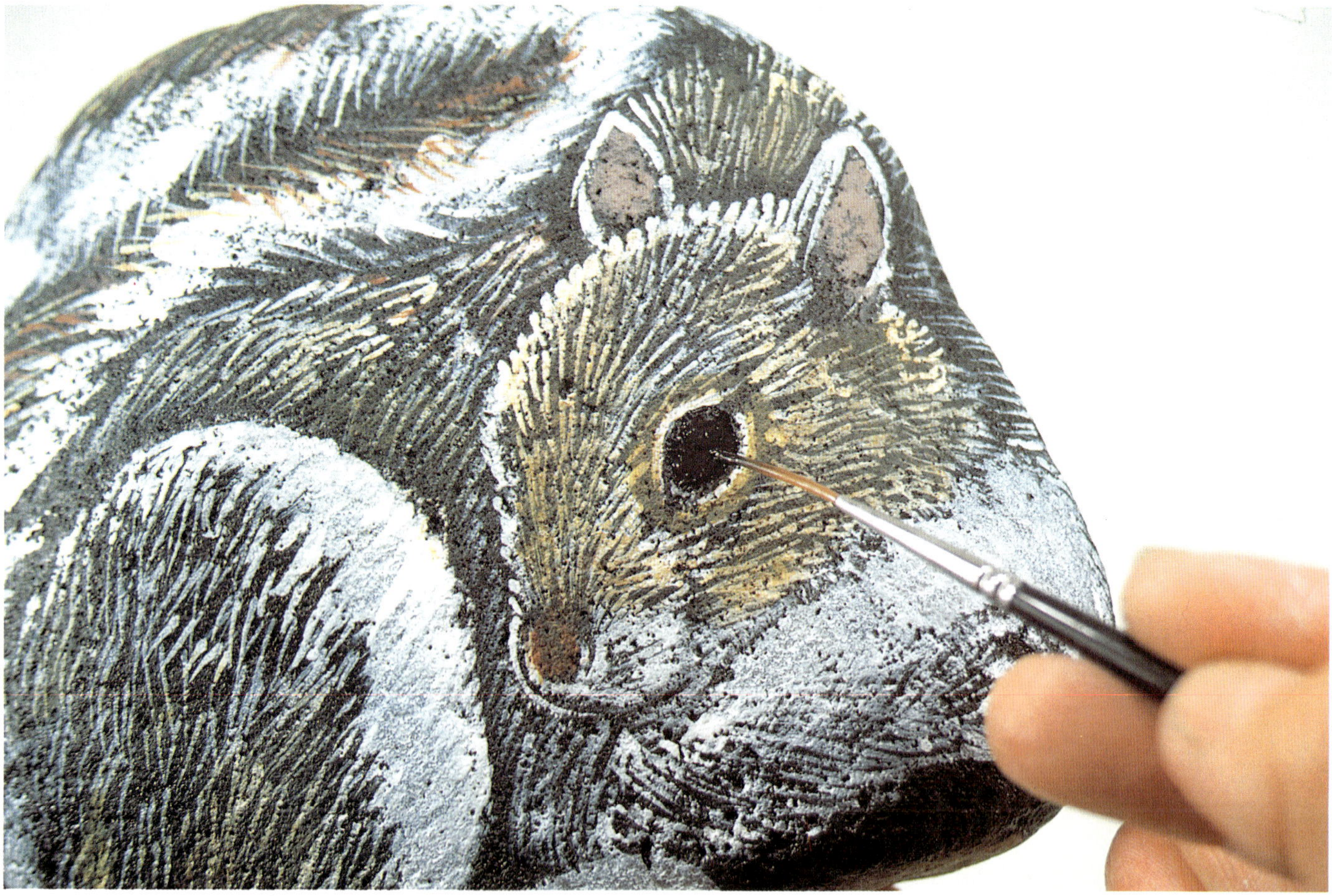

Fill in the eye with solid black paint.

5 Finishing Touches

While you have black on your brush, work on areas of your squirrel that may need more emphasis or definition. When in doubt, it does not hurt to add a few dark accents to clean up white fur lines that look too thick, or to add emphasis. Look for places where fur strokes may have obscured the underlying features. For example, add dark lines of fur to the top of the front leg and paw to create more distinction between that and the white chest area. Also, add more detail to the curve of the haunch and the tail.

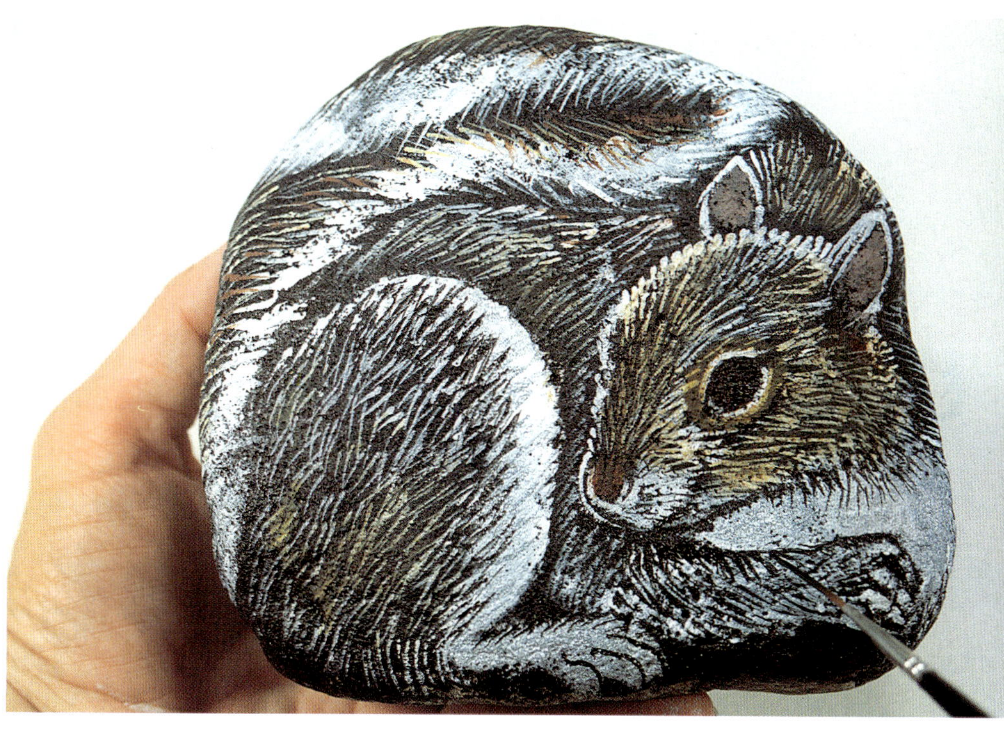

Apply a few dark strokes to sharply redefine the front leg.

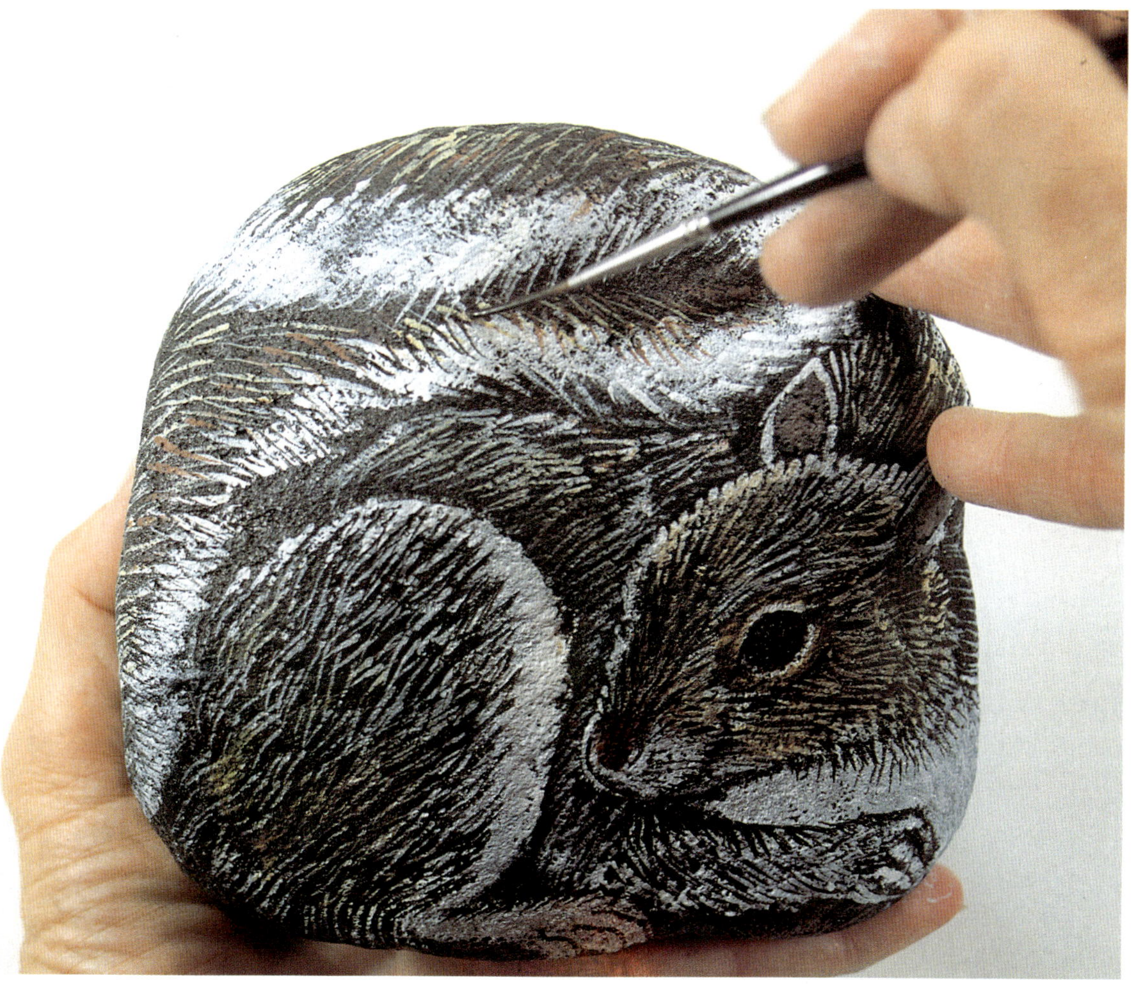

Scatter additional dark fur strokes to create more realistic detail. Pay attention to the inside edges of white that border the tail.

Add a touch of burnt sienna to the black on your brush and use this deep shade to make a semicircle around the side and bottom of the eye. Leave the centre black to create the iris.

Returning to black, add just enough water to ensure that the paint flows easily without becoming transparent. Carefully stroke in five or six slightly arching whiskers, beginning inside the muzzle area and flowing gracefully outward. Add two tiny dots of white to make the eye sparkle.

Leave to dry, then apply a coat of varnish to seal the surface and bring out the rich colours.

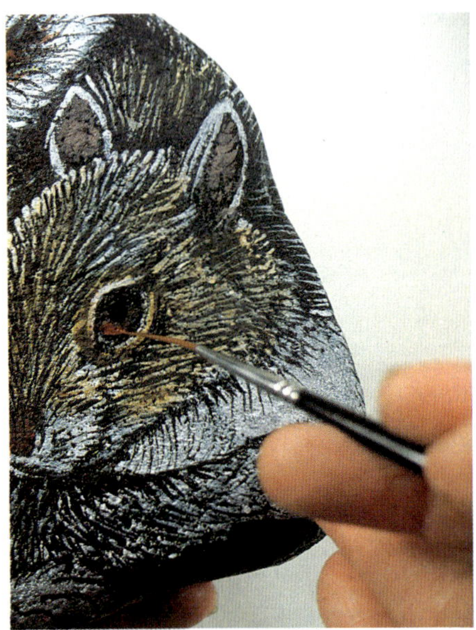

Apply a small semicircle of dark brown to add realistic depth to the eye.

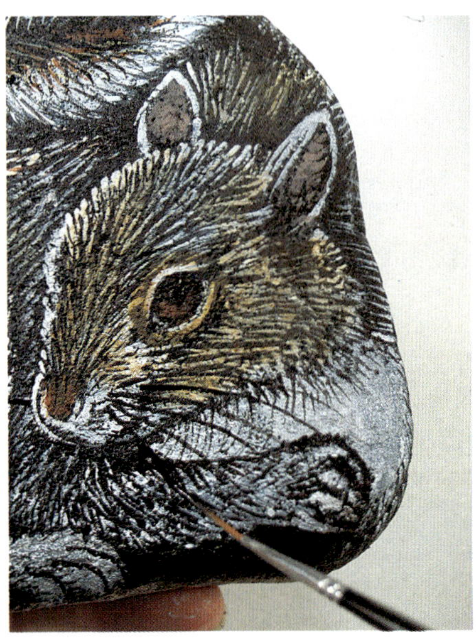

Add narrow black whiskers to frame the squirrel's face.

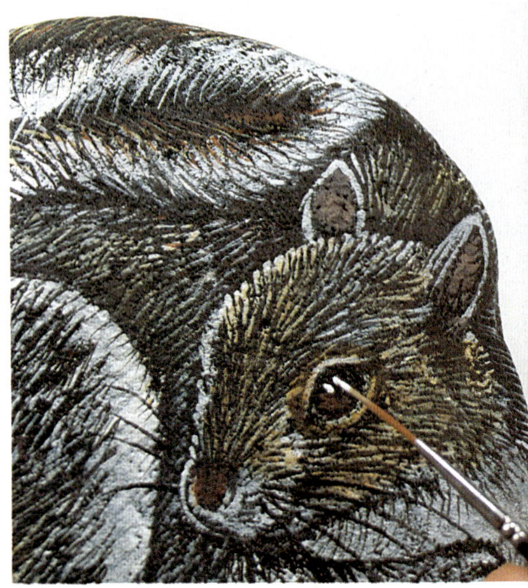

Paint in two tiny dots of white to add a mischievous glint to the squirrel's eye.

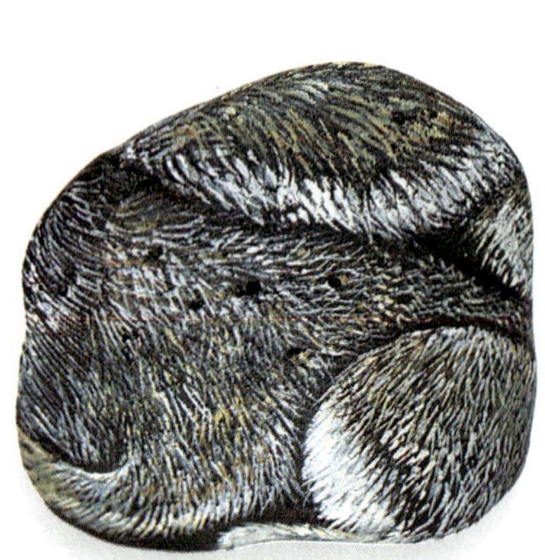

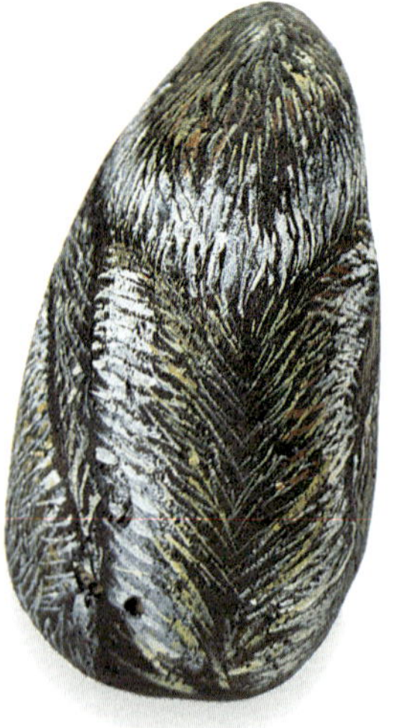

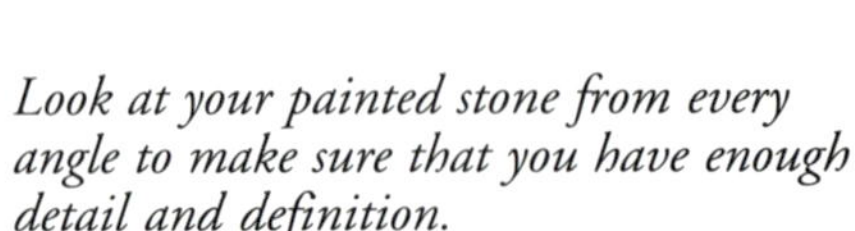

Look at your painted stone from every angle to make sure that you have enough detail and definition.

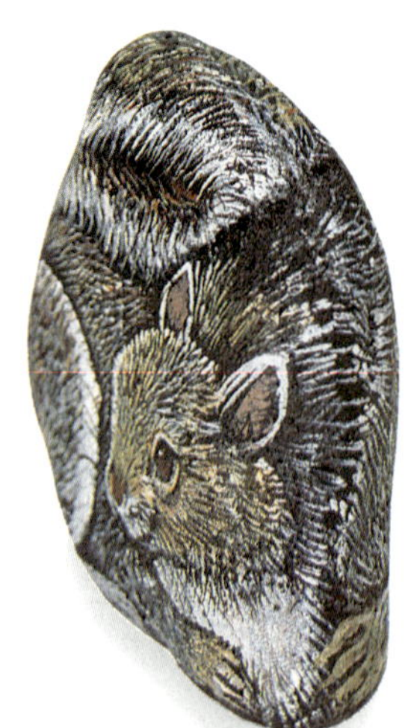

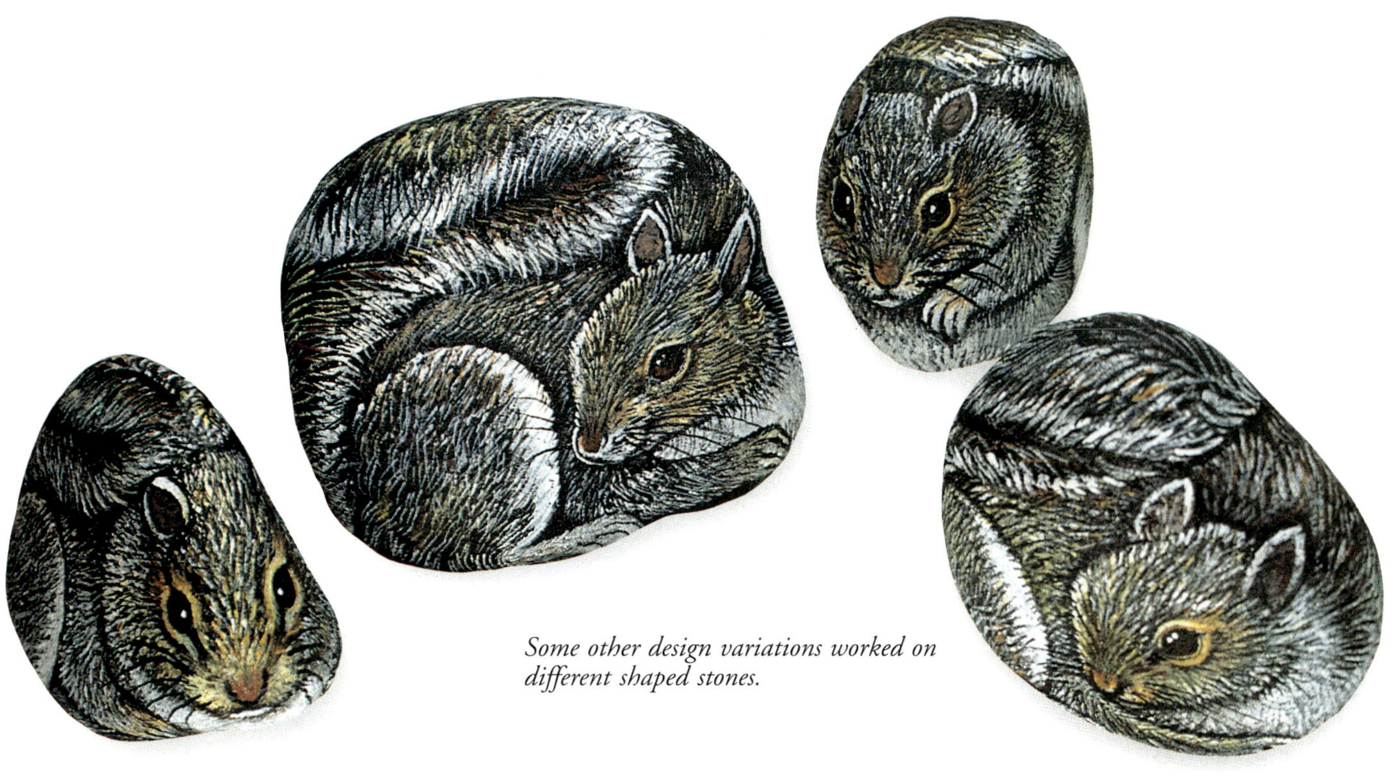

Some other design variations worked on different shaped stones.

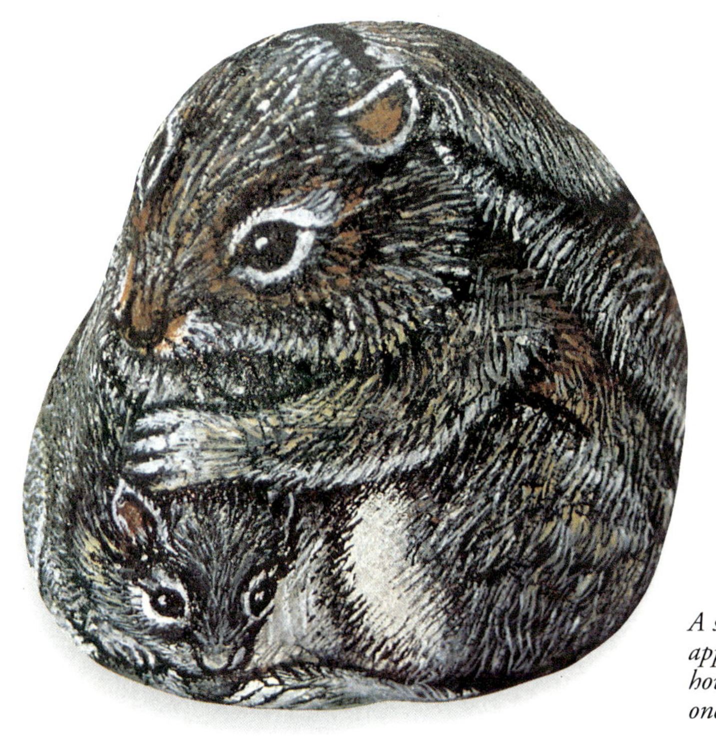

A squirrel posed with her baby makes an appealing subject. Further details on how to paint two animals together on one stone can be found on pages 92–95.

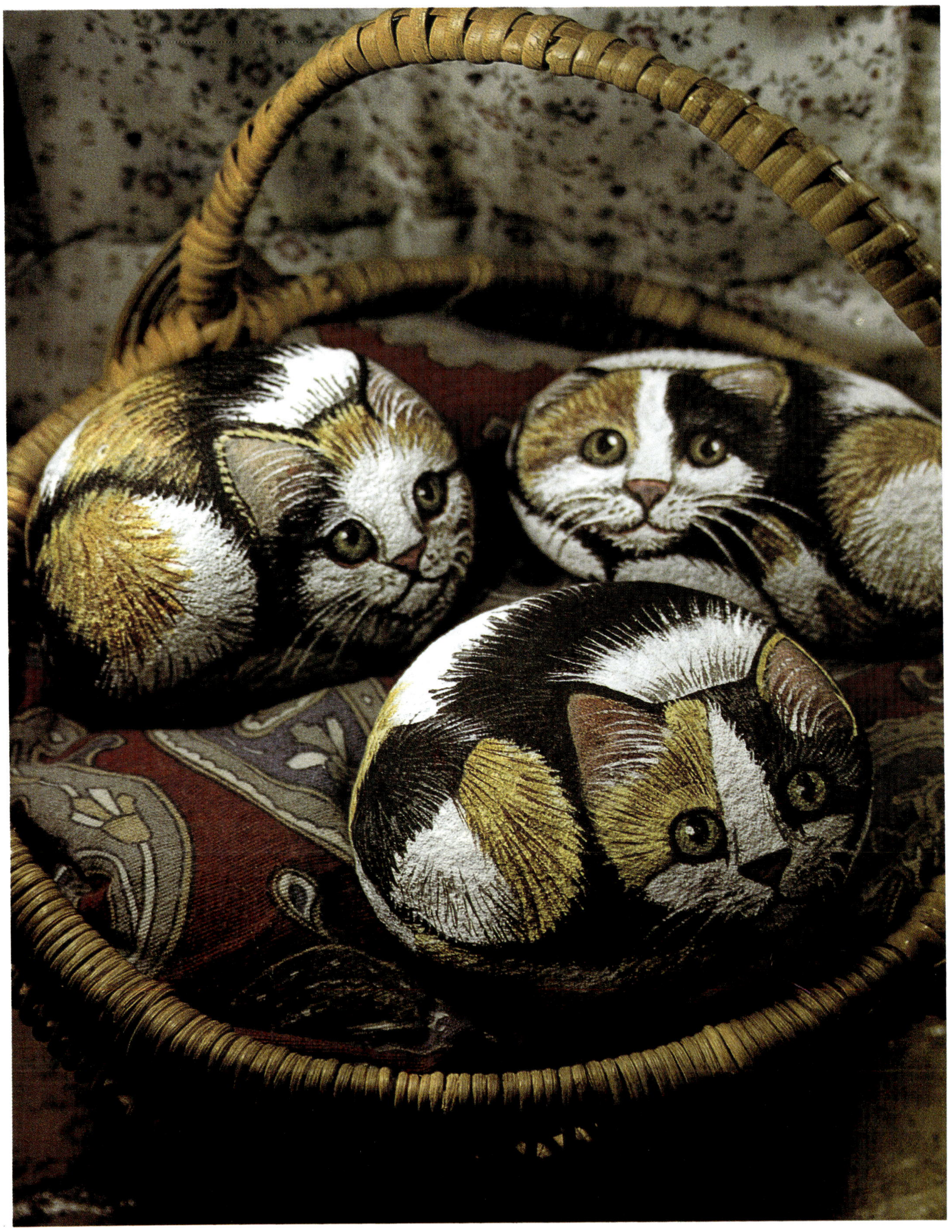

How to Paint a
KITTEN

With their wide, innocent eyes, stone kittens are nearly as irresistible as the real thing. People cannot resist picking them up or stroking them just to see what they are made of.

Stone kittens can be rendered in an incredible variety of colours and breeds, and they make ideal gifts. This project is designed especially for painters with a knack for creating delicate fur lines. However, the pattern of tortoiseshell patches should allow even those with moderate skills to achieve results they can be proud of.

A number of stone shapes are suitable. The most common choice is an oval stone, but round ones work well, too. A plump, kidney-shaped stone is practically made to order if you happen to find one. Kittens can also be worked in a more upright, crouching position, but for this project, I concentrate on the curled-up pose. Look for a stone that is between 13 and 18cm (5 and inn long, and one that is neither too flat nor too rounded.

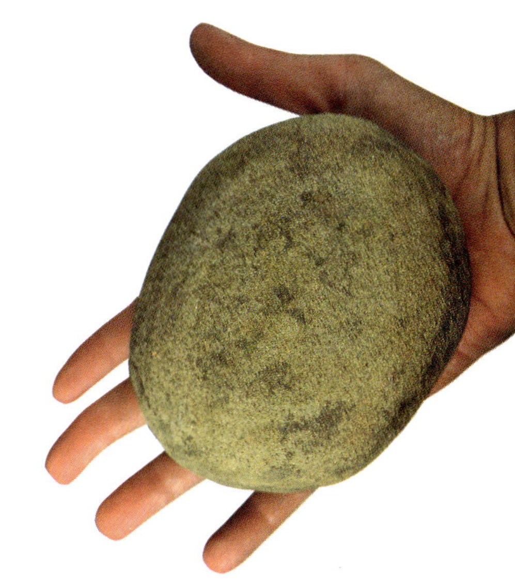

A perfect kitten stone should fit in the palm of your hand.

Measure the length of your stone across the top.

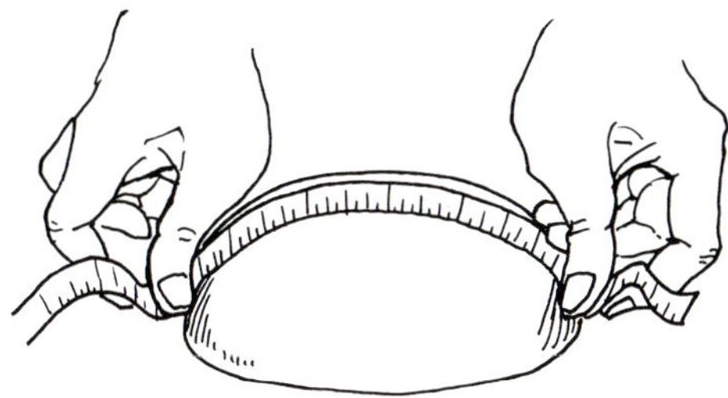

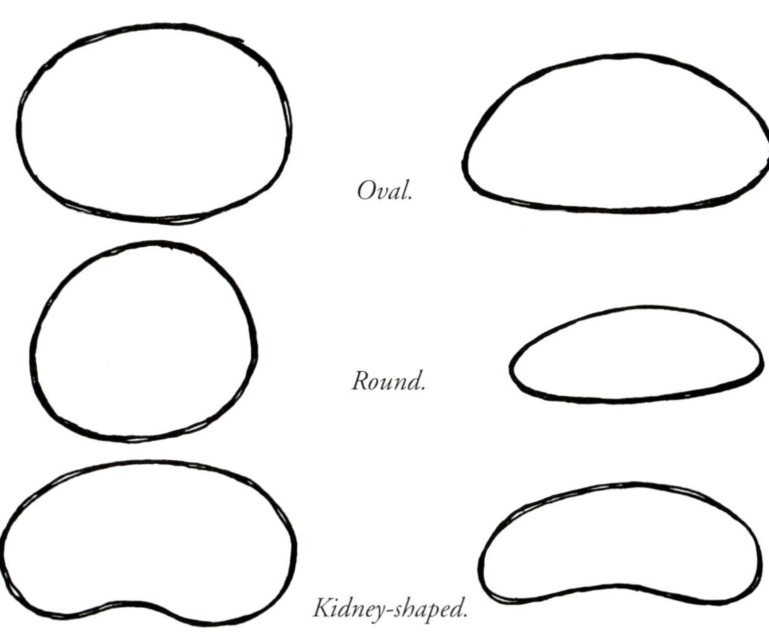

A selection of stones, seen from different angles, that would all be suitable for this kitten project.

Oval.

Round.

Kidney-shaped.

You Will Need
- acrylic paint: black, white, burnt sienna, gold, red and medium green
- selection of brushes
- pencil
- measuring tape (optional)
- oil-based or acrylic clear varnish

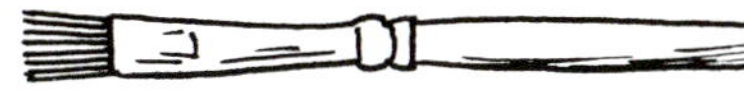

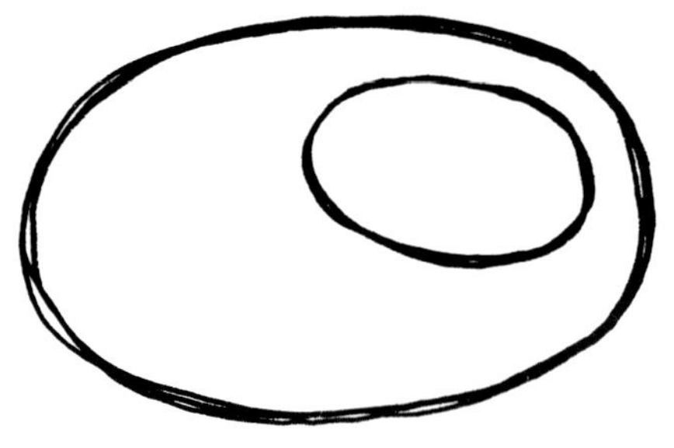

This head is too small.

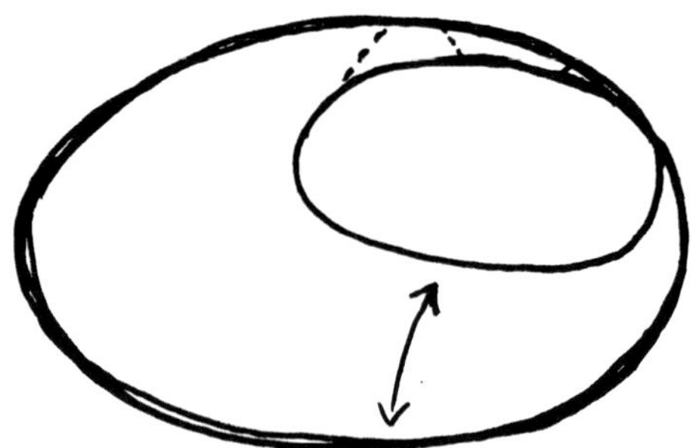

This head is too far back.

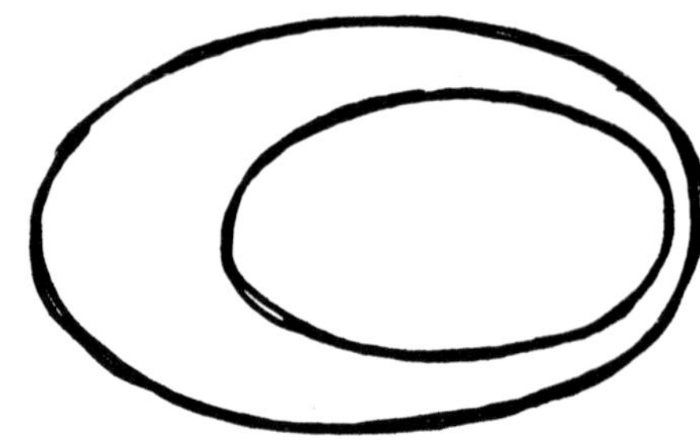

This head is too large.

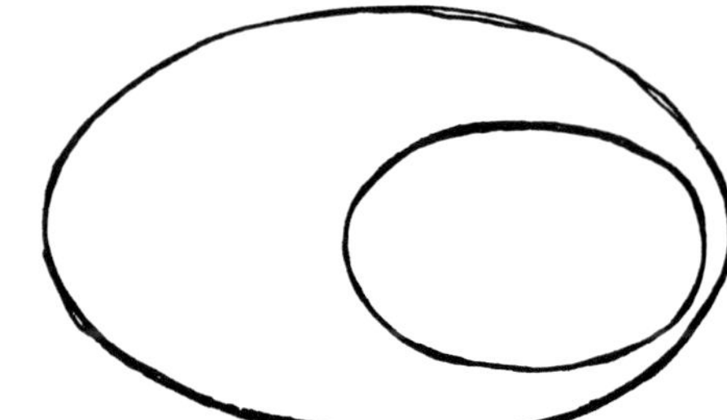

This head is in the correct proportion and location.

1 Head Placement

When your stone is scrubbed and dry, set it on a flat surface and decide on the best place for the head. The stone should sit solidly on one flat side. To give you an idea of proportion, on my 15cm (6in) stone kitten, the head spans approximately half the length of the stone.

When positioning the head, bear in mind that the ears will extend a little way above the basic oval shape of the head, so set the head low enough to keep the ears from disappearing around the curved edge of the stone. Also, leave room beneath the head for the front paws to show. A good rule of thumb is to locate the head as far over to one side as the contours of the stone will allow, and just high enough to leave room for the paws.

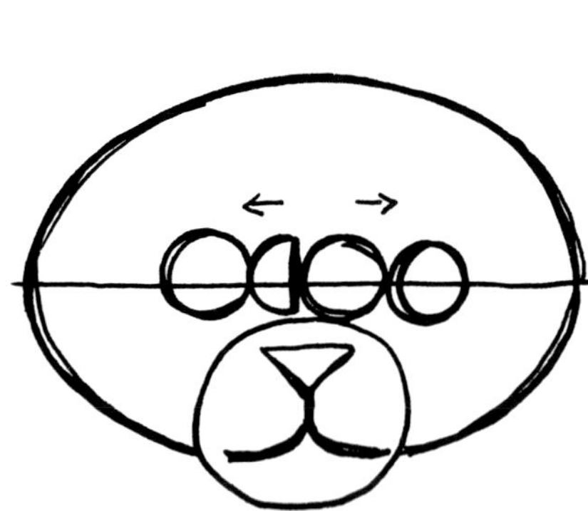

The eyes should be 1¹/₂ eye widths apart.

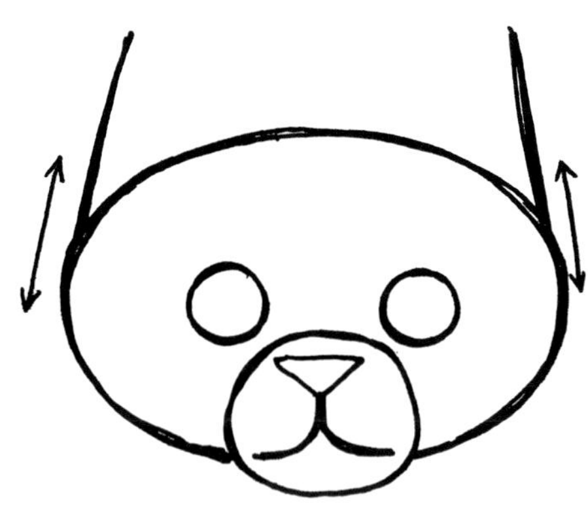

The ear lines should extend from the side of the head.

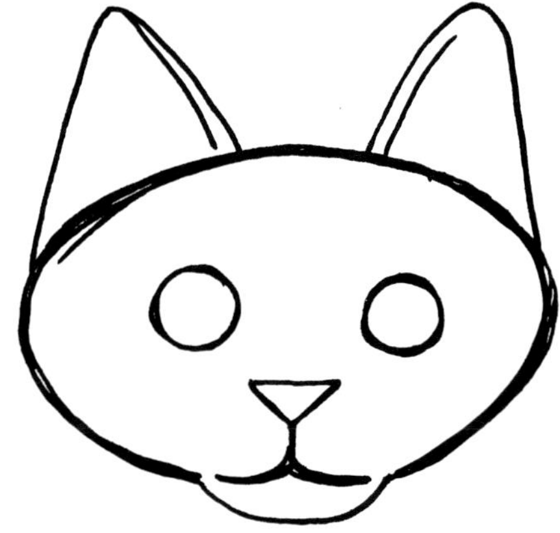

On a 15cm (6in) stone, the ear triangles should be about 2.5cm (1in) high.

2 Facial Features

Form the muzzle by drawing a circle approximately 2.5cm (1in) in diameter in the bottom half of the face oval. Allow the lower third of the circle to dip below the bottom of the oval. At the top of the muzzle, sketch in a small triangle for the nose, then add lines for the mouth as shown.

Now sketch the eyes. Bisect the head oval horizontally and draw eye circles on this line. Leave a space between the eyes, equal to one-and-a-half eye widths.

Extend a line up from each side of the face to form the outer edge of each ear. Kitten ears can vary in size depending on breed and age, but 2.5cm (1in) long is a safe choice. The inside edge angles back down to the head to create a triangular shape. The space between the ears should equal the width of one ear at its base.

1 Haunches, Paws and Tail Layout

With the head in place, it is fairly simple to complete the layout. The haunch is also an oval, laying at an angle to the head shape. Leave at least 5mm (¹/₄in) between the inside edge of the haunch and the curve of the face oval.

Curve the tail up from below and behind the haunch until the tip reaches almost to the face edge. Again, leave at least 5mm (¹/₄in) between the two features. By allowing the tip of the tail to curl slightly, you will help distinguish it from the front paw.

The paws are formed from two long, narrow ovals below the kitten's chin. Situate them so that the space between the paws is slightly off centre, not directly in line with the chin.

When you are satisfied with your sketch, outline the features with black paint and a medium brush. Blacken the areas around the front paws, tail and between the head and haunch all the way up to the tip of the ear. With a small brush, paint the outlines for the eyes. Try to make the outside edges neatly rounded and the same size on both eyes.

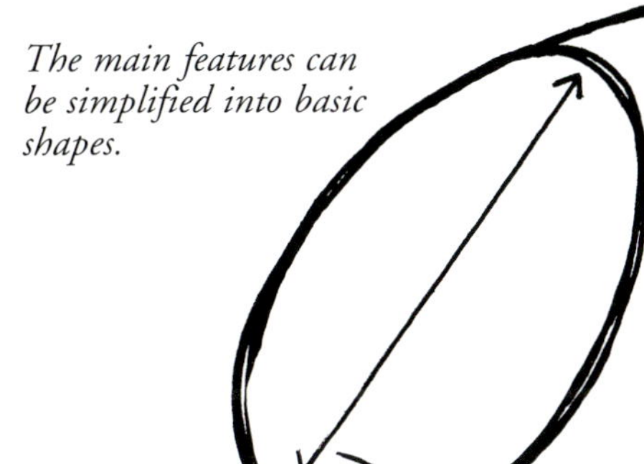

The main features can be simplified into basic shapes.

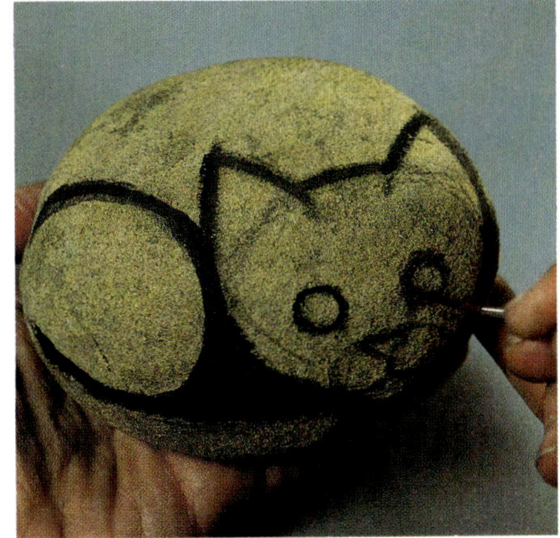

Outline the facial features in black.

4 The Tortoiseshell Pattern

Tortoiseshell kittens come in many combinations of colours and patterns, but I have arranged the patches in this pattern to show off the kitten's features. Begin by sketching a blaze between and above the eyes that covers both sides of the cheeks and the whole muzzle. Next draw in a raggedy band between the ears, and then sketch longer curving bands behind that one. Sketch in the pattern on the haunch – this is divided into three parts like an inverted Y. Also mark off the last couple of centimetres of the tail and a similar-sized half-circle patch on the tail just below the haunch.

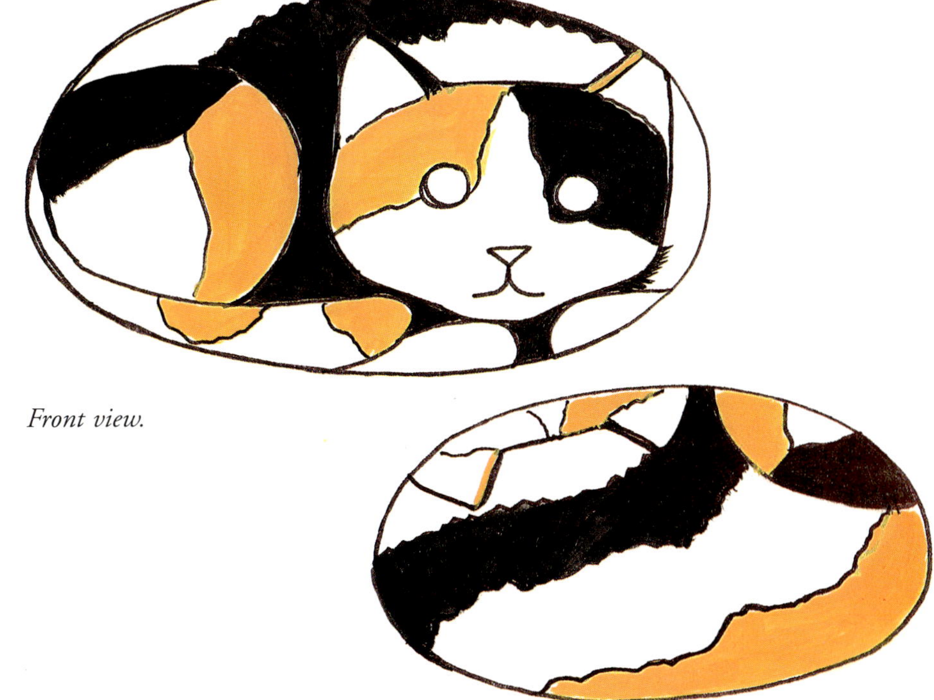

Front view.

Rear view.

5 Filling in the Pattern

Use a clean, medium brush and white paint to fill in the white areas as shown. These include the blaze and lower half of the head. Be careful not to go over your guidelines as you paint around the nose and mouth. Next, fill in the front paws, the band between the ears, the band along the back, the middle haunch section and all of the tail except for the tip and the half-circle patch.

Clean your brush and change to golden yellow to paint in patches on the side of the head nearest the haunch, the section of the haunch facing the head, the tip and half-circle patch on the tail, and the lowest band on the kitten's backside. Change to your smallest brush and carefully paint a slender golden yellow line around the kitten's outside ear. Do not cover the black outline around the ear. You will need this to make the ear stand out.

Complete your base coat by filling in any remaining areas with black (with the exception of the eyes, nose and ears).

6 Nose and Ears

For the insides of the ears, mix two or more drops of white paint with one drop of red to get a deep pink. Use this colour with a small brush to fill in the nose triangle and the mouth guidelines. Now add just enough golden yellow to soften the pink to a flesh tone. Use this colour to fill in the triangle shape of the ears.

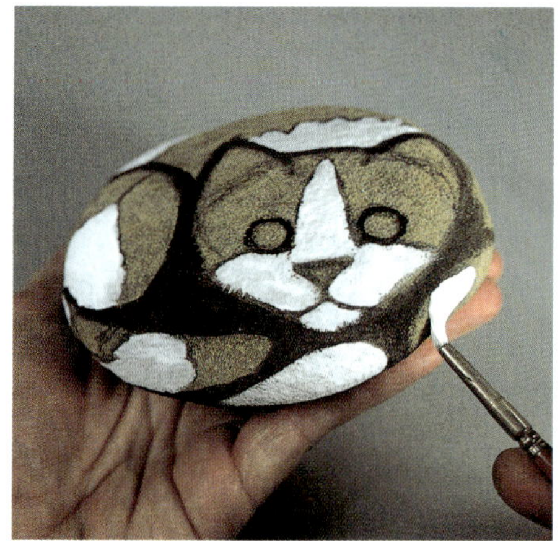

Apply white patches.

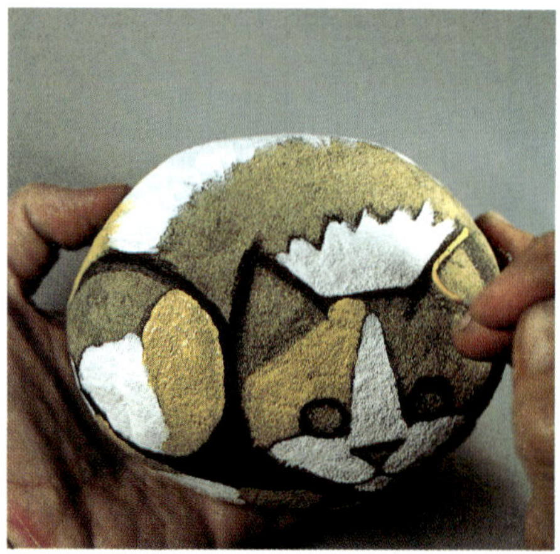

Paint a golden yellow line around one ear.

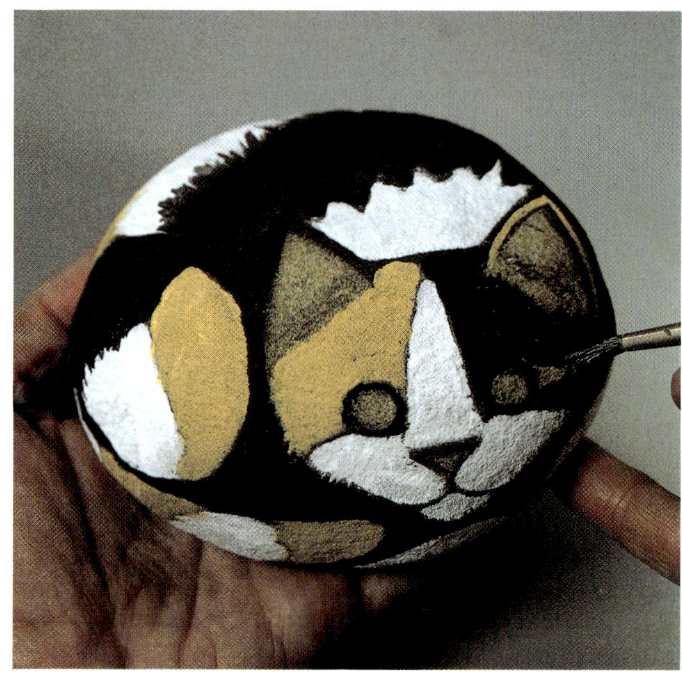

Fill in remaining areas with black.

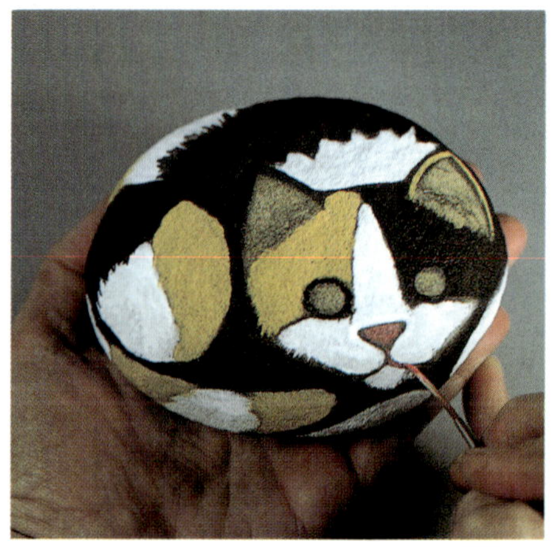

Paint the nose deep pink.

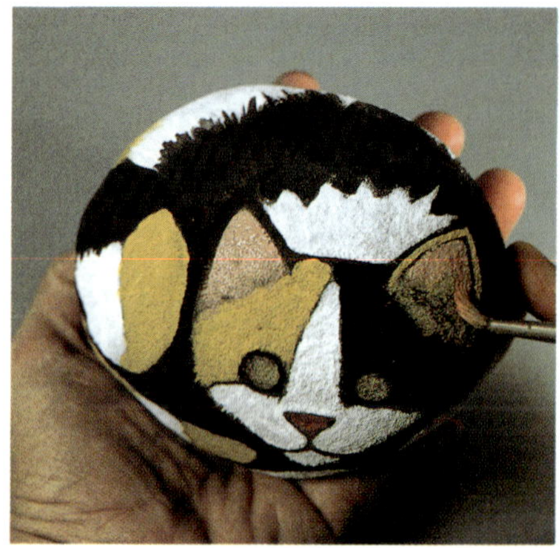

Fill in the ears with soft pink.

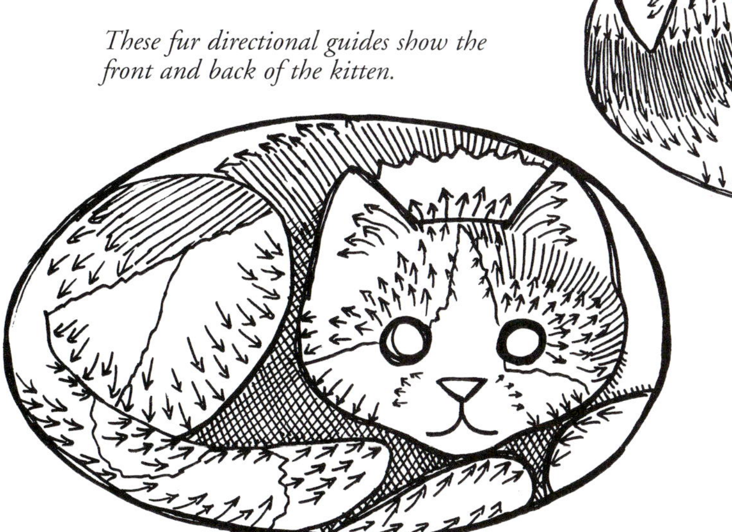

These fur directional guides show the front and back of the kitten.

7 Adding Fur Lines

You are now ready to begin the delicate fur lines that will give your kitten its fluffy look. Follow the fur directional guides above to create realistic fur lines. Begin with the golden yellow section of the haunch, and use a small brush and burnt sienna to work a series of short, fine fur lines. Work from inside to outside in layers. Do not be afraid to vary the stroke direction, allowing strokes to cross or overlap.

Stroke long, contrasting fur lines in the ears. Next, turn the stone and stroke in a series of short, fine lines radiating outward from around the eye on the golden yellow side of the face. Add fine fur lines on the golden yellow areas of the tail and down the patch on the back.

Rinse your brush and mix golden yellow with white paint to get a pale straw colour. Use this to go over the same patches you just touched up with burnt sienna. Use this paler colour sparingly, mainly to highlight and soften the edges of the golden yellow patches. Make short, delicate strokes around the eye. Draw out slender tips of colour along the edge of the cheeks and across the top of the head. Paint the curve of the haunch with the same kind of spiky strokes, keeping them perpendicular to the line of the haunch. Finally, highlight the edges of the tail, and add fuzz to the outlined ear.

Clean your brush and mix a small amount of black with white to create a pale grey. Highlight the black patches on your kitten. On the black side of the face, radiate lines out from around the kitten's eye and along the top of the head. Apply fur strokes sparingly along the lower half of the black portion of the haunch.

Continue to cover all the black areas in this fashion. Use this same pale grey sparingly to soften and add texture to the white areas (without making these patches look more like grey patches). Leave the tops of the paws totally white but create a shadow by making grey fur strokes along the bottom edges. Use fine, dark grey lines to smooth the transition between white and black bands of fur.

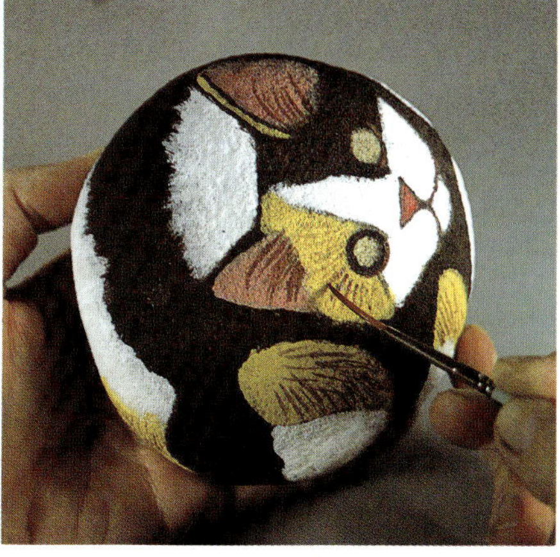

Radiate brown lines around the eye.

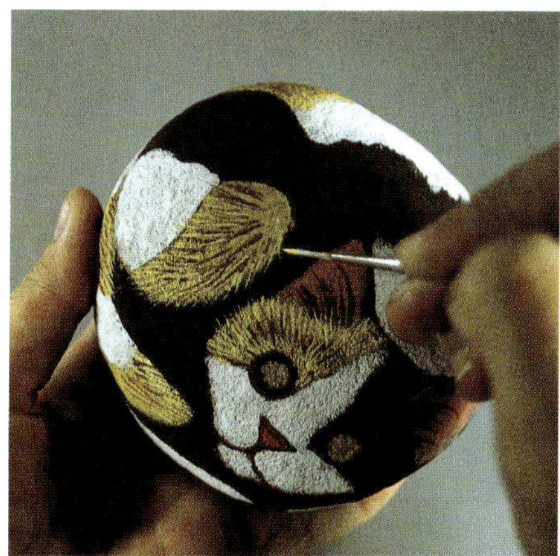

Texture the haunch with spiky strokes.

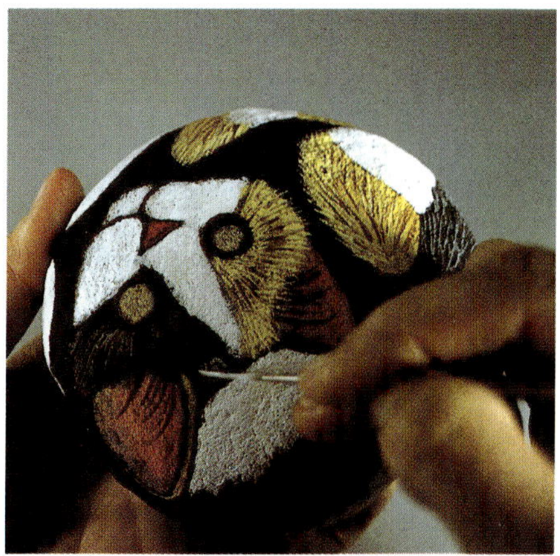

Highlight black patches with grey fur lines.

8 Muzzle and eyes

Add more black to the dark grey to get an even deeper shade. Use this colour to define the muzzle with a series of short, spoke-like strokes. Add a few lines of small dots across each muzzle to resemble follicles for the whiskers.

Now you are ready to fill in the eye colour. Most kittens' eyes range in colour from milky blue-grey to yellow-green. For this kitten I have used a medium green softened with burnt sienna. Remember to leave a black rim all the way around each eye. While the eyes are still wet, dip your brush into a drop of golden yellow paint and make an inner ring. Clean and dry your brush and use the tip to draw spikes of gold, like sunrays, out into the green. Allow the eye colour to dry before painting black oval irises in the upper part of each eye circle, to create the impression that the kitten were looking up at you.

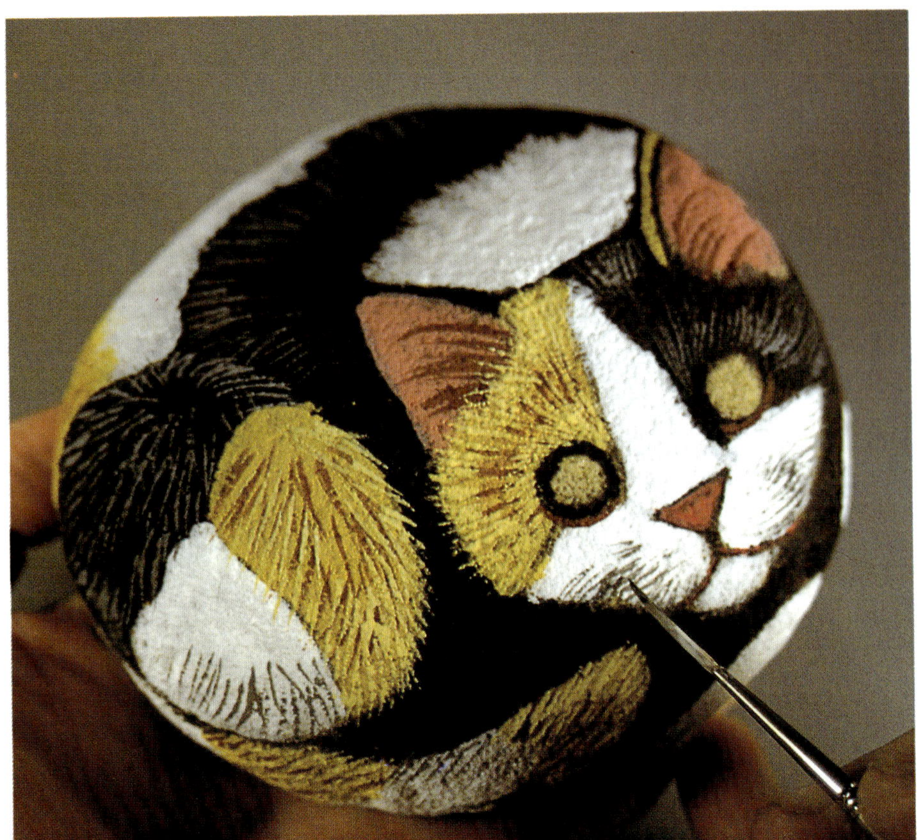

Define the muzzle and add the whisker follicles.

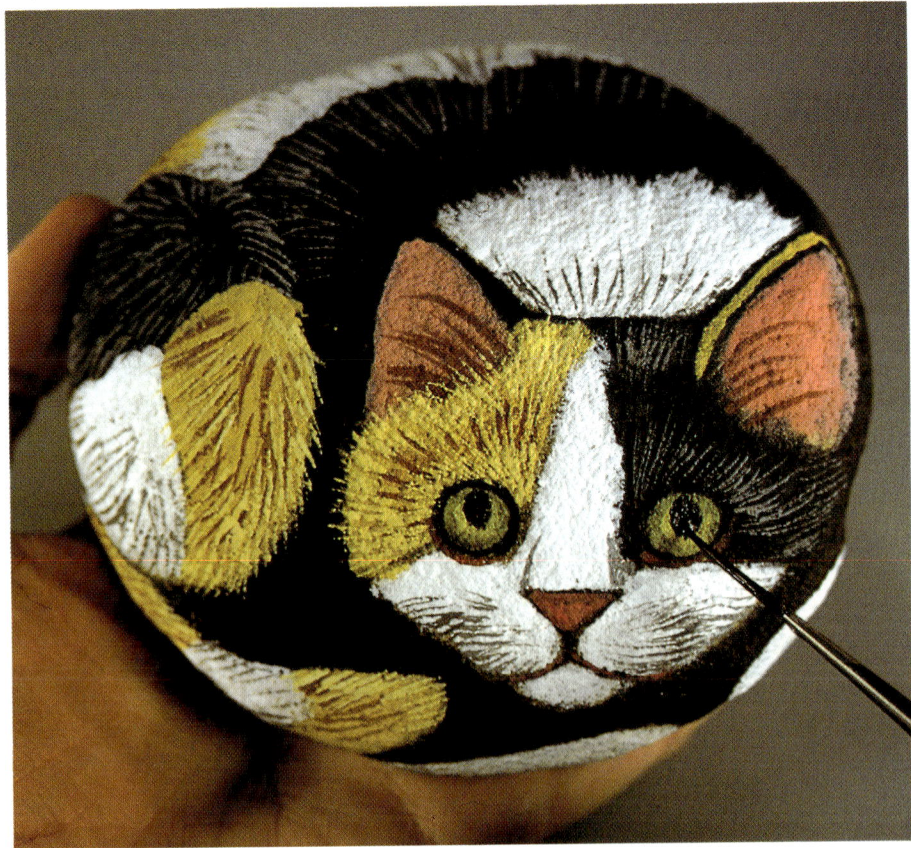

Paint in the black irises.

9 Finishing Touches

Clean your brush once more and change to white paint. Fan delicate white ear whiskers out over the darker set you made earlier. Next, soften the blaze between the kitten's eyes by feathering little fur lines along each side. You may find it easier to do these strokes if you turn your kitten around.

To make the whiskers, you may need to dilute the white paint slightly to ensure it will flow in long, unbroken lines. Start your whiskers just inside the muzzle area and pull them out in graceful curves. Three or four whiskers per side should be enough.

Finally, add a dot of white at the edge of the iris in each eye. When dry, apply a coat of varnish.

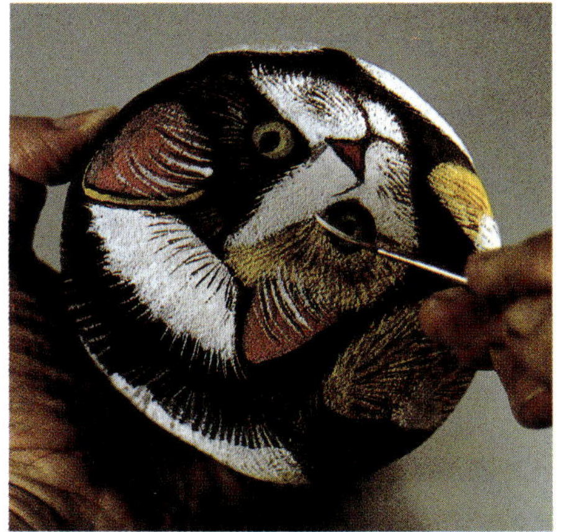

Soften the blaze with tiny lines.

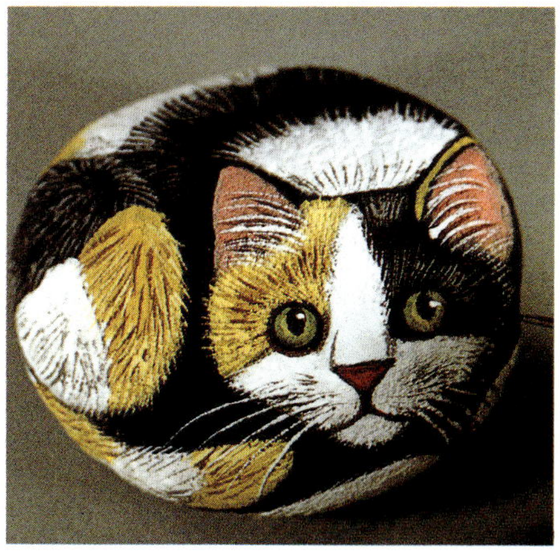

Add a white sparkle to each eye to bring the kitten to life.

While single kittens are endearing, two or three kittens in a basket or posed on a pillow are even more enchanting. Once you have mastered this first design, try making up variations. You can paint a variety of breeds using the techniques shown in this project.

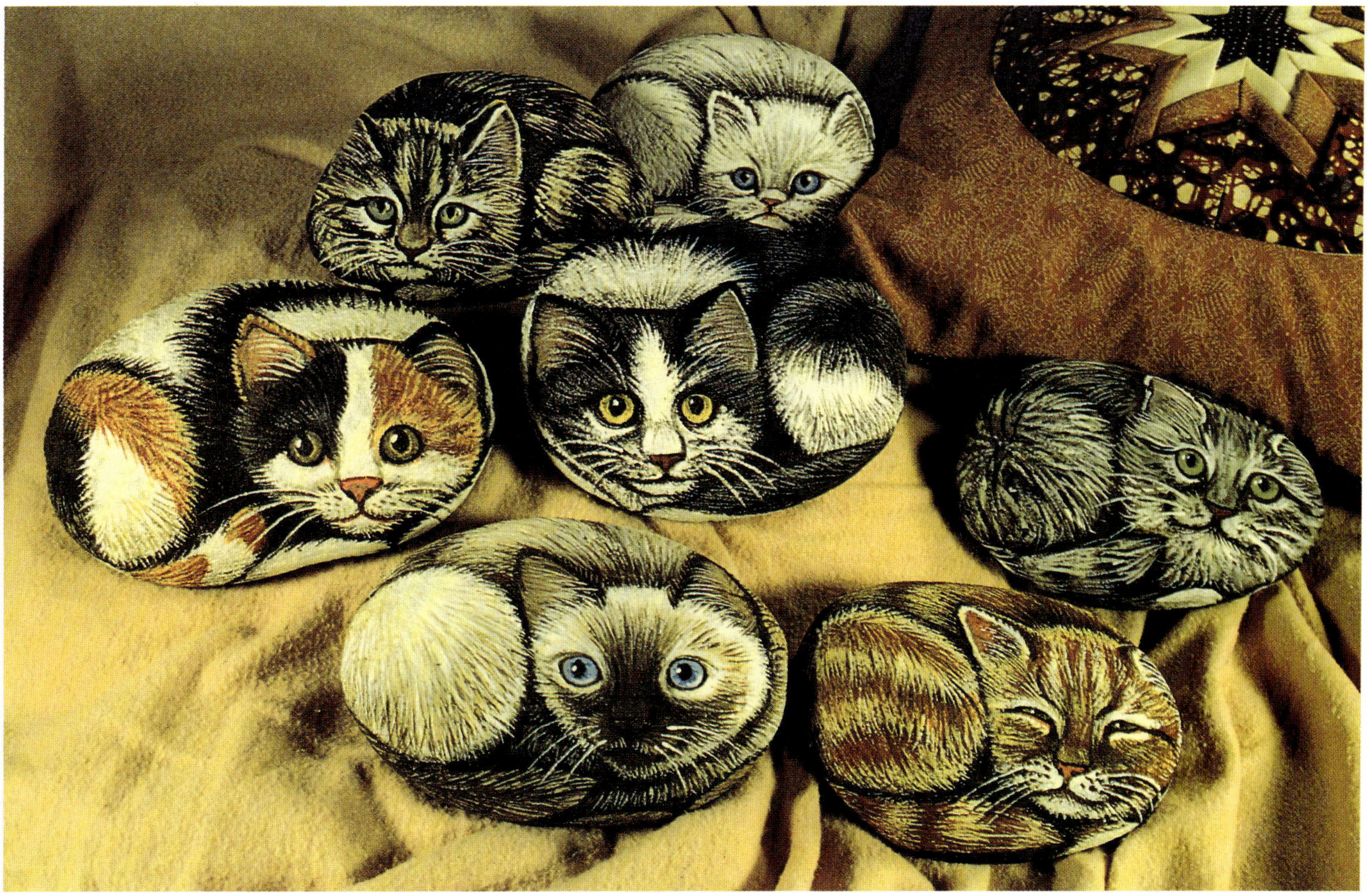

You can now apply all the skills you have learnt in this book to create exciting variations. Families of lots of different types of animal can be painted on to stones.

Animals with their young look adorable, but brothers and sisters also work well. Depending on the animal you choose and the shape of the stone, you may be able to fit on more than two animals. The example shown below features a fox with two cubs.

When painting a mother and baby, sketch the mother in the same way that you would a single animal, then add the baby; this is usually tucked behind the tail.

Make sure your babies look like babies, and not simply miniature versions of adults. Usually this means giving them shorter muzzles and ears, and larger eyes.

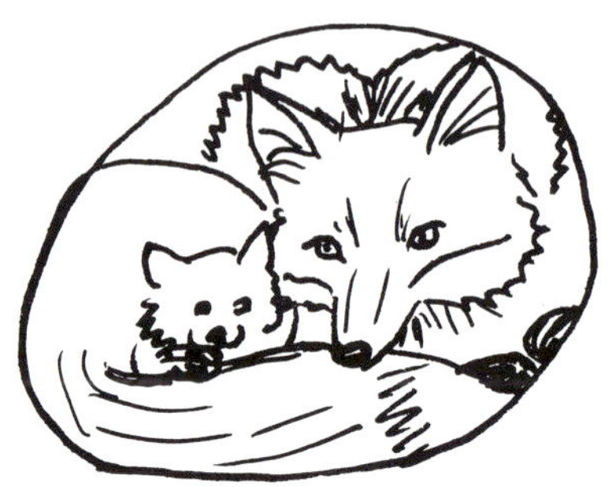
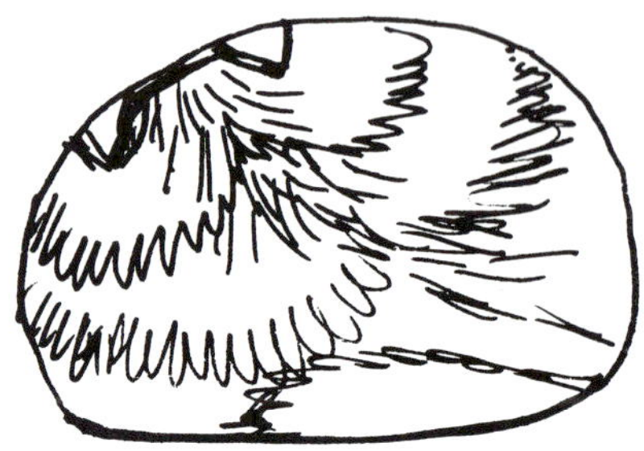
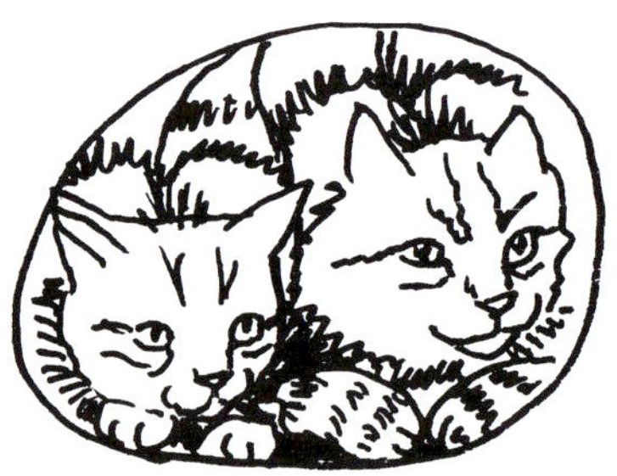
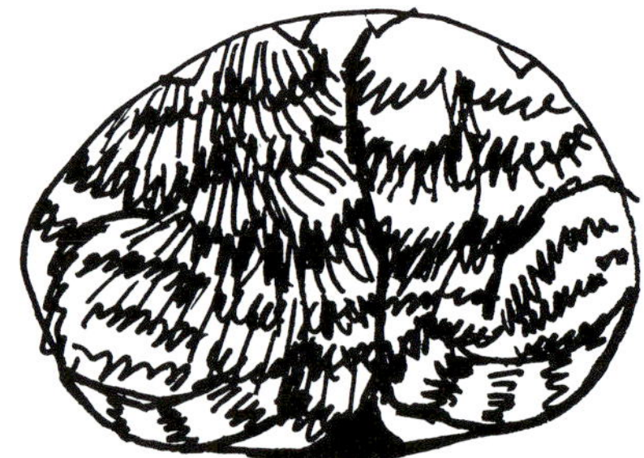

Sample arrangements of animal families, showing front and rear views.

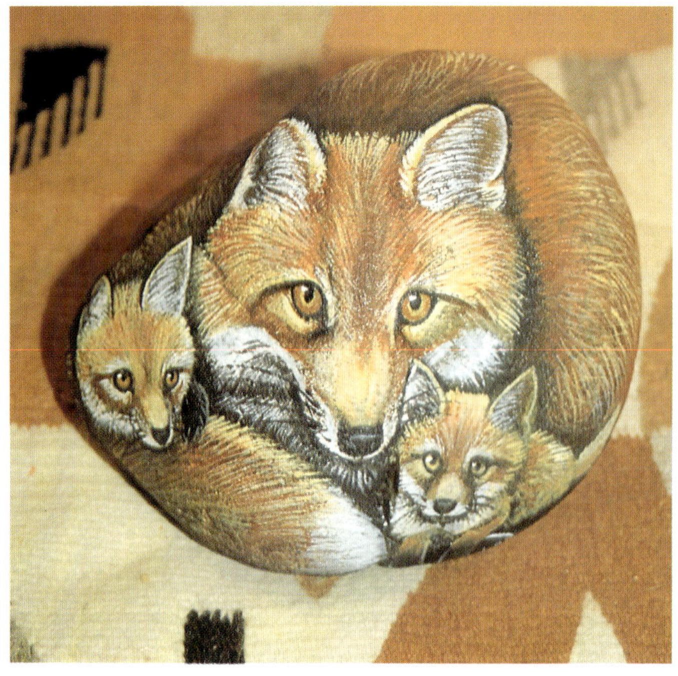
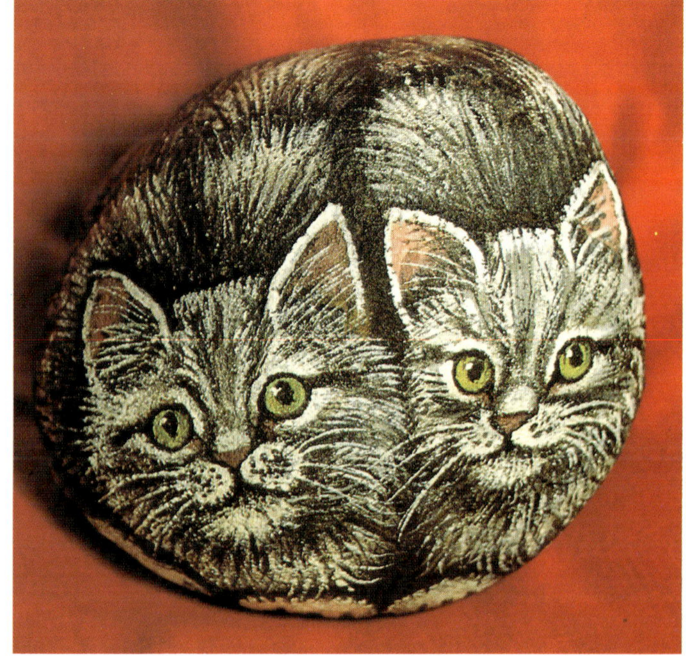

These animal families feature mother-baby combinations and twins.

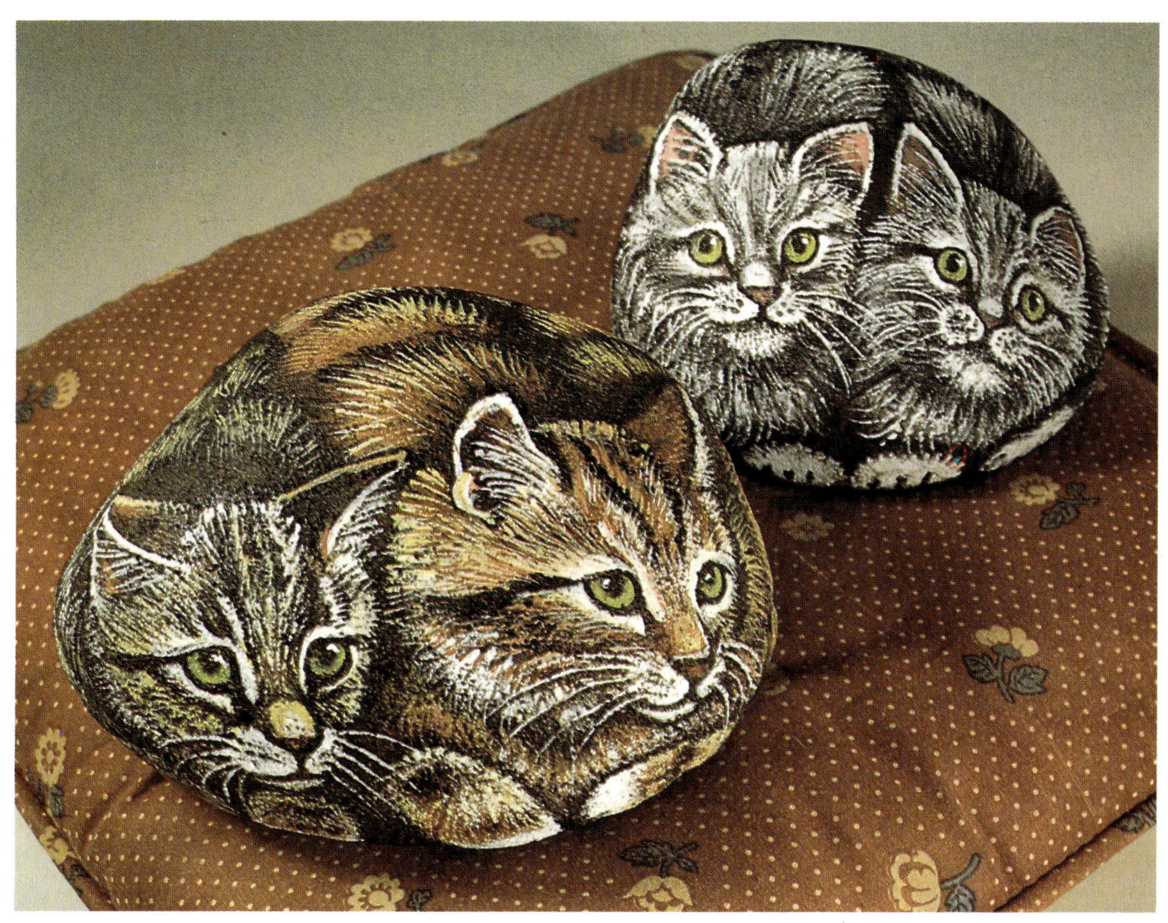

Not only are families of cats and kittens fun to create, they can be painted on a wide range of stone shapes. You can make identical twins by painting the same animal twice, or you can vary the position, expression and coloration for an even more dramatic look. Cat families can also be worked with one facing forward and the other(s) facing backward.

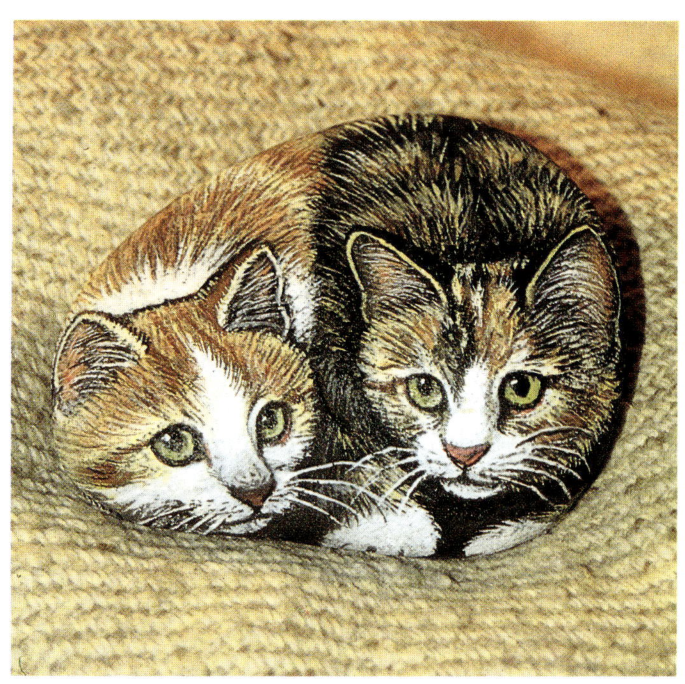

I have painted these baby squirrels a number of times since coming across a photograph that helped me see how I could fit them on to a stone. The photographs on these pages show the same stone viewed from different angles. Ordinarily, squirrels are difficult subjects because their fluffy tails do not readily conform to stone shapes. However, these two, clinging to one another with their tails wrapped around their feet, are made to order for painting on stone. Approach them in the same way as shown on pages 72–83, beginning with a black base coat. Note that squirrels' front paws have very distinctive claws.

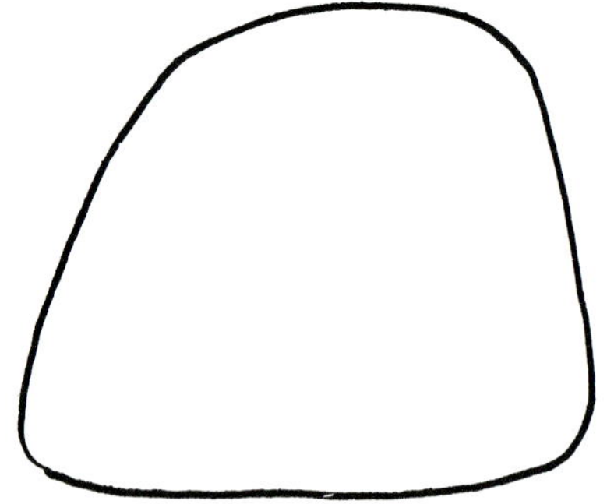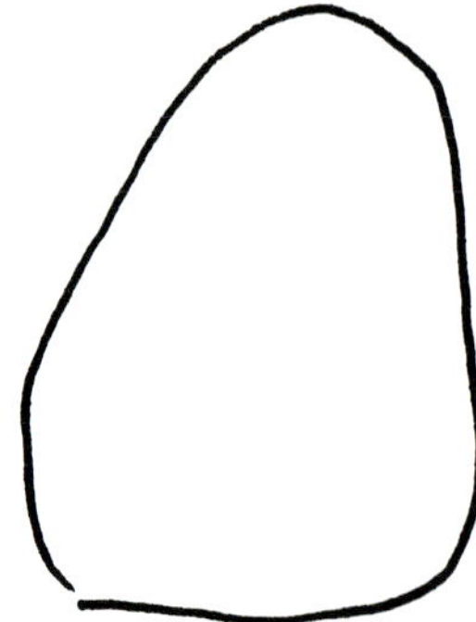

Sample arrangements of double squirrels.

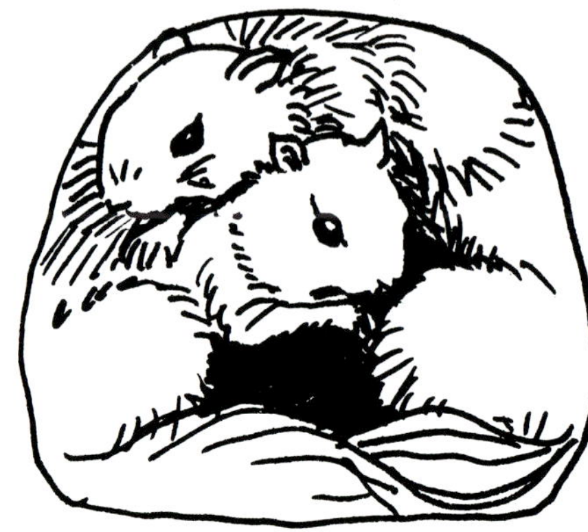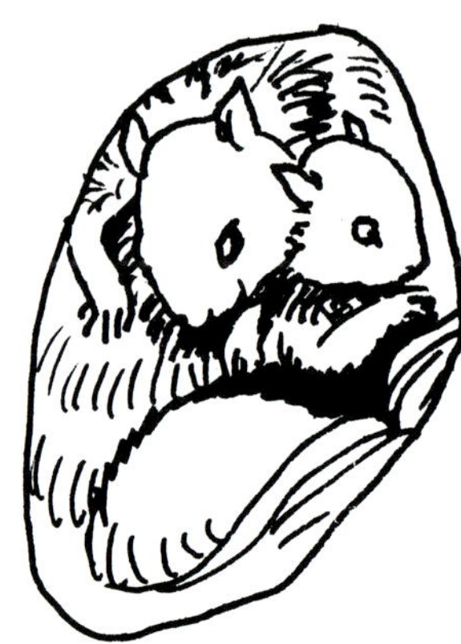

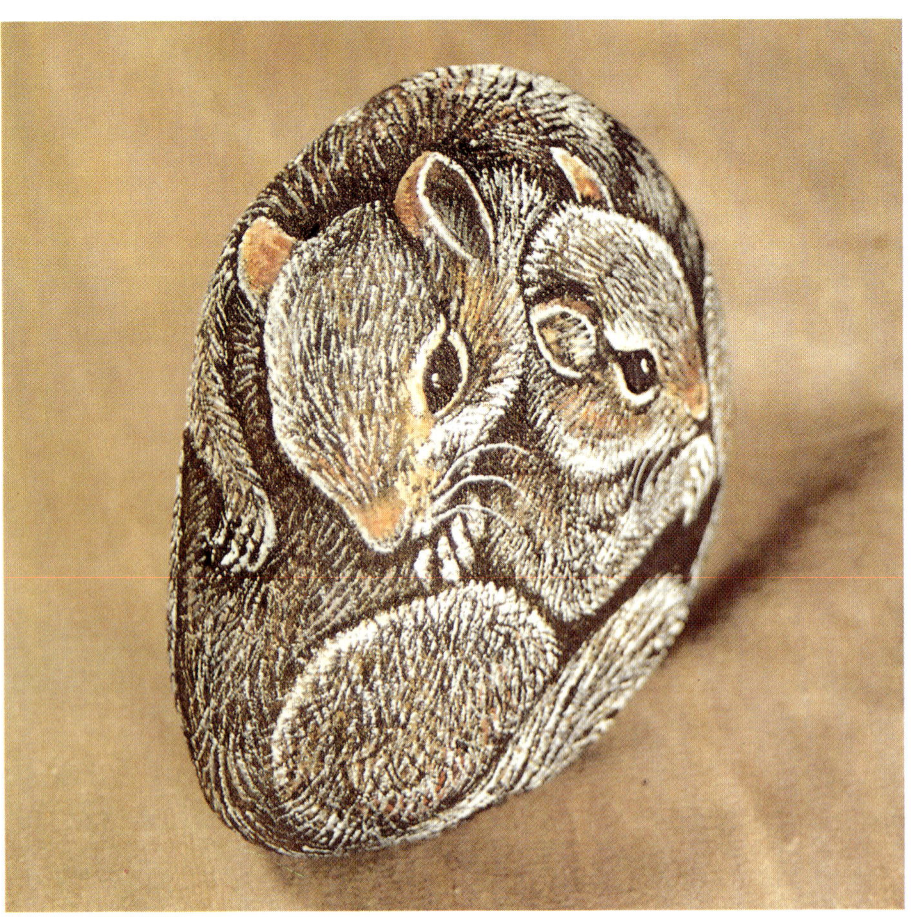

Side view of a pair of squirrels.

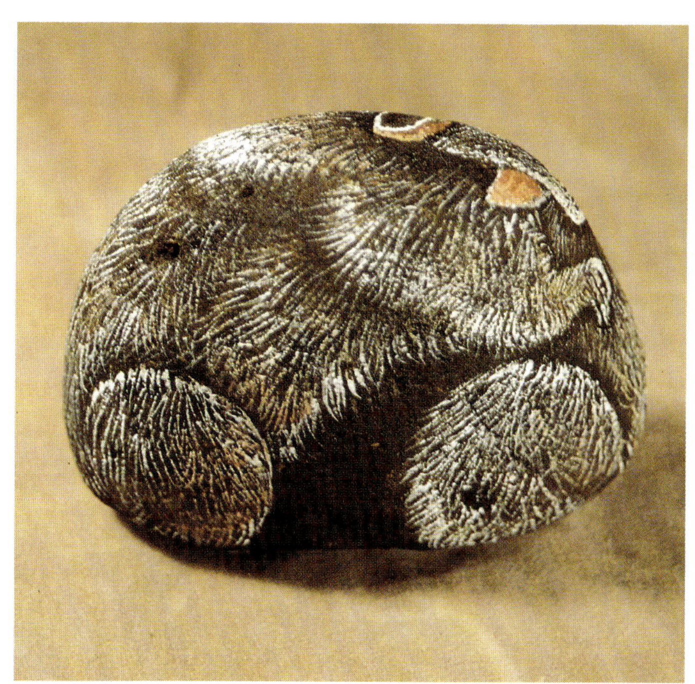

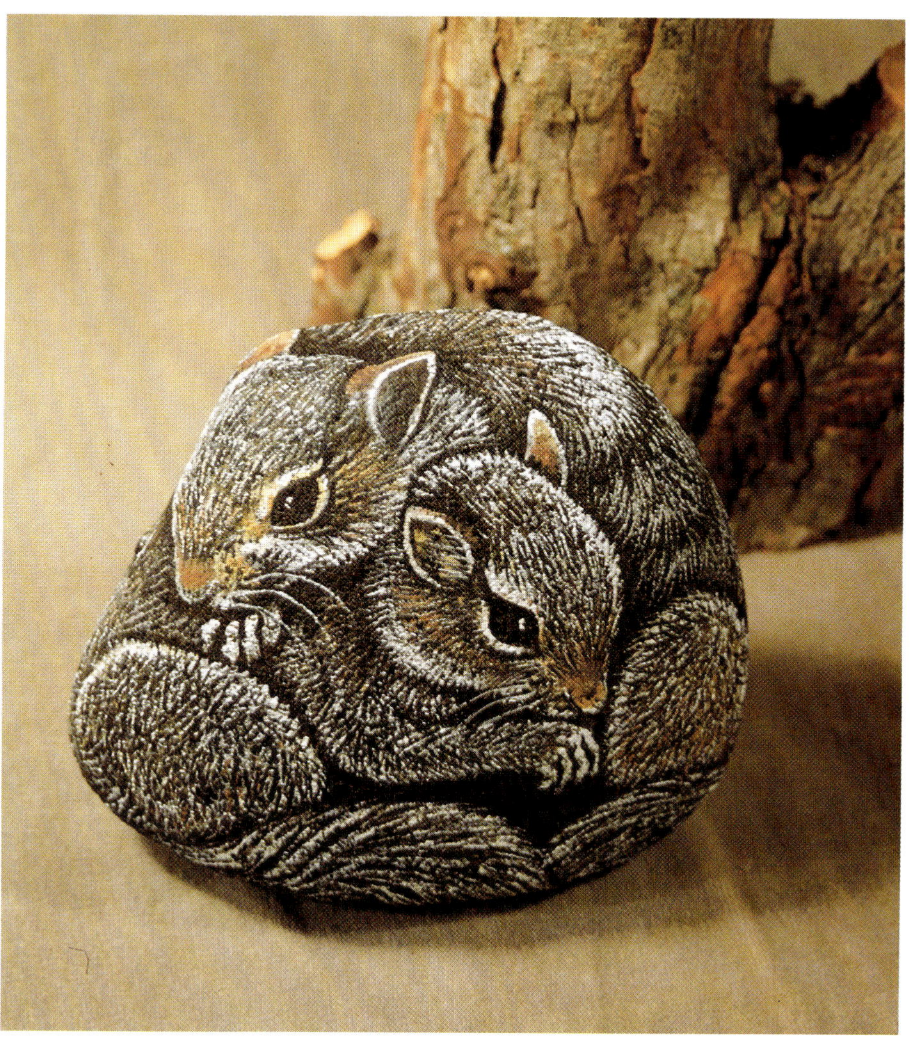

Front view of a pair of squirrels.

Index

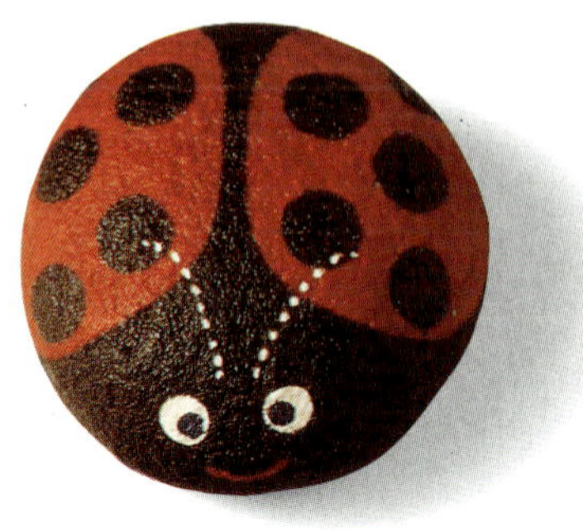